THE NATIONAL FRONT ANI

'Civilisation is in danger. The white race risks being submerged by the Third World and shouldn't we defend ourselves?'
(Germaine Burgaz, vice-president F.N.)

Source: *Le Monde Diplomatique*, March 1984

The National Front and French Politics

The Resistible Rise of Jean-Marie Le Pen

Jonathan Marcus

To Gordon,
with many,
many thanks

Jonathan.
July 1995.

MACMILLAN

First published 1995 by
MACMILLAN PRESS LTD
Houndmills, Basingstoke, Hampshire RG21 6XS
and London
Companies and representatives
throughout the world

ISBN 0–333–58816–9 hardcover
ISBN 0–333–64648–7 paperback

A catalogue record for this book is available
from the British Library.

10   9   8   7   6   5   4   3   2   1
04 03 02 01 00 99 98 97 96 95

Printed in Great Britain by
Mackays of Chatham PLC
Chatham, Kent

To my Father

Contents

Preface

This book results from my long-standing interest in both contemporary France and the history and politics of the European Far Right. These interests were developed during my studies at the University of Leeds and at the London School of Economics and Political Science. My thanks are due to my teachers, David Bell and the late Peter Sedgwick at Leeds, and Professor Gordon Smith, Howard Machin, and John Madeley at the LSE.

I have benefited from interviews and discussion with several leading members of the National Front, and I would like to thank the following for their help and their time: Jean-Marie Le Pen, Carl Lang, Bruno Mégret and Marie-France Stirbois. I would also like to thank the Front's Press Officer, Alain Vizier, for his help in obtaining documents and Party publications. From the Socialist Party, Jean-Christophe Cambedelis and Gérard Fuchs gave their time to be interviewed. I am also grateful to Pierre Aidenbaum, the President of LICRA, who also granted me an interview.

Several French academics provided invaluable help. Professor Serge Hurtig has given me the benefit of his knowledge of the French political scene for several years, and has frequently been interviewed by me for radio programmes. I must thank Jean Charlot, Gérard Grunberg, Nonna Mayer, Pascal Perrineau and Colette Ysmal for sharing their expertise and insights. I would also like to thank Susan Dolamore and Susan Oldfield of the Modern Languages Library at Leeds University for their help in tracking down some rather obscure publications, and my colleague, Andrew Bell, of the BBC, with whom I shared a day 'at the fair'.

This project would not have seen the light of day, but for the help and support of three people. To David Bell who first aroused my interest in French politics several years ago, I owe a major debt of thanks. Not only has he supervised a related PhD thesis with wisdom and humour, but he has read and commented on successive versions of this draft. Gina Burgess has provided invaluable assistance, helping with the translation of material, the transcription of interviews and generally acting as a sounding board as work progressed. Above all, I am indebted to my wife, Dr Fiona Macintosh, for her constant support and encouragement. It is customary to absolve such people from responsibility for any inaccuracies, which I gladly do. However, if the book does have strengths, then I am more than willing to share the honours accordingly.

JONATHAN MARCUS
November 1994

viii

List of Abbreviations

CDS	Centre des Démocrates-Sociaux
CNIP	Centre National des Indépendants et Paysans
EPEN	Ethniki Politiki Enosis (National Political Union).
FANE	Fédération d'Action Nationale et Européenne
FEN	Fédération des Etudiants Nationalistes
FN	Front National
FPÖ	Austrian Freedom Party
GRECE	Groupement de Recherche et d'Etudes pour la Civilisation Européenne
HLM	Habitations à Loyer Modéré (Public Housing)
LICRA	Ligue Internationale Contre le Racisme et l'Antisémitisme
MSI	Movimento Sociale Italiano
PCF	Parti Communiste Français
PFN	Parti des Forces Nouvelles
PR	Parti Républicain
PS	Parti Socialiste
RPR	Rassemblement pour la République
SOFRES	Société Française d'Enquêtes par Sondages
SMIC	Salaire minimum industriel de croissance
UDF	Union pour la Démocratie Française

Introduction: The National Front's World

The Fair has come to town. It is September 1993, the late summer sun is shining and the various factions of the French far Right have gathered for a family day out. The National Front is holding its thirteenth annual Fête Bleu Blanc Rouge at the Pelouse de Reuilly, itself a small corner of the Bois de Vincennes, a vast, green wooded area, south-east of the centre of Paris. Once a royal hunting ground, the land was given to the City of Paris by Napoleon III to create a park for public use. There is a boating lake, flower gardens and the capital's largest zoo. But today, a menagerie of a rather different kind is on display.

Around the entrance barriers loiters a detatchment of the Front's *service d'ordre*, its own security force, cropped hair, black lace-up army boots, black bomber jackets. One holds an alsatian dog on a leash. They pose and posture, their uniforms and behaviour a parody of the Fifth Republic's own guardians of public order – the CRS riot police – on whom they are clearly modelled. However, there is no problem about getting in. Pay for your ticket (70 francs for the two-day event) and you can sample all the fun of the fair. Nothing in the National Front is free; admission is charged at all meetings and the Fête is no exception.

The Fair is laid out on a grand scale, two avenues of tents meeting in the form of a cross. There's cause for excitement; the Front may be marking time in electoral terms, but this year's Fête celebrates the Party's twentieth birthday. There are different marquees for each of the regions of France, manned by local Front activists. Inside each, tables and chairs are set out and regional food and drink can be purchased. Eating and drinking seem to be the principal activities for most visitors; from all sides, the fairgoer is assailed by oysters, *charcuterie*, armagnac, and cider. One vineyard in the Vaucluse is even offering specially labelled wine, *Cuvée du Front National*, each bottle bearing Le Pen's smiling face, superimposed over an outline of France.

By mid-morning the tented restaurants are doing a good trade. Crowds of people are strolling between the various attractions. There are pony rides, dodgem cars and a coconut shy, with, predictably, targets bearing the faces of Mitterrand, Chirac, Fabius and other leading members of the big political battalions, who (the Front insists) are trying to exclude it from office. The stall-holders are also doing good business, selling things that no self-respecting Front supporter could be without. There are badges calling for the reintroduction of the death penalty, cloth shoulder flashes bearing the Front's slogan '*France d'abord*' and every possible novelty carrying the Party's emblem of the tricolour flame. The face of the Front's President, Jean-Marie Le Pen, is everywhere, on T-shirts, book covers and buttons. Those with a taste for political futurology (and a good dose of optimism) can read an account of Le Pen's first hundred days in the Elysée, penned by Jean-Claud Martinez, one of his senior lieutenants.

The crowds thronging the stands are a bizarre mixture of the archetypes that make up the National Front's audience. Middle-class families, fathers in sports jackets and ties, mothers in summer dresses, rub shoulders with a sprinkling of skinheads. There are respectable-looking army veterans, wearing the red or black berets of the paratroops or the marine infantry, and people dressed in a variety of traditional country costumes. The Front's own stand, where you can join up, or buy posters and publications, is manned by smartly dressed young people, eager to explain and persuade – the sort of cadres who would not disgrace any of the formations of the mainstream Right. 'See,' says one Party worker I talk to, 'we are not monsters with two heads, just ordinary people.' He is right; it is the very normality of much of the National Front's world that surprises. Buy a copy of the Front's political yearbook and you can see passport-size photos of all its national and local officials and elected office-holders. Again, the faces that stare back from the pages are men and women who, for the most part, might occupy the ranks of any political formation.

A brief tour of the stands nonetheless provides clear evidence of the things that matter to the Front and its supporters. The past is everywhere. But it is a very particular past; a past which is by no means shared by many French men and women, and one that is certainly not celebrated by the Republic in which they live. One of the most potent visible symbols were the bright-red sacred hearts, each with a cross at its top: the badge of *Les Chouans*, the Vendéennes peasants who rose up against the French revolutionary armies in 1793, and who were slaughtered mercilessly. For the far Right as a whole, the Vendéean revolt symbolises opposition to the universalist values of those who overthrew the old order in1789.[1] The subsequent massacres are seen as the first crimes perpetrated in the name of progress by a revolutionary regime.

By far the largest of the sacred hearts were on the stand of the Catholic fundamentalist group, Chretienté solidarité. Le Pen himself is always eager to court the faithful. On the second day of the Fair, a Sunday, a special mass was held at an improvised open-air auditorium. In his closing speech – the grand finale of the Fair – Le Pen was in a religious frame of mind. 'Our values', he told the audience, 'are those of the Ten Commandments. We want to re-establish what is true, beautiful and good in all areas of life.' Le Pen switched between Old and New Testaments at will. Citing St John, the Apostle, he noted that 'truth was the criterion for liberty'. Chretienté solidarité has a significant position in the National Front's world, since it controls the only far-Right daily newspaper, *Présent*. The paper provides a platform for some of the most reactionary elements of the far Right, including monarchists and Catholic ultra-nationalists.

Elsewhere, more recent history was remembered. On the stand of the Cercle Nationale des Combattants, there were reproductions of colonial army posters and reminders of the heroes of the struggle to keep Algeria French. Such Circles, closely associated with Le Pen's movement, are an important part of the Front's activities – a way of spreading their message into areas where overt party-political action may be less appropriate. About a dozen such groupings were represented at the Fair, including a Circle of French Farmers, the grandly titled Cercle National des Gens d'Armes, concerned with military matters, a Circle for European Women, and a National Circle for Education, involving both teachers and parents. Each had its own literature, bulletins and newsletters.

While there were many rides and side-shows to attract children, younger aspects of the Front's activities were also well represented. The Party's youth wing, the Front National de la Jeunesse, had its own stand and there was even a scout-like organisation for nationalist-minded children, complete with its own uniform that looked much like that worn by the Vichy milice during the Second World War. There was a special exhibition of Asterix cartoons. Indeed, it was possible to buy a postcard caricature of Le Pen, represented as the mighty Obelix carrying a huge stone. You could even send it to your friends via a National Front post-box, bearing a special cancellation commemorating the Fair. There was also a good deal of music. A procession of folk groups and singers entertained the crowd, including one bizarre troupe who appeared dressed in a panoply of French military costume through the ages, ranging from a medieval knight, to a First World War infantryman.

Paradoxically, the Fair was reminiscent of a similar event run each year by the French Communist Party, the Fête de l'Humanité. Indeed, the various National Front Circles, associated journals, children's activities and so on, have created a sort of far Right counter-culture, almost a mirror image of that created by the Communists, and for very similar reasons. By establishing this web of interlocking organisations, a whole world is created in which the activist can feel at home.

However, the creation of a counter-culture is not an end in itself. The Fair contained a good deal of straightforward politics. Throughout most of the two-day jamboree, a Forum was held in a massive marquee, where leading Front politicians were quizzed by a panel of far-Right journalists, as well as taking questions from the floor. The climax was of course Le Pen's own speech on the Sunday afternoon.

At one end of the tented avenue there was a large open space. Here several hundred chairs were set out in rows, facing an elevated podium covered in light blue cloth. All this was set off by a backdrop comprising a massive French tricolour flag. Le Pen was billed to appear at half-past-four in the afternoon. People took their seats early, the air of expectation building up to a generalised euphoria when the National Front President appeared. For a time he was lost in the crowd of well-wishers. People were on their feet, clapping and shouting. The mood was carefully orches-trated, Le Pen choosing the right moment seemingly to rise out of the crowd, as he mounted the long flight of steps up to the podium.

Nonetheless his speech was a disappointment to the uninitiated. This was not the bravura performance that I, for one, had expected. True, it touched on all of the Party's long-standing concerns: the corruption of the political order, opposition to a federal Europe and immigration. But Le Pen's pre-sentation was strangely flat; perhaps he was tired. Ritual denunciations of mainstream politicians drew whistles and cat-calls from the audience, as if on cue, with the strongest condemnation being reserved for the leaders of the centre-Right Government. The speech ended in the traditional manner with the Front's President leading the crowd in singing the *Marseillaise*.

Perhaps the most bizarre episode during the Fair came after the Sunday morning mass, when Le Pen presided at the presentation of a cheque for eighty thousand Francs, to a woman whose case had become something of a *cause célèbre* to the Front. In February 1989, Marie-José Garnier, the so-called 'baker of Reims', had fired on a group of attackers – *Présent* described them as 'a horde of ethnic assailants' – mortally wounding one of them.[2] According to the paper, while acquitted by the courts, she still had to pay damages to the family of the dead youth. The cheque was to help her make a fresh start.

Perhaps her trade was an appropriate one. Her very title, *la boulangère de Reims*, conjured up memories of another name, that of General Boulanger – no baker, but the far Right's champion in the 1880s. After a string of election victories, Boulanger seemed ready to march on the Elysée and seize power, but 'indecisive, intimidated and distracted by a passionate love affair, he fled the country'.[3] Le Pen, like Boulanger, is very much a larger-than-life figure. But here any similarity ends. For the National Front President is undoubtedly one of the great survivors in French politics. And he is made of much sterner stuff than the errant General.

FROM 'LE SEIZIEME' TO STRASBOURG

The National Front's headquarters are situated in the rue du Général Clergerie, in the Sixteenth Arrondissement, not far from the Arc de Triomphe.* Compared with the political nerve-centres of some of the other major parties – and certainly those on the Left – it is a modest affair. Its address commemorates neither a great Resistance hero – as does that of the Communist Party's modern glass-and-concrete structure at Place Colonel Fabien; nor does it have the grand historical echoes of a famous French victory, like the Socialist Party's headquarters, not far from the National Assembly, in rue Solférino. General Clergerie may not be one of France's best-known commanders of the First World War. But as a young officer he took part in the campaign that established a French protectorate in Tunisia – a decisive moment in the Third Republic's colonial expansion – an enterprise which Jean-Marie Le Pen might well regard as giving his address a certain appropriateness.[4]

Just as at all the other political parties' headquarters, security is tight. The Front's offices are protected by an outer wire-mesh gate and a remotely-locked door. Once inside, the small, congested lobby has a rather spartan appearance, relieved only by a lighted display case on one side of the room containing Party publications and enamel badges and pins. The contrast with the plush, modernised offices of the Socialist Party – accommodation that would suit a thrusting advertising agency or public relations firm – continues as you head upstairs. There's no lift at the Front's headquarters, there are no pictures on the wall of the stairwell and, at the top, there is little more than a landing with an old hat-stand and two leather arm-chairs, that have seen better days.

But appearances can be deceptive. The Party machine itself is far from dilapidated. The Front believes that its advance is continuing and that its best times are still ahead. The offices of the Party's leading figures are tastefully decorated; there is a charcoal drawing of Venice and prints of

*In January 1995 the National Front moved its general headquarters to Saint-Cloud, in the Paris suburbs. The party's main operations are now housed in a long, low-rise building, dubbed by Le Pen 'Le Paquet-bot'.

Napoleon's retreat from Moscow. Computers hum, televisions and video-recorders stand ready. And from behind a black ash-veneered desk, Bruno Mégret, effectively the Party's number two, seeks to explain that the Front is indeed a new force, for a new political age. Mégret is a small, dark-haired man with a piercing gaze. Now in his mid-forties, he ran Le Pen's Presidential campaign in 1988 and has served as both a Deputy in the National Assembly and as a Member of the European Parliament.

Bruno Mégret discounted suggestions that the Front was stuck on an electoral plateau, unable to make further advances, even if it was able to retain its current level of support. However, he did hold out an alternative strategy to a slow electoral progression towards power, what he termed a '*phénomène de rupture*', a crisis in the political life of the nation at which point the Front would be called on to take over.[5] So, here at last, was the mask slipping? What price the Front's claimed democratic credentials? 'There was no question of anything illegal or insurrectionary', said Mr Mégret. What he meant was that the Front could 'suddenly arrive at the threshold of power,' propelled by the forces of political circumstance, just like the Gaullist wave of 1958. 'They arrived in office legally, as a result of the popular vote, but in a very rapid way.' According to Mégret, the current political system was disenfranchising the people: 'The National Front's voters along with those of the Ecologists are being denied parliamentary representation', he said. But it was worse than that. Mr Mégret is not without a sense of humour and he argued that the methods of the Prime Minister, Eduard Balladur, were actually putting people to sleep. 'I believe', he warned, 'that there could be a rude awakening, a bit like what happened in 1968.'

There is no doubt that the electoral system does not work in the Front's favour. The Communist Party, for example, won some 9 per cent of the first ballot vote at the 1993 Legislative election. It emerged with 23 seats; the National Front, whose first ballot tally was over 12 per cent, emerged with none.[6] Indeed, apart from local office-holders, you have to travel all the way from Paris to Strasbourg to find a parliamentary stage on which the Front's national figures can perform.

Strasbourg, December 1993. The door to Jean-Marie Le Pen's offices at the European Parliament is ajar. Inside, he can be heard talking, issuing instructions to a string of assistants and colleagues who seem to arrive at regular intervals. Though our meeting has long been scheduled, his press secretary shakes his head doubtfully. 'The agenda means little', he explains. 'If Le Pen chooses to fit you in, he will.' On the wall facing one of the secretaries in the outer office, there is a bizarre juxtaposition of images: a poster, in English, proclaims 'Rugby League is about winning', while beneath it Le Pen himself smiles down, with his anti-corruption slogan 'clean hands and head held high'. But I am given little time to muse on a possible connection.

With a flurry of departing courtiers, the door opens fully and I am ushered into Le Pen's office. This is clearly a port of call, rather than a home-from-home. There is little about the room's modern furnishings to betray anything of its occupant's character. Le Pen is business-like, but affable; relaxed at the end of a long day and clearly flattered that his movement has provoked interest on this side of the Channel.

There seemed little point in tackling the National Front President head-on. For twenty years he has denied all charges of racism, claiming that it is not immigrants, but the politicians who brought them into the country who are his real targets. I choose the indirect approach. Why, then, did Le Pen believe that his Party attracted such opprobrium? 'It was all rumour and scandal,' he insisted, 'created by our adversaries. You see examples of this all the time,' he went on. 'Why, only this morning, I saw the reports about Zhirinovsky. The new Hitler has arrived they said. But I remembered that much the same thing was said about Yeltsin.'[7] Le Pen clearly felt some sympathy with the leader of the ultra-nationalists in Moscow, whose success had been one of the more noteworthy aspects of Russia's recent general election. 'Each time a character who is a bit anti-conformist arrives in the world of politics, he is immediately dubbed a second Hitler', explained Le Pen. 'It's a great honour for Hitler', he added ironically.

But if the press and media had stirred up anti-Front sentiments, the Party's President was now feeling the absence of their attention. 'For more than a year now,' he complained, 'we have been subjected to a real boycott. I have never been invited on to any of the big television programmes, nor for that matter have my lieutenants, although we represent more than three million voters.'

What about Bruno Mégret's idea of a political rupture, I ask: a break in continuity, a crisis that would propel the Front into power? Le Pen leaned over and tapped my knee for emphasis. 'Let me remind you of something,' he said. 'The so-called democratic parties are trying to exclude us from the game. But one small episode, the so-called Headscarves Affair, and the following Sunday, Madame Stirbois [the Front's candidate in a parliamentary by-election] was elected with 63 per cent of the vote.[8] Madame Roussel in Marseilles received 49 per cent. This means she really won 54 per cent', claimed Le Pen, 'for in Marseilles 5 per cent of the votes are

forged. On the same day one of our young candidates in a cantonal election defeated a Socialist who had been there for thirty years!' Le Pen
paused for effect. 'In other words,' he went on, 'with a simple episode
like the Headscarves Affair, in virtually three constituencies we broke into
the majority parties' stronghold. It's at that moment that the establishment
parties took fright.' In Le Pen's view there was a clear message here.
'There is a risk that if a serious event happens – if a million Algerian
refugees arrived in France for example – it could sweep away the electoral
barriers that have been raised against us.' There was a certain irony here,
in that a man who campaigned so fervently against immigration, could
raise the idea of a massive influx of foreigners as one of the best hopes for
a springboard to allow his own Party to leap the electoral hurdles and to
arrive in power. But any irony seemed to be lost on Mr Le Pen himself.

What would happen, I asked the National Front leader, if he did not win
the Presidency in 1995? 'That was possible', he acknowledged. In that
case, what would have been his contribution to French politics? Le Pen
thought for a moment. 'We have re-built the Right,' he argued, 'we have
given this political family something that it didn't have, continuity and
durability.[9] That's assured by an apparatus, a structure, which is capable of
filling in the gaps, between bursts of sentiment and fervour. In the past,' he
explained, 'the Right was devoted to its cause and courageous, but it
couldn't sustain itself over time.' But in its President's view, the Front
had also played another significant role, albeit a thankless one. 'We have
been the look-out in the tower, warning of impending danger. We know
that a Cassandra is never much liked, but that's the part we will have
played. And if we don't get into power we will have re-orientated French
politics to face new dangers.'

Chief among these dangers, at least in Le Pen's view, is the threat posed
by immigration. He denied absolutely that he was a xenophobe. And then
he turned to one of the great simplifying metaphors for which he is
famous: 'The flourishing of nations,' he argued, 'is best accomplished on
their own territory, in their own country. It's a bit like in an apartment,' he
went on; 'one doesn't just let anyone in. For family life to remain stable, it
needs a nucleus, a father, a mother, children and grandparents. Then there
are friends to whom one opens the door from time to time. And then there
are the bandits, against whom one bolts the doors and shutters, because
they are a threat. If you like, I extrapolate from this, to the national level.
But it's not a closed view of things at all.' As evidence of how open the
National Front is, Le Pen cited its leadership's domestic arrangements.
'It's amusing,' he said, 'when the Party's administrative team is accused
of narrow-minded nationalism, because almost all of its leaders are either

sons of immigrants or married to foreigners. It is true,' he insisted; 'for example Bruno Gollnisch, one of our stars, is married to a Japanese woman and as for me, my wife is half-Greek.'

DREUX: WHERE THE ELECTORAL MARCH BEGAN

The town of Dreux, some 70 kilometres west of Paris – easily within commuting distance of the capital – has a significant place in the National Front's electoral history. It was the site of its first dramatic emergence on to the political scene. It was here that one of Le Pen's chief lieutenants, Jean-Pierre Stirbois, established his political base during the late 1970s. At the Municipal elections of 1983, this grassroots work achieved its first significant results: Stirbois was elected to the town council. After his death in 1988, his widow, Marie-France Stirbois, took the Dreux parliamentary seat at a spectacular by-election victory in November 1989.

Some four years later, in March 1993, Madame Stirbois is back on the hustings, defending her seat in what looks set to be a close-run race. However, Dreux has some surprises. The town has suffered from rapid expansion, high immigration, and rising unemployment; Jean-Pierre Stirbois chose his political power-base well. Beyond the town-centre, grim barrack-like blocks of public housing attest to the hopelessness of many of the Drouais.

But the town-centre itself is a total contrast. It still looks much the same as it once did in the years before the expansion of the1950s – a charming market town. Most of the main streets are pedestrianised. Squares are newly-paved and set-off with *fin-de-siècle* lamp standards and flower-beds. Overlooking the town from a wooded hill is the ornately-domed Chapel of Saint-Louis; built in the early nineteenth century, it was the last resting-place for many of the princes of the House of Orléans.

However, some two-thirds of the constituency and probably half its voters live in the countryside. I drove towards the village of Chateauneuf-en-Thymerais. It has some two-and-a-half thousand inhabitants, and lies to the south-west of Dreux. The countryside was flat; rolling plains of modern agro-industry, barely a hedgerow or fence, with only the spires of the country churches in the distance marking out the various hamlets and villages. It is a France dear to the political salesmen: a spire like those piercing the horizon figured prominently on François Mitterrand's posters during his Presidential campaign in 1981. This image of *La France profonde*, the underlying or essential France, has also been much used by Le Pen.

Some five kilometres outside the town National Front posters began to appear. They carried Marie-France's picture, set against a yellow-flowered field of oil-seed rape, the mandatory church spire over her left shoulder. None of the other candidates' posters were much in evidence. Maybe it was apathy on their part, but the National Front's teams had clearly beeen up early and done their work well.

Chateauneuf-en-Thymerais's market was the typical mixture of cheap clothing on racks, live chickens in crates, *charcuterie* counters and cheeses. The National Front candidate had come to press the flesh of early morning shoppers. Looking like a Tory lady down from Westminster and accompanied by a small team of supporters, all solid citizens, she did the round of the stalls. Marie-France offered encouragement here, exhortations to vote National Front there. Asked by one stall-holder if she had any doubts about the the vital second round, she claimed her campaign was motoring along and moving into even higher gear. 'We're into fifth,' she quipped, 'and the turbo-charger is on.'

On the face of it you wouldn't think Chateauneuf was encouraging territory for the Front. It has a Socialist mayor and only some 3 to 4 per cent unemployment, many people working in Chartres, some 22 kilometres to the south-east. But in these rural *communes* the National Front does seem to gather support. Dreux is not so far away and the local newspapers are full of the 'terrible things' that go on there: mugging, crime and delinquency. Agriculture faces an uncertain future – the Front's strongly anti-Maastricht and anti-GATT message evoking considerable sympathy among many farmers.

Later in the day, Madame Stirbois visited the farm of one of her leading activists, Jean-Luc Martin, himself a Front candidate at the last regional elections. Martin's farmhouse and outbuildings in the village of Bailleau-l'Evêque are ranged around a large courtyard. The family dining room was the setting for an impromptu press conference for local reporters.[10] After a glass of red wine and a slice of cake, we took our seats around a large oak table. Marie-France Stirbois was flanked by Marie-Renée Maissen, another Front candidate who had won through to the second round of voting.

This was the starting-point of the meeting. Two Front candidates present and both women! The Front is not noted for its feminist line, but Marie-France would have none of it. 'The National Assembly is a semi-circle of men,' she noted, 'and it is good that we will be there for the 53 per cent of women in this country.' The outgoing Deputy went straight on to the offensive, launching into the mainstream Right. Referring to her Gaullist opponent, she commented that 'another old boot in Parliament won't serve any purpose; we want to provide an incentive for people to vote against single-party dominance. What is needed are Deputies with the courage to speak out.' Marie-France spoke of her hopes that Marie-Renée too would defeat her opponent, whom she described as 'an eminent member of the mainstream Right's Departmental *nomenklatura*'.

The two women then moved on to discuss the Front's agricultural programme, which provoked some lively exchanges between the candidates and the journalists present. Just what was the Front's policy, they asked? Jean-Marie Le Pen, it seemed, would offer hope, as he would in virtually every other area of policy. The first step, according to Madame Stirbois, would be a moratorium on agricultural debts. But both candidates wouldn't be drawn about what would come next. There was a lot of talk of corruption, Third World debt and so on. 'We are in a war,' claimed Marie-France Stirbois, 'an economic war pitting France, and Europe as a whole, against the Americans.' What was needed, she insisted, was firmness. Few of the journalists were convinced. But the press conference was a typical example of the Front's strategy: it offered seemingly simple solutions to complex problems. But many of the Dreux voters were convinced. Marie-France Stirbois failed to retain her seat by only the narrowest of margins – a mere 105 votes.

1 The Emergence of the National Front

Ever since its formation in 1972, the National Front has been associated with the name of one man, Jean-Marie Le Pen. When the Party obtained its first electoral successes during the early 1980s, it was Le Pen who personified its message and it was his rhetoric that, in large part, gained the Party a following. Le Pen and the Front have become so closely associated that it is now hard to imagine the Party in the absence of its charismatic and ebullient leader. However, at the outset, and for much of the1970s, Le Pen's position was by no means assured. The National Front was not his creation. It was established by the leadership of France's most important postwar neo-fascist organisation, Ordre Nouveau. Its aim was to create a movement that would bring together the disparate and often feuding families of the Extreme Right to amplify their message. But the National Front was also to be a 'front' organisation in the literal sense, providing a respectable political facade, behind which the more traditional activist and street politics of the Far Right would continue.

There had been earlier attempts to federate the Far Right's splinters, all of which had come to nothing. Indeed, for most of its first decade of existence there was no sign that the National Front itself would be any more successful. However, the late 1970s were to be a turning-point. Though marked even to this day by its origins, the Front nonetheless underwent an ideological and organisational renewal. Many of the old neo-fascist cadres were either expelled or isolated. Others made their peace with the movement largely on Le Pen's terms. The result was that the National Front was able to divest itself of much of the old political baggage that the Far Right had carried with it during the long crossing of the political wilderness since 1945. It emerged from the 1970s as a more modern political force which, though eager to maintain its sectarian base, sought to present its populist message to a much wider audience. Le Pen may not have been the first to recognise that the Far Right needed a new political strategy. But he alone was able to carry out this transformation. Throughout the postwar years, despite a few brief attempts at pursuing an electoral path, the Far Right remained largely an army of the shadows. Le Pen's achievement was to leave the shadows behind, turning the National Front, in the process, into the fourth largest political force in France.

FROM THE LIBERATION TO ALGIERS

In the immediate aftermath of the Second World War, the extreme Right inevitably suffered from its association with collaboration and with the Vichy regime of Marshall Pétain. In what the French lyrically term *l'épuration*, the purification, many collaborators were summarily shot. Others were tried and sentenced to death or imprisonment. Vichy's head of state, Marshal Pétain himself, was given a life-sentence, and his Prime Minister, Pierre Laval, was executed by a firing-squad. Often, however, and certainly at a local level, the search for justice was mixed with an equal desire for revenge. From June 1944 onwards, as each successive part of France was liberated, there was a good deal of settling of old scores. Statistics are inevitaby difficult to come by, but the figure of some 10 800 summary executions, given by De Gaulle in 1959, remains a reasonable estimate. At the time, De Gaulle himself noted that this figure was 'quite limited ... considering the number of crimes committed [during the Occupation] and their frightful consequences'.[1]

It is perhaps easy to overestimate the extent of the postwar purges of collaborators and Nazi sympathisers. France's appetite for retribution was limited. By the early 1950s, many of those imprisoned were receiving amnesties, and the painful years of Occupation soon became shrouded in a purposeful cloak of obscurity. The resistance myth became part of the Republican pantheon. The other side of the coin – co-existence with the Nazi occupiers at best, collaboration at worst – was rarely a subject for public debate.[2] The postwar political climate, the revulsion against Nazi crimes, and the restoration of democratic institutions, meant that the far Right was effectively marginalised. Nonetheless, while deprived by *l'épuration* of most of the leading figures of the Vichy era, it sought both to survive and to regenerate itself. One French historian describes the extreme-Right during this period as 'the fire beneath the cinders'.[3]

Despite the purges and the trials, there were still enough former collaborators to keep the far Right alive. Maurice Bardèche, Vichy's most prominent intellectual survivor, became the principal theoretician of a neo-fascism in French colours. He condemned both *l'épuration* and the Nuremberg trials as 'the victors' justice'.[4] He articulated aspects of what would later become the 'revisionist' view of the Nazi era – that the crimes of the Nazi regime were not unique and that such crimes occur in all major conflicts. Furthermore, these excesses were not, in Bardèche's view, necessarily an inherent part of the fascist scheme of politics, but rather an aberration, and a German one at that. Bardèche was a disciple of Italian fascism rather than German Nazism.

During the early 1950s, he sought to spread these ideas both through a fascist international – the *Mouvement social européen* – and through a journal, *Défense de l'Occident*. Publications such as this were important in spreading the far Right's message to a new generation of activists, attracted by a strident anti-communism as much as by some of the more traditional clarion-calls of the French Right. The weekly paper *Rivarol,* which first appeared in January 1951, played a significant role in providing a platform for the various elements of the postwar Far Right: the neo-fascists, the supporters of Vichy, and the heirs of the fascist leagues of the 1930s. From the outset, *Rivarol* was firmly in the Vichy tradition – among its leading writers was Maurice Gait, the former Commissioner for Youth in Pétain's regime. Another was François Brigneau, one of the most barbed and able polemicists of the far Right, and a former member of the Vichy paramilitary milice. Brigneau was later to join Ordre nouveau, where he played a significant role in campaigning for the creation of the National Front. He stood as a Front candidate at the 1989 Municipal elections though his principal activity has been as an editorial writer for *National-Hebdo*, which is effectively the Front's weekly paper. Brigneau personifies a number of the traditions that go to make up the National Front: opposition to Algerian independence (which led to his first encounter with Le Pen), Catholic fundamentalism, a primitive anti-semitism, as well as a strong anti-Zionism.

If individuals like Brigneau were able to articulate different aspects of the far Right's message, journals like *Rivarol* provided them with a platform for discussion. It began in the 1950s as a vehicle to try to rehabilitate the Vichy regime. In the 1970s it drew close to the principal neo-fascist organisation of the day, Ordre Nouveau. Indeed, François Duprat, the formation's leading ideologist and an important political influence on Le Pen himself, was a regular contributor. *Rivarol* strongly supported the National Front during the Party's early years, while more recently, its editorial line has championed a radical anti-Zionism and revisionist historiography.

However, the semi-clandestine coteries and intellectual groupings of the early 1950s were beset by schisms and personal rivalries. They were unable to gather a mass appeal; and until the political emergence of a repackaged version of the National Front in the early 1980s, the far Right's electoral success was minimal. Nonetheless, during the 1950s two new factors appeared to offer the heirs of Vichy some hope of an election breakthrough. The first of these was the revolt of the small businessmen that crystallised around Pierre Poujade. This anti-tax, anti-capitalist protest movement, was in large part a reaction against the forces of economic modernisation. But despite registering significant initial successes, the

Poujadist wave receded almost as quickly as it had arisen.[5] The second factor was the colonial struggle in Algeria. Beset by political problems at home, the war in Algeria proved the final straw for the parliamentary regime of the Fourth Republic. The Algerian conflict seemingly provided the far Right with its best mobilising theme since the Liberation, and its best opportunity to influence national political events. A variety of associations were formed to campaign on behalf of keeping Algeria French. Here at last was a contemporary issue capable of raising significant passions. Algeria provided a focus for many of the far Right's concerns: their hostility to the Left, their belief that France's historic destiny was being undermined, and their concern at France's diminishing status in a world increasingly dominated by two rival superpowers.[6]

However, the struggle over French Algeria, rather than demonstrating the far Right's strengths, ultimately served to illustrate its abiding weakness. General De Gaulle's grip on power and the creation of a strong Gaullist movement extending from the centre to the right of the political spectrum, effectively created a barrier to the far Right's advance. The cause of *Algérie française* may have stirred passions, but it was not the issue to federate the far Right or to give it widespread appeal. The April 1962 Referendum – which effectively demonstrated popular support for Algerian independence and ending the war – represented a success for the General. Nearly 65 per cent of the electorate backed De Gaulle's proposals. The 'No' camp – the supporters of *Algérie française*, won just over 6.5 per cent of the electorate, some 1 800 000 votes.[7]

The Far Right hoped to build on this base, pursuing both a strident anti-communism and a bitter anti-Gaullism. It sought to use the Presidential election of 1965 to demonstrate its electoral strength against the Gaullist monolith. The mechanics of a Presidential contest – the need to rally around a single candidate – would also help to encourage some sort of unity in the far Right's fractious ranks. In 1963, Jean-Marie Le Pen was instrumental in creating a *Comité d'initiative pour une candidature nationale*. Its chosen Presidential candidate was Jean-Louis Tixier-Vignancour, a fervent nationalist and supporter of *Algérie française*. Tixier-Vignancour had been Deputy General Secretary for Information in the Vichy regime, and in the postwar period he had flirted with several neo-fascist organisations. This *curriculum vitae* enabled his campaign to generate widespread support from the different families of the far Right.

Tixier-Vignancour's Presidential campaign, in large part orchestrated by Le Pen, called for the tearing up of the Evian agreements which had ended the war in Algeria. In his rhetoric there were clear references to the problem of immigration. He declared that while he was a supporter of

'French Algeria', he did not back the idea of an 'Algerian France'. He railed against the dangers of an invasion by the starving, the sick and those without training – an early articulation of what was later to become one of Le Pen's own favourite themes.[8]

In the event, Tixier-Vignancour obtained a mere 5.3 per cent of the votes cast. The far Right's hopes for an electoral surge were dashed. One phase of the far Right's postwar political struggle, therefore, effectively ended in 1965. What had begun in 1956 with the explosion of Poujadisme, was prolonged by the struggle over *Algérie française*. This 'colonial nationalism' thus enabled the far Right to emerge from isolation. But once the colonial issue was removed from mainstream political debate, the far Right lost its best mobilising issue. This electoral strategy had run its brief course, and Tixier-Vignancour's Presidential result confirmed its failure.

During the succeeding years a variety of neo-fascist groups emerged, coalesced and then split apart. All this activity, despite the considerable ideological and intellectual effort that was invested in it, was essentially marginal. The far Right had two principal problems. The apparent stability of the Gaullist regime afforded little hope of the sort of crisis or chaos that might provide an opening for an insurrectionary neo-fascist or reactionary force. But the far Right's very marginality, its divisions, and above all its bully-boy image, precluded any more legitimate approach towards political power.

Over the second half of the 1960s, this negative image was further strengthened by the activities of Occident. Founded in 1964, at its peak Occident probably had no more than six hundred activists, mainly based in Paris. But it was known for the extreme violence of its activities, and it was finally banned in 1968. Whilst its notoriety would earn it little more than a footnote in France's postwar political history, its young guard included several leaders, like François Duprat and Alain Robert, who were soon to figure prominently in Ordre Nouveau. Later still, they were to be instrumental in establishing the National Front itself.[9]

THE QUEST FOR A PARALLEL STRATEGY

In November 1969, one year after the dissolution of Occident, many of its leading figures helped to form a new grouping, Ordre Nouveau. This was quickly to become the most significant neo-fascist movement in postwar France. But it was also much more than this. From the outset, the New Order included representatives from all the generations of the Far Right:

supporters of the Vichy regime, former Poujadistes, neo-fascists, and advocates of *Algérie française*. The extreme Right had watched with horror as the 'events' of 1968 unfolded. Gaullism's hand had ultimately been strengthened. Their own division and ideological confusion seemed to offer them little hope of broadening their appeal.

During the spring and summer of 1969 there was a growing debate within far Right circles on the need for a new 'front' organisation, behind which the various factions and splinters could sink their differences.[10] New Order was one of the first responses to this growing desire for a new sort of political vehicle. It emerged at a time when the far Right in Germany, Italy and Britain seemed on the verge of making electoral headway and New Order explicitly took the Italian neo-fascist organisation, the Movimento Sociale Italiano, or MSI, as its model.[11] Its goal was to emulate the MSI's success. It wanted to become a significant political force in its own right.

However, New Order's rhetoric continued to insist on the need for revolutionary change. Despite claims that it opposed terrorism and insurrection, it sought to pursue a double strategy – street-violence against the Left on the one hand, with a professed electoral approach on the other. The two parallel aspects of its approach to politics were clearly displayed in March 1971, when the movement presented its list of candidates for the Municipal elections at a sports stadium in the Paris suburbs. News of the gathering provoked threats of a strong counter-demonstration, but New Order was ready to defend itself. It mounted guard at the stadium with its own paramilitary security force, young men in helmets, equipped with iron bars and shields.[12] The rhetoric from the podium was equally threatening, with François Duprat asserting that New Order's mission was to cleanse the country of all those who represented a threat to the safety of its citizens.

The electoral progress of New Order was limited. In the March 1971 Municipal elections in Paris it obtained some 2.6 per cent of the vote. Its leaders were now looking towards the Legislative elections due in 1973. Indeed, elsewhere on the far Right, the debate on forming some sort of broader-based grouping to fight the campaign was continuing. New Order was an active participant in these discussions and sought to take advantage of its position as the strongest and best-organised movement on the far Right to influence the proceedings. In June 1972, New Order held its second Congress which was to set in motion the formation of the National Front. To further its dual strategy, and with the parliamentary elections beckoning, the movement was eager to turn itself into a political party. However, there were differences as to how broadly based this should be.

François Brigneau argued strongly for a national front that would bring together the various tendencies of the far Right, while still respecting their differences. He also entertained hopes that such a front could reach out towards a broader audience, on the conservative Right and even towards the centre of the political spectrum. New Order's own publications stressed the need to moderate the organisation's hard line, at least in public. The prevailing view was that it was vital to create a current of opinion that would give the far Right's message the appeal it deserved. New Order militants were enjoined to work within this front organisation, eschewing revolutionary purity and setting aside any rivalries between the various families and traditions. New Order's hopes for the new organisation couldn't have been clearer: 'For us', said the movement's weekly paper, 'the National Front represents an opportunity to break out of the political ghetto.'[13]

THE NATIONAL FRONT'S FIRST INCARNATION

The National Front was founded on 5 October 1972. While it gathered together a heterogeneous collection of far Right groups, including supporters of the Vichy regime, of *Algérie française*, and monarchists, it was the neo-fascists of Ordre Nouveau who initially held the reins of power. Nonetheless, New Order's leadership was well aware that the ambiguity of its double language – the attempt to pursue a violent activism, in parallel with electoral politics – had not paid off. Accordingly, they chose a leader for the new National Front who might give it a more respectable public face. Jean-Marie Le Pen was well-known in far Right circles. He was, relatively speaking, a moderate. He had not been directly involved in the neo-fascist groupings of the postwar years. His career had taken him from Poujadisme, via support for French Algeria, to a position as one of the principal backers of Tixier-Vignancour's presidential campaign. The fact that he had not sprung from the ranks of New Order was seen by many as a positive advantage, making him better able to play the role of federator. Jean-Marie Le Pen became the National Front's President.

New Order's grip on the new formation was strong. Its leading figures played a prominent role in the political bureau that presided over the Front's affairs. François Brigneau was the National Front's vice-President and Alain Robert its General Secretary. But each position was paired with an assistant's post held by a figure from a different tradition. Brigneau was deputy to Le Pen himself. Roger Holeindre and Pierre Durand – who were seen as supporting Le Pen – were made Assistant Secretary-General and

Assistant Treasurer, respectively.[14] The Treasurer's post itself was given to Pierre Bousquet, whose supporters were grouped around the magazine *Militant*, which peddled a stridently Eurocentric nationalism that was, in a sense, the political equivalent of the *nouvelle droite's* cultural project.

Once again the model for the National Front was to be the Italian neo-fascist Party, the MSI. The Front even copied its emblem of the tricolour flame. The Front also hoped to emulate the MSI's electoral success: in the Italian general election of 1972, it had obtained 8.7 per cent of the vote, winning 56 parliamentary seats.[15] However, such results were to prove elusive for the National Front. At the French general election of 1973, it was able to field only a little over one hundred candidates, well short of the figure of four hundred that it had promised to support. Some two-thirds of those carrying its colours into the contest were concentrated in the Paris region. The Front campaigned under the slogan of 'Defending the French'. Considerable stress was placed on the need to support the family: there was a call for a programme to encourage an increased birth-rate. The Front's economic policy contained a strong dose of corporatism, that went hand in hand with support for small-business. While the Party's economic policy was to change considerably, many aspects of the Front's later, more populist appeal were already present, not least its anti-immigrant message. Immigration was seen as a clear danger to France. In the Front's view it was linked to crime and urban insecurity; it was a drain on the social services. Any immigrant who put a foot wrong was to be expelled immediately.

The election outcome, a mere 2.3 per cent of the votes cast in those constituencies where it ran candidates, was a major disappointment for the Front. And the results provoked serious repercussions within its ranks. There had been considerable uneasiness in sections of New Order about pursuing a broadly-based front strategy. The National Front's poor showing only heightened these concerns. There was a growing division within New Order, between those who wanted to consolidate its position within the National Front, and those who sought to end the whole experience, once and for all. These strains were evident at a special Congress of the Front, held at the end of April 1973. Le Pen argued that three options were now open: everyone could go their own way; the Front could proceed as a federation of different groups; or, his own preference, it could fuse its various factions into a single party.[16] The meeting was not able to come to any clear conclusion, and New Order's own Congress, a few weeks later in June, also failed to outline a clear strategy for the future. Nonetheless, in an effort to win back the support of its more activist wing, the movement embarked upon a strident and often violent anti-immigrant campaign. A rally in Paris, on 21 June, provoked fighting between New

Order supporters and those of the Communist League. New Order militants then turned on the police. Many were injured and police vehicles set
on fire. By the end of the month, the authorities had banned both groups.

Le Pen sought to take advantage of New Order's dissolution to consolidate his position at the head of the National Front. Le Pen sacked Alain
Robert and replaced him as Secretary-General with one of his own close
collaborators, Dominique Chaboche. For a brief period there were effectively two National Fronts, with both Le Pen and Alain Robert claiming to
speak on behalf of the Party. Le Pen went to the courts, and secured for
himself the sole right to use the label National Front. In November 1974,
Alain Robert and François Brigneau founded a rival movement, the Parti
des Forces Nouvelles (PFN), which, throughout the late 1970s, was to
contest the Front's claim to be the principal political force on the far
Right.

The differences over strategy which caused the split between Le Pen
and many of his erstwhile New Order allies, did not result in a tidy distinction between the neo-fascists and the other families of the far Right.
Throughout the 1970s, both the National Front and the Parti des Forces
Nouvelles continued to draw support from neo-fascist activists. Indeed,
one of the most significant figures in French neo-fascism, François Duprat,
opted to remain with Le Pen, when most of his New Order colleagues
broke away. Some have even argued that Duprat was effectively Le Pen's
number two; what is clear is that he exercised a significant influence over
the National Front's President.[17] At the same time, Duprat continued his
involvement with a network of neo-fascist organisations, acting as a link
between such groups (both at home and abroad) and the Front itself.
Duprat continued to personify the far Right's dual strategy and double
language; openly acknowledging in his writings that despite the integration of many New Order supporters into the National Front, they had not
lost, what he termed, their 'national-revolutionary' aspirations.[18] Duprat
played a significant role in 'popularising' revisionist literature about the
Nazi Holocaust. He was also an admirer of the Nazi army – especially of
the volunteer SS units, that played an active role on the Eastern Front –
and he sought to rehabilitate the image of these units that had fought, as he
saw it, not so much for the Nazis, but against Bolshevism.

It was Duprat's 'national-revolutionary' connections that brought
the neo-Nazi organisation FANE (Fédération d'Action Nationale et
Européenne) into the National Front's orbit. This group was headed by
Marc Fredriksen, who himself stood as a National Front candidate at the
1978 Legislative elections. Fredriksen's movement was virulently anti-
semitic and was suspected of carrying out a variety of attacks against

Jewish and other targets. While he himself had neither the intellectual ability nor the significance of Duprat, Fredriksen's supporters were useful to the National Front, especially in providing activist manpower at election times.

Duprat was killed in a car-bomb explosion in March 1978. His death greatly weakened the neo-fascist element within the National Front. As we shall see in the next chapter, other elements of the far Right were already moving closer to Le Pen's formation. New leaders were emerging, not least Jean-Pierre Stirbois, who was to take on the 'national-revolutionaries', effectively removing them from the National Front's leading circles. The National Front's message was changing too. During the late 1970s, the struggle against immigration was given added salience. A special edition of the Party's journal *Le National* was devoted to the problem, setting out an early version of a formulation that has subsequently been regularly updated by the Front's propagandists, 'One million unemployed is one million immigrants too many'.[19] The Front's presentation of its economic policies was greatly expanded. A detailed programme, *Droite et démocratie économique*, was published in 1978. This turned its back on the corporatism that had long tempted many sections of the postwar far Right. The keynote was now economic liberalism; the aim was to reduce the state's involvement in the economy wherever practicable.[20]

The Front was starting to learn some of the lessons of the far Right's experiences over the course of the mid-1970s. However, the two rival political formations continued to campaign over the same narrow ground. For a time it looked as though the PFN of Pascal Gauchon was doing marginally better than Le Pen's party. Its desire to become the rightward element of the existing majority – effectively radicalising the mainstream Right in the process – had little impact, but it at least seemed to offer a more realistic approach than the 'go it alone' approach of the National Front. The PFN also seemed better able to forge links with like-minded formations elsewhere in Europe. For the 1979 European election campaign it struck a deal with both the Italian MSI and the Francoist Fuerza Nueva in Spain to campaign under a single flag – the Euro-Right.

An attempt was made – largely by journals such as *Rivarol* – to get the National Front and the PFN to put forward a joint list, though after some progress, this idea collapsed amid bitter recriminations. The Presidential election of 1981 highlighted the marginalisation of the far Right. Neither Gauchon nor Le Pen could obtain the 500 signatures from elected Deputies or Councillors necessary to stand. But if 1981 marked the beginning of the end for the PFN, it paradoxically heralded a new era for the National Front.[21] For during 1980–81 a series of factors helped to lay the foundations for the National Front's renewal. The 'national-revolutionaries' were largely marginalised by the so-called *solidaristes*, whose leading figure, Jean-Pierre Stirbois, gradually brought his organisational talents to bear on the Front's local and national organisation.[22] Moreover, the defeat of the mainstream Right, and the arrival of the Left in power, gave a broader audience for a more radical Right-wing message.

Indeed, the ground had already been prepared for just such a message. The so-called *nouvelle droite*, the intellectual movement that emerged during the 1970s, certainly saw its battleground as the field of culture rather than that of partisan politics. But their activities were important for two reasons: they provided a cultural bridge between the mainstream conservative and liberal parties and the world of the far Right, over which several prominent figures in Le Pen's movement passed. And the popularisation of the *nouvelle droite's* ideas, through the mass-circulation *Figaro-Magazine*, slowly drip-fed the far Right's poisonous intellectual brew into the political system. Ultimately, this not only made Le Pen's message appear more respectable; it also made it easier for the mainstream Right to emulate his rhetoric in an attempt to limit his rise.

THE *NOUVELLE-DROITE'S* CULTURAL OFFENSIVE

The so-called 'New Right' in France which gained prominence during the late 1970s was centred around the activities of an organisation called the Groupement de Recherche et d'Etudes pour la Civilisation Européenne, better known by its less unwieldly acronym, GRECE. This was essentially a far-Right intellectual think-tank, having its own magazines, like *Eléments* and *Nouvelle Ecole*, and its own publishing house, Copernic. It also staged various conferences and seminars.[23] The style and approach of the organisation was unashamedly elitist. For much of the early part of its existence, its activities were confidential, aimed at influencing a relatively small group of people close to the centres of national power. However, GRECE and its principal thinkers, like Alain de Benoist, gained a much wider audience for their views by writing in *Figaro-Magazine*, the supplement of the conservative daily newspaper, *Le Figaro*. Louis Pauwels, the Director of the magazine, was closely associated with Alain de Benoist and GRECE. And for a period during the late 1970s, *Figaro-Magazine* became an important mainstream platform for spreading the 'New Right's' ideas.

Initially, the principal ideologues of the *nouvelle droite* resisted attempts by their critics to mark them down as being on the Right of the political spectrum. However, in due course, the right-wing label was accepted, and the anthology of Alain de Benoist' s work – a central text in defining the 'New Right's' ideology – appeared in 1977 under the title *Vu de droite*.[24]

However, the label 'New Right' is potentially misleading. For the French *nouvelle droite* has little in common with the political New Right that emerged in the English-speaking world at around the same time. This New Right posed a fundamental critique of social democracy and of the postwar political consensus. It opposed the interventionist role of the state in economic affairs, and it combined 'the traditional liberal defence of the free economy with a traditional conservative defence of state authority.'[25]

The French 'New Right' was both different and distinctive. Its critique of existing society was much more fundamental, rejecting not only Communism and the Left, but also capitalism and indeed the value-system of the Christian world as well. Perhaps its most original aspect – at least for a Right-wing movement – was its choice of strategy. The French 'New Right's' cultural approach to politics, its desire to conquer the intellectual high ground in society – thus preparing the way for a political transformation – was heavily influenced by the work of the Italian Marxist thinker, Antonio Gramsci.[26]

Gramsci, who died of ill-health after enduring imprisonment by the Italian Fascist regime, believed that the working class would only come to power by imparting its values and beliefs to other classes who were its potential allies. Thus, for Gramsci, the establishment of a cultural hegemony was a prior condition for the attainment of political power. The French 'New Right' sought to put this idea into practice for a very different political project. Indeed, the realisation that the political struggle might have to be waged in the realm of ideas, rather than on the streets or through the ballot box, had been slowly percolating through sections of the Far Right for some time.

As early as 1962, Dominique Venner, writing in *Défense de l'Occident*, called for a new elaboration of the nationalist camp's doctrine in an attempt to end its seemingly infinite tendency to fragment. The article also asserted that the political struggle must be waged more through the use of ideas and artfulness, rather than by force.[27] And the 'New Right's' strategy of a cultural, indirect approach latterly received the blessing of the grand old man of French neo-fascism, Maurice Bardèche, who in 1979 wrote that 'this *realpolitik* of the Right, which the generation of Alain de Benoist offers us, is perhaps the only route which remains open to us to leave the ghetto in which the Right finds itself trapped'.[28]

Seen in this light, the label 'New Right' is itself something of a misnomer, suggesting novelty and a break with past traditions of far-Right thinking. In fact, many of the leading figures in GRECE have a clearly-defined political pedigree, stretching back through a variety of far-Right-groupings. And the 'New Right's' ideology was a confection of elitist, pseudo-scientific and mythical ideas that have long figured in the panoply of European far-Right thought. But although the emergence of the 'New Right' in France may seem to be linked chronologically with the upheavals of May 1968 – a right-wing reflection of the political and ideological forces that conjured up the 'New Left' – it was in fact a continuation of something much older. GRECE itself was actually founded in January 1968; the review *Nouvelle Ecole* in March of the same year.

The real roots of the French 'New Right' date back to the early 1960s and the realisation that the far Right, as then constructed, had virtually no hope of achieving any real political influence. Its origins lie among the disillusioned young intellectuals of the neo-fascist sub-culture and the world of *Algérie française*. The team that coalesced around Nouvelle Ecole and GRECE was essentially made up of activists from organisations like Jeune Nation and the Fédération des Etudiants Nationalistes or FEN, which broke away from the main student union in 1960 after it expressed its support for the Algerian independence movement. The breakaway Federation's journal, *Cahiers universitaires*, provided a political nursery where the future leadership of GRECE could hone their political skills. *Défense de l'Occident*, a journal more rooted in the neo-fascist sub-culture, also played a significant role in forming this new intellectual elite, as did the monthly magazine of Dominique Venner, *Europe Action*, which linked far-Right nationalists of various persuasions and helped to forge links with similar groups elsewhere in Europe. Indeed, one expert has suggested that these three journals formed 'a triangle of common connections for most of the people who would later become significant figures in GRECE'.[29]

The ideology that emerged from this sub-culture was strongly influenced by social Darwinism: it was anti-egalitarian and fundamentally opposed to the doctrine of the Rights of Man. Alain de Benoist, in *Vu de droite*, sought to challenge head-on what he saw as the myth of equality. 'The enemy as I see it', he noted, 'is not "the Left" or "communism" or even "subversion" but that egalitarian ideology, whose formulations, religious or lay, metaphysical or pseudo-scientific, have never ceased to flourish for two thousand years, and in which "the ideas of 1789" are nothing but a stage, and of which the current subversion and communism are the inevitable outcome.'[30] For the 'New Right', society is much like the natural world: the animal kingdom is unequal and the pack contains both those who lead and those who are led. In the debate between nature and nurture, GRECE was firmly on the side of nature, the 'New Right' believing that there are inherent inequalities between people and that these are in large part transmitted genetically. The cruder biological racism of its earlier years gave way to a more sophisticated formulation – a sort of ethno-cultural racism which celebrated different societies' right to affirm their differences.[31]

One of the more bizarre aspects of the 'New Right's' thinking is its animosity to the Judeo-Christian world and its exaltation of pagan antiquity. Christianity is seen as an alien (i.e. Jewish) mode of thought imposed on a noble Indo-European culture. What is required, according to the 'New Right', is a sort of mental decolonisation and a return to the roots of European civilisation. Often this view of Europe's origins has strong nordic overtones, not unlike some of the mythology associated with German Nazism.[32] The Judeo-Christian outlook is seen as sharing with Marxism a linear view of history as a progressive journey. This too, the 'New Right' rejects, preferring a cyclical view of history and opposing the idea, inherent in monotheism, of a single, universal good.

Much of this ideology was unlikely to find favour with a more traditional, often Catholic audience. Growing unease at the salience of neo-paganism in the 'New Right's' message contributed in 1981 to the loss of its platform in *Figaro-Magazine*. While the rupture was by no means complete, it was clear that the popular diffusion of the 'New Right's' ideas was likely to be limited. Paradoxically GRECE and its associated reviews and organisation did not prosper after the arrival of the Left in power. The mainstream Right did not turn to it for intellectual leadership, and it became increasingly marginalised.

How then should we measure the 'New Right's' impact? It never sought to become a mass-membership organisation. The very nature of its activities meant that it reached a restricted audience. But at its peak, its influence was considerable. For one thing it appeared respectable; its intellectual seminars and publications attracted contributions from people who would by no means be regarded as having links with the far Right. Its eclectic, dare one say catholic, intellectual borrowings, from Gramsci, Nietzsche and Wagner, to name but a few, added to this aura of intellectual credibility.

While the 'New Right' sought to pursue a cultural strategy, there were those who sought to give its activities a more conventional political dimension. During the 1970s, the Club de l'Horloge, an elitist right-wing political circle, helped to infiltrate elements of the 'New Right's' thinking into the mainstream conservative parties. The Club was founded in 1974 and took its name from the room in the Ecole Nationale d'Administration where it held its early meetings, in which there was an ornate clock. While the Club appears to have had no formal links with GRECE, there was a significant overlap in membership, and some leading Club members ultimately played an important role within the National Front itself.[33]

It is clear that many aspects of the 'New Right's' ideology – its anti-egalitarianism and its opposition to the spirit of 1789, for example – are shared by most of the other families of the French Far Right, and have been longstanding themes in Jean-Marie Le Pen's own discourse. Thus it is difficult to trace a direct line of influence between the 'New Right' and the National Front's own ideology. Certainly links are there, often due to the personal political itineraries of some of the Front's principal actors. Yet equally, many elements of the 'New Right's' thinking – its neo-paganism, for example – would find little favour with Le Pen, who is eager to court the fundamentalist Catholics among the Front's diverse constituency. In fact, as we shall see later, the Front's ideology is a reflection of its own composition – an amalgam of different currents of thought, which do not always sit easily together.

2 Le Pen: The Man and His Party

The Gaullist legacy means that French politics are in large part Presidential politics. The outcome of the referendum of October 1962 – which established the direct popular election of the President – has had a fundamental impact upon both French politicians and political parties. The presidential politics of the Fifth Republic has placed an enormous emphasis on the personality of party leaders. For political success you need at least two things: an attractive candidate and an efficient party machine to secure victory.

General de Gaulle created a disciplined political force of the mainstream Right which remains (despite successive changes of label, and a bewildering array of acronyms) the foundation for its current incarnation, the Rassemblement pour la République of Jacques Chirac. During the 1970s, François Mitterrand's great achievement was to have established a new Socialist Party and to forge a successful electoral vehicle from its fractious currents.

This message has not been lost on the Far Right. As we have already seen, the creation of the National Front in 1972 was an explicit attempt to establish a vote-winning formation from the ideological remnants, coteries and splinters on the extreme Right of the French political spectrum. In Le Pen, the National Front found its own Presidential candidate, and through the 1970s and into the mid-1980s a party machine was gradually constructed to serve his Presidential ambitions. In its local and national organisation, and its apparently democratic structures, the National Front is unlike any other previous formation on the French Far Right. The public face of the Party – its shop-window – suggests that it is much like any other. There are its bulletins (*La Lettre de Jean-Marie Le Pen*); its ideological pamphlets; an intellectual magazine (*Identité*); and a network of Departmental Federations around the country. But, as we shall see, despite appearances, the Front is not like any other party. It is a highly disciplined vehicle for Le Pen himself. Its democratic institutions, which replicate those of other French parties, are largely a facade. Decisions are taken at the top, by Le Pen and those in his immediate entourage, and opposition to these decisions generally results in expulsion. (However, many 'dissidents' simply leave before they are expelled.) Indeed, the Front's internal

27

life evokes strong parallels with the Leninist democratic centralism of Le Pen's hated enemy, the French Communists.

In the National Front there is almost a cult of personality centred on Le Pen; his face and name are everywhere. Party publications present little more than a hagiography: Le Pen, the son of a Breton fisherman; Le Pen, the paratrooper in Indo-China and Algeria; Le Pen the youthful Poujadist Deputy; and Le Pen, today, the potential saviour of the nation. In effect two currents have combined to elevate Le Pen to this dominant position within his movement. On the one hand, there is the relatively recent pres-identialisation of French politics; and on the other, there is a more long-standing factor – the French Far Right's traditional predisposition to a strong leader, a man of destiny. However, Le Pen's own political skills should not be underrated. For once in control of the National Front, he has maintained his iron grip on its helm. And his undisputed rhetorical ability – a free-style form of speaking reminiscent of American charis-matic evangelists – has done much to consolidate his hold over the Party faithful.

THE 'MAN OF PROVIDENCE'

The events in Jean-Marie Le Pen's life have been carefully packaged by the National Front to present the image of a man from humble origins, who after fighting for his country in the Resistance and in Indo-China, became its youngest parliamentary Deputy, and then went on to volunteer for military service in Algeria.

The National Front President's own autobiographical writings paint a picture of a patriot and longstanding anti-Communist, whose political journey took him from a poor Breton childhood, via the Maquis to Paris, first as a Right-wing student activist, and then in January 1956 to the very centre of French political life, the chamber of the National Assembly. Great emphasis is placed by Le Pen on the fact that he is allegedly a self-made man – someone who had to work for his living. Indeed, in these ret-rospective and sympathetic accounts, his whole life seems to have been carefully organised to mark him out as the providential figure of the Far Right.

This is the Le Pen myth or legend: the ex-'para', dubbed the 'menhir' by his supporters, after the tall, prehistoric, standing stones of his native Brittany. (Hence the postcards on sale at the Party's annual fair showing a smiling Le Pen in the guise of the cartoon character Obelix, cheerfully carrying a huge menhir stone.) And like all myths there are elements of truth. However, many aspects of Le Pen's life are rather murkier and the facts more difficult to establish.

Le Pen was born in the fishing village of Trinité-sur-Mer, in Brittany, on 20 June 1928. His mother came from a family of small farmers and his father was a fisherman. Le Pen presents his boyhood in lyrical terms: it seems to have been spent dreaming of the sea and the glories of the French fleet and its maritime empire. At the start of 1940, Le Pen was sent to the Jesuit college of Saint-François-Xavier at Vannes, where (according to his political autobiography, published in 1984) he recalls being visited by his father, now mobilised into the French Navy. Le Pen was 14 when his father was killed, leaving him a *Pupille de la Nation*, which, in his own words, gave him 'additional rights and duties'. In his view, his status as a war orphan made him 'more French' than his contemporaries, giving him a double claim on French nationality.[1]

Le Pen recounts how, as a teenager, he kept a rifle, an automatic pistol and ammunition in his home – a crime punishable by death had the Nazi occupiers found out. In due course, Le Pen claims to have run away to join the Resistance. In his own writing he modestly plays down his wartime role: 'It was no great thing', he comments, but it clearly remained an important credential in Le Pen's future political armoury.[2] As far as his war record is concerned, Le Pen believes that he has need of lessons from nobody, least of all the Communists. As he comments: 'The name of Le Pen is inscribed on the war memorial at Trinité-sur-Mer' while that of the Communist leader Georges Marchais 'is only on the pay-roll accounts of the Messerschmitt factory at Augsberg.'[3] (A reference to the veteran Communist leader's wartime work in a German aircraft factory, and, Marchais' unsuccessful denial that he went as a volunteer worker.)

Le Pen not only claims to have been active in the Resistance but to have participated in a significant engagement – the battle at Saint-Marcel in June 1944, when a unit of over two thousand resistance fighters was discovered by German troops. However, there are considerable doubts about Le Pen's claimed wartime role. In 1987, the newspaper *Libération* ran a long investigative article under a banner headline 'The Untraceable Resistance of Le Pen'. The article carried interviews with several local resistance leaders who (while admitting that teenagers as young as 16 or 17 were present, running messages and so on) insisted that nobody by the name of Le Pen took part.[4]

With the war behind him, Le Pen passed the *baccalauréat* and was eager to pursue a naval career. In *Les Français d'Abord*, he notes that during his childhood he had collected postcards of warships. 'Even today,' he comments, 'I think that the image that best symbolises France, is the French flag flying at the stern of a warship.'[5] However, the whole-sale destruction of the French fleet during the war seemingly thwarted his plans. At 19, Le Pen headed for Paris and life as a law student in the Latin Quarter. He was an active student politician, and became President of the Law Students' Union (Corpo de Droit). His strident anti-Communism was reinforced during his time at university. After a student trip to Berlin, he says that he was shocked by the contrast in the political climates of East and West.[6] But Le Pen's student activism had another side: it is clear that he was also something of a streetfighter, not averse to using his fists when necessary, and his behaviour led to brushes with the law on at least two occasions.[7]

Le Pen was as eager to fight the enemy abroad as he was his political opponents at home. He was already a strident defender of France's colo-nial mission and saw the war in Vietnam in global terms. In his view, the fighting in Indo-China was nothing more than the active theatre of a world-wide and generally clandestine campaign, waged by international Communism against the free world.[8] Le Pen abandoned his law studies and volunteered for military service, as an officer in the elite First Parachute Battalion of the Foreign Legion.

Despite the hagiographic portrayals of Le Pen in uniform as a man of action, his military service was rather less glorious. By the time his unit finally arrived in Vietnam, the siege of Dien Bien Phu was virtually over and French troops were being pulled out of Tonkin to defend the south of the country. When his battalion was withdrawn to Tunisia, Le Pen stayed on with the French forces in Saigon working as a journalist for the military newspaper, *La Caravelle*.

Le Pen's experiences in Indo-China confirmed his strident anti-Communism and he returned home, in his own words, 'an angry young man',[9] France's humiliation in Indo-China and the first shots of insurrec-tion in Algeria confirmed his developing desire to pursue a political career. Reunited with his old Law School associates, Le Pen was introduced to Pierre Poujade. Le Pen claims that he saw much in Poujade's campaign on behalf of small shopkeepers and artisans that reflected his own views.[10] At any rate Poujade was against the politicians' regime of the Fourth Republic and was an advocate of *l'Algérie française*. The Poujadist move-ment provided Le Pen with an institutional home, albeit a temporary one, and Poujade was quick to recognise the abilities of the young firebrand street-orator.

In January 1956 the Poujadist electoral tide swept into the National Assembly: 52 deputies were elected, among them Jean-Marie Le Pen. At 27, he was the youngest member of the French National Assembly. Le

Pen draws parallels between the hostile reception accorded to the new Poujadist deputies by the established political elite, and the exclusion suffered by the National Front at the hands of the so-called 'gang of four' mainstream parties, some thirty years later.[11] Within six months Le Pen broke with Poujade, citing the latter's failure to act in support of French Algeria. In Le Pen's view, Poujade could have played a critical role in the crisis since he had good links with the French settlers – the *pieds-noirs* – and his support for the small shopkeepers and artisans gave him a potential audience among the more affluent Muslim commercial class. In Le Pen's view, Poujade had not lived up to expectations; he had fallen short of his destiny and was not the 'man of providence' that Le Pen had imagined him to be. Indeed Le Pen seems to have fundamentally misjudged Poujade from the start. Any chronicle of the rapid rise and equally rapid fall of the Poujadist movement illustrates Poujade's rather basic political skills, and his inability to turn a simple protest movement into an entrenched political force.[12]

Since the mid-1960s the paths of Poujade and Le Pen have occasionally crossed, most recently in March 1993, when a Paris court condemned Poujade for defamation, following remarks made on a television programme broadcast in 1992. Poujade, referring to Le Pen's military experiences in Indo-China, had said that the National Front leader had only met the front-line soldiers [*soldats de la boue*] in the brothels of Saigon. This remark cost Poujade 15 000 francs in damages.[13] The episode is but one example of Le Pen's litigious nature. The National Front President is a frequent plaintiff, eager to secure redress for what he regards as the regular slurs on his character. But his frequent anti-semitic outbursts, as we shall see in the next chapter, have also landed him in the dock on several occasions.

When the Government lengthened the duration of national service because of the Algerian crisis, Le Pen decided to take leave from the National Assembly and rejoin his old regiment to demonstrate his solidarity with the fighting men. He arrived just as his unit was preparing for the Suez operation. Le Pen took part in the landings in Egypt, after which his unit was sent to Algeria. In his political autobiography he speaks with pride at having participated in the Battle of Algiers. But here again, myth and reality are difficult to separate and Le Pen's specific duties remain unclear.

By early 1957, Muslim bomb-attacks and shootings, and *pieds-noirs* reprisals, had made it impossible for the civil authorities to maintain order in Algiers. The job was entrusted to General Jacques Massu's Tenth Parachute Division which included Le Pen's battalion. By the use of informers, massive round-ups of suspects, and a good dose of brutality, the 'paras' imposed order in Algiers. But it was effectively a pyrrhic victory. As one historian of the French Foreign Legion notes: 'the defeat of the FLN [*Front de Libération Nationale* – the Algerian independence movement] was more apparent than real, for the methods employed by the paras to win the battle had probably done more than anything to discredit the cause of *Algérie française* in the eyes of both French and world opinion'.[14] The torture of Muslim suspects was commonplace, almost institutionalised; and there were allegations that Le Pen himself was involved.[15]

In April 1957, a police investigation was conducted into claims by a young Algerian that he was tortured by Le Pen. According to the report of Police Commissaire Gilles, the young man alleged that two electric wires were attached to his ear lobes and that (the then lieutenant) Le Pen operated a small transformer to administer electric shocks.[16] The allegations first came to light in 1962 and were largely forgotten until Le Pen's rise to prominence in the early 1980s, when the newspaper *Libération* published interviews with Algerians who claimed to have suffered at Le Pen's hands. Le Pen has repeatedly insisted that he was decorated for his service in Algeria and that his behaviour was honourable.[17] He claims that the newspaper interviews were lies and that interrogations were not part of his duties.[18] However, Le Pen does acknowledge that torture did take place. After comments at a private dinner in 1957, he was quoted as stating that in the anti-terrorist operations in Algeria there was no place for the rules of warfare and even less for the niceties of civilian legality. He argued that if it was necessary to torture a man to save a hundred lives, then torture was inevitable, and, in the circumstances, just; but he insisted that he himself had had nothing to do with it.[19] And Le Pen has regularly had recourse to the law to defend his war record, notably suing the former Socialist Prime Minister, Michel Rocard, for describing the National Front leader as a torturer in a television programme in 1992. Le Pen won his case.[20]

On completion of his tour of duty, Le Pen returned to Paris convinced that the political battle to keep Algeria French would be won or lost in Metropolitan France and not in Algiers. During the summer parliamentary break, he organised a touring road-show visiting beaches and seaside resorts throughout France to campaign on behalf of *l'Algérie française*. (This was a precursor of the National Front's own summer tours of the holiday beaches.) He also spoke out in the National Assembly, warning once again that Algeria was but one battle in the broader struggle against Communist domination. And in a line which prefigured his later concerns with immigration, Le Pen remembers telling his parliamentary colleagues: '*si vous ne faites pas l'Algérie française, vous aurez la France algérienne*'.[21] His rhetoric in the National Assembly also heralded some of his later, highly personalised, criticism of Jewish political figures. In a debate in February 1958, for example, he attacked Pierre Mendés-France, saying: *Vous cristallisez sur votre personnage un certain nombre de répulsions patriotiques et presque physiques.*[22]

Le Pen was re-elected to parliament for his Paris constituency in November 1958. He was deeply suspicious of General de Gaulle during this period, and remembers being in Algiers when the General gave his famous speech of 16 September 1959 raising the idea of self-determination for the Algerian people. Le Pen was briefly held in custody during the Algiers insurrection of January 1960, though he seems to have kept his distance from both the more radical *pieds-noirs* leaders and from the Generals' putsch one year later. However, Le Pen's strident opposition to de Gaulle probably cost him his seat in the General Election of 1962.

Le Pen was now out in the political wilderness. To earn his living he established a small recording company, specialising in military music and historical records, chronicling the works of a catholic selection of twentieth-century political figures, including, Pétain, De Gaulle, Churchill, Hitler and Lenin. Le Pen was taken to court for the sleeve-notes on one record of Nazi songs which maintained that Hitler's rise to power was the product of a popular mass movement, and that his triumph was the result of a democratic electoral process. For Le Pen himself, the court-case was merely one of the early examples of what he calls 'the intellectual terrorism' to which he has fallen victim.[23]

In 1965 Le Pen was the Presidential campaign manager for the far-Right candidate Jean-Louis Tixier-Vignancourt. And Le Pen is convinced that Tixier-Vignancourt's Presidential bid was the real target for his detractors. The campaign was by no means a total disaster but Tixier's failure left Le Pen once more on the political margins.

In 1972 Le Pen became the leader of a new organisation – the National Front – which he soon forged into a highly personalised political vehicle. But this was by no means the end of the controversy. In September 1976, Le Pen inherited a fortune from Hubert Lambert whose family money came from a highly successful cement business. Lambert's wealth was estimated at some 24 million francs; and, in addition to a large house outside Paris at Saint-Cloud (now lived in by Le Pen himself), valued at the time of his death at around four million, he left shares and other assets worth an additional 20 million francs.[24] Lambert had joined the National Front in 1973 and changed his will to favour Le Pen some nine months before his death.

Lambert's cousin Philippe, the beneficiary of an earlier will, decided to contest the issue, claiming that Hubert had been manipulated by Le Pen,

who, it was alleged, had taken advantage of the 42-year-old cement millionaire's failing health and mental weakness. Despite threats of court
action, Lambert and Le Pen came to an arrangement in 1977 to end the
dispute, and subsequent press reports claimed that a sizeable Swiss bank
account had been discovered in Hubert Lambert's name, and that this
account had helped to facilitate a compromise.[25]

The story was given an additional twist in 1985, when the former
Poujadist deputy and long-time colleague of Le Pen, Jean-Maurice
Demarquet, rounded on his one-time friend and revealed that Hubert
Lambert's cousin's concern was not without justification. Demarquet, a
physician, was called in by Le Pen to advise on Lambert's health. He
claimed that the millionaire was in a lamentable state of health and was
indeed heavily influenced by Le Pen. And in a devastating interview with
Le Monde, Demarquet went on to claim that Le Pen had indeed been
involved with torture in Algeria, and that he was also obsessively and
crudely anti-semitic.[26] Not surprisingly, Le Pen denied everything, threatened legal proceedings and argued that Demarquet was just a pawn in a
campaign being waged by the Front's opponents. The National Front
leader clearly implied that, in his view, elements in Jacques Chirac's RPR
hoped to prosper from Demarquet's attack.[27] After claiming that he had
long had doubts about his former friend's integrity and political record, Le
Pen was asked why, in that case, he had kept Demarquet in his circle for
so long. To this Le Pen replied that 'You don't throw out an old dog even
if it does have fleas.'[28]

The new mansion at Saint-Cloud, inherited from Lambert, was more
than welcome, when in November 1976, Le Pen, his wife and their three
daughters escaped injury after their Paris apartment was totally wrecked
by a bomb blast. This was the first of two bomb-attacks against leading
Front figures. Two years later, another explosion killed François Duprat, a
member of the Front's Central Committee. In neither case were the
authors of the attack identified.

By the 1980s, his anti-semitic outbursts apart, Le Pen was strenuously
trying to cultivate a more respectable image. His appearance had certainly
changed. The black eye-patch of the mid-1970s, worn to cover an eye lost
during a fight at an election meeting during the late 1950s, had long gone. Le
Pen now sported smarter suits, he was better groomed, and it is said that his
second wife was an important factor in the National Front leader's new look.

His first marriage had broken up during the mid-1980s, and in an
attempt to embarrass the National Front President, his ex-wife, Pierrette,
had posed semi-naked for the French edition of *Playboy* magazine,
dressed as a chamber-maid. (Le Pen had wryly commented in an inter-

view that if she was short of money, she should get a job doing cleaning.)
More significant was the far from flattering interview she provided to the
magazine, concerning Le Pen's egoism and arrogance.[29] The couple's
three daughters sided with their father; and two of them remain active in
Front politics: Marie-Caroline is a Regional Councillor in the Hauts de
Seine, and her sister Yann works in the Party's Paris headquarters.

The image of Le Pen, the family man, surrounded by his daughters, was
heavily played upon during his presidential bid in 1988. By now both Le
Pen's personal circumstances and those of his Party had changed dramatically. During the 1970s, Le Pen had secured both a financial and a political base. By the late 1980s, the National Front had changed significantly
from the marginal grouping founded in 1972. It had secured election victories, obtaining seats on local and regional councils, in the National
Assembly, and in the European Parliament. It had also developed the com-
bination of a nationwide political machine, building upon clear local roots,
something that was unique in the history of the French Far Right. Above
all else, Le Pen had succeeded in holding together a disparate collection of
groupings, overcoming the traditional rivalries and antipathies within the
extreme-Right camp.

ALL THE PRESIDENT'S MEN

The National Front does not recognise any official factions or currents
within its ranks. It insists upon rigid internal discipline and loyalty to the
line pursued by its President, Jean-Marie Le Pen. However, like many
political formations, its leadership is drawn from a variety of different
groupings and traditions on the Right, each of which brings a distinctive
element to the party's image and outlook. Bruno Mégret, the Front's
délégué géneral, the man responsible for honing the Party's ideological
message, characterised these various traditions as follows:

There are those who, above all, are upholders of the Catholic tradition,
grouped around Bernard Antony, the organisation Chrétienté Solidarité
and the newspaper *Présent*; there are those who, on the contrary, on the
religious level have a more ancient view of things, the *nouvelle droite*;
there are those who have a more policy-orientated view of things, the
Club de l'Horloge; and there are those who are for the most part the
heirs of a more militant Right, one might say that of *Algéries Françaises*
and those who supported the presidential bid of Tixier-Vignancourt.
There are also those who joined the Front principally because of their

opposition to socialism, and those who one might say have joined from the Poujadist tradition, who favour the economic independence [and protection] of the professions.[30]

To this description could be added a number of other strands – the Monarchists for example, the Far Right's oldest tradition, and various neo-fascist elements, who in more recent years have kept out of sight. But what is interesting about Mégret's thumbnail sketch of the Front's constituents, is that many of these elements and their leaders, including Mégret himself, were not present at the National Front's birth in 1972. Indeed, during the late 1970s and the early 1980s, three important groups of actors joined Le Pen's movement, changing its internal balance of forces and adding significant new accents to its appeal. It could be argued that during this period the Front experienced something of an ideological rebirth, as it drew support from diverse elements on the Far Right and also attracted converts from the mainstream Right, especially from the Republican Party and the neo-Gaullist RPR. This second formative phase was critical in shaping the National Front as it appears today, and many of its leading figures are drawn from these recruits.

The first significant group to join Le Pen during the late 1970s were the so-called *solidaristes*, advocates of a 'third way' between communism and capitalism, strongly anti-Marxist, anti-Zionist, and anti-American. One of the leading figures in this group, Jean-Pierre Stirbois, who joined the Front in 1977, quickly became the chief architect of its new organisation. Until his death in a car crash in 1988, he was, to all intents and purposes, Le Pen's number two. Stirbois became the strong-man of the party machine, who was often accused by local activists who fell foul of him, of having 'dictatorial' or even 'Stalinist' tendencies.[31] He was a useful figure to Le Pen, who needed to maintain order over his diverse troops. Early on, the *solidaristes* were used by the National Front President to eclipse the neo-fascist elements within the Front's leadership. Stirbois recognised that such elements posed a considerable threat to the Party's electoral credibility.

Stirbois believed in the need to promote a strident anti-immigrant message. The slogan 'One million unemployed is one million immigrants too many' was first used in 1978. He also insisted on the need for the Front to put down local roots. During the late 1970s, Stirbois established a personal political base in the town of Dreux, west of Paris and he was in the vanguard of the Front's electoral rise during the early 1980s, being the first of its leaders to cash in on the electoral value of a strident anti-immigrant message. After his death, his widow, Marie-France Stirbois, inherited his political mantle in Dreux, though not his position in the Party hierarchy.

Stirbois' career is interesting in that it displays a feature common to many of the Front's leading figures. For although he belonged to a specific camp or splinter – the *solidaristes* – he nonetheless had political roots that were common to many of his other National Front colleagues. He was, for example, drawn into politics by the cause of *Algérie Française*. He too was a supporter of Tixier-Vignancourt. During the late 1960s in a variety of groupings, he rubbed shoulders with many of the Front's future leaders. His career illustrates the fact that the ideological strands within the Front are by no means exclusive; they are frequently intertwined, and individuals can draw upon them to varying degrees.

In 1984, Bernard Antony (also known as Romain Marie) joined the National Front after leaving the smallest of the groupings of the mainstream Right, the Centre National des Indépendants et Paysans (CNIP). Antony personifies the Catholic fundamentalist tradition in the National Front.[32] It is a grouping which has only a limited appeal among the Front's electorate – the National Front's voters tend to be less observant than those of the other mainstream parties – but the fundamentalists have an important influence in the Party's hierarchy, since they control *Présent*, the only daily newspaper on the Far Right, and one which is widely read by the Front's members and officials.

Antony's departure from the CNIP was precipitated by the Party's contacts with Simone Veil concerning its participation in the centre-Right list she was to head in the European elections.[33] Veil, as Minister of Health during Giscard d'Estaing's presidency, was responsible for the introduction of legislation for the liberalisation of abortion; and both her liberal views and her Jewish origins made her something of a *bête noire* for the Far Right, and for the Catholic Far Right in particular. But Antony had been flirting with the National Front for some time. Founder of the organisation Chrétienté-Solidarité, a fundamentalist Catholic pressure group with ambitions to promote an international Catholic counter-revolution, Antony was already in bad odour with the CNIP for the pronouncements made at the so-called *Journée d'amitié française*, which he organised in Paris in October 1983. During this conference, which gathered together various right-wing Catholic and political groups, including the National Front, several speeches were delivered containing explicitly anti-semitic comments.[34] Antony himself is well-known for peddling his own brand of traditional Catholic hostility towards the Jews. Le Pen had been at the first of these *Journées d'amitiés* in 1980, and the National Front President takes considerable care to cultivate the Catholic fundamentalist community. In 1991, for example, Le Pen attended the memorial service for Monseigneur Marcel Lefebvre, the traditionalist right-wing cleric whose followers retain the Latin mass, and who split with Rome in opposition to the liberal reforms of Vatican II. Bernard Antony did not follow the Lefebvre schism, but he and his supporters co-exist in the National Front with those like Roland Gaucher, the director of the weekly right-wing paper, *National Hebdo*, who did take the Lefebvriste line.

The third group to join the National Front and take an active role in its leadership came from the mainstream Right, via intellectual circles, like the Club de l'Horloge, or associations on the margins of the mainstream parties, like the Comités d'action républicaine established by Bruno Mégret, in the autumn of 1981.[35] The National Front's initial electoral successes in 1983 encouraged many middle-ranking officials in the RPR and, to a lesser extent the UDF, to jump ship.[36] Le Pen made it clear that National Front candidates need not necessarily be longstanding members, and it is clear that the Party's ambitions to widen its appeal at the local elections of 1985 required a significant increase in the number of candidates it needed to put forward.[37] The National Front's developing organisation and its explosion on to the electoral scene during the early 1980s promised rapid advancement, especially for those who, for whatever reason, were unable to fulfil their ambitions within the mainstream camp.

These converts helped the Front to establish itself on the ground, but a parallel movement, at a rather higher level, gave the Front a new element in its leadership. Here the role of the Club de l'Horloge, or 'Clock Club' is critical. This elitist think-tank was established in 1974, largely centred on Paris. Yvan Blot, then an influential member of the Gaullist Party, became its President and Jean-Yves Le Gallou, then in the Republican Party, its Secretary-General. Both subsequently joined the National Front (in 1989 and 1985 respectively), and began to play a significant role in its activities.

The Club de l'Horloge served as an important conduit through which the ideas of the French 'New Right' passed into the mainstream liberal and conservative camps. Le Gallou has always insisted that the Clock Club had no links with GRECE.[38] However, it is clear that many of the themes of the *nouvelle droite* – the interest in socio-biology, the attack on the doctrine of equality, and its organic view of society – were all reflected in works published by the Clock Club's leading figures. And while GRECE and the Club de l'Horloge have certainly parted company in more recent times, it is clear that the Clock Club was an influential element in this new intellectual climate.[39] Moreover, given GRECE's avowed Gramscian strategy of intellectual colonisation – its goal of creating a new ideological hegemony based upon its ideas – it is quite unnecessary to demonstrate firm institutional links between the two organisations when assigning them to the same intellectual constellation.

As well as being one of the conduits through which the ideas of the *nouvelle droite* reached an audience in the mainstream Right, the Clock Club also acted as a bridge over which people like Le Gallou and Blot passed into the National Front's camp. Bruno Mégret, though also a member of the Club de l'Horloge, took a slightly different route to join Le Pen's formation. A member of the RPR's central committee, he served in the ministerial private office of Robert Galley, prior to the Socialist victory of 1981. The Right's defeat prompted the creation of various political clubs and associations, whose aim was both to renew the mainstream Right's ideology and to prepare for the reconquest of power. In 1984, his 'Republican Action Committees' coalesced with a variety of other clubs on the Right and Far Right to form the Confédération des associations républicaines or CODAR.

Following Le Pen's success in the European elections, Mégret decided to throw in his lot with the new political formation. At CODAR's second annual conference in 1985 he announced his plan to merge his loose association of clubs with the National Front. The marriage was consecrated at a National Convention in December 1985. The two formations would go into battle together, under the banner of the Rassemblement National – a 'national grouping'.[40] Mégret himself was asked to head the Party's electoral list in the Department of Isère and he was subsequently elected to the National Assembly in 1986. The use of the term *rassemblement* or rally made good electoral copy, but in reality, Mégret and his supporters were simply incorported into the National Front. Nonetheless, Mégret was soon to play an important role within the Party's leadership. He was determined to give the Front a more modern and less abrasive image, something that would inevitably bring him into conflict with the more hardline views of Stirbois. Mégret, along with Stirbois' successor Carl Lang, also set about completing the Party's still unfinished organisational machine.

THE PARTY MACHINE

While the National Front's initial electoral success in Dreux in 1983 owed much to Jean-Pierre Stirbois' grassroots work, its early progress was generally achieved without either a significant national party machine, or a strong local base. Its performance in the 1984 European elections, for example, when it sent ten deputies to the European Parliament in Strasburg, was in no sense a product of its developing organisation. On the contrary, according to the former National Front Deputy, Yann Piat, there was an almost total lack of organisation in many areas, a dearth of members, and especially, of money. She was forced to start the Party's departmental Federation in Landes as a backroom operation; its headquarters were in her home, and its posters and tracts were provided without charge, by a sympathetic printer.[41]

Clearly this situation could not continue. The Front needed to put down local roots and establish a disciplined party machine if Le Pen's soaring political ambitions were to have any chance of realisation. During the mid-1980s Stirbois, as Secretary-General, set about building a nationwide organisation with Departmental Federations throughout France. Once again, Yann Piat provides an insight into his methods. Stirbois was eager not only to build up the Front's organisation, but to ensure that each of the Departmental Secretaries – the local patrons of the Party – owed their positions to him personally. Piat, on Stirbois' orders, was to take over the Var Federation, replacing Bernard Mamy, an old friend of Le Pen himself.[42] Stirbois' insistence overcame the bonds of friendship and Mamy and his supporters left the Party to set up a rival faction.[43]

This was by no means the first or last time that local Front supporters took exception to Stirbois' methods. Piat paints a rather sinister picture of him: there were rumours inside the Party that he kept files on his opponents.[44] Stirbois emerges as a Richelieu-like figure: cool, calculating and ruthless. He appeared deeply suspicious of those who had joined the Front from the mainstream Right during the 1980s and was unwilling to accept their view that the Party should have the aim of incorporating as wide a grouping as possible on the Right of the political spectrum. It is clear that Le Pen watched the rise of his powerful, hardline lieutenant with some unease. In due course the National Front President employed the classic tactic of 'divide and rule', elevating Bruno Mégret to the newly-created post of délégué général, in October 1988.[45] Mégret, who in an attempt to improve the Party's public relations image had directed Le Pen's Presidential campaign team, was now charged with turning this body into a permanent secretariat, the délégation générale, close to Le Pen, and responsible for coordinating and developing the Party's message, its policy studies, and training. Stirbois would retain his responsibility for the party apparatus, though it was clear that Mégret's new team would act as a counterweight to the Secretary-General's own political ambitions.

Following Stirbois' death in a road accident in November 1988, Carl Lang, a former head of the Party's youth wing, took over the post of Secretary-General. He had joined the National Front in 1978, at the age of 21 and represented a new generation of activists whose political experience has been almost totally gained within the Front's own ranks. With the demise of Stirbois, the balance of political advantage inside the Party shifted very much in Mégret's favour. He and Lang were able to develop a more amicable division of labour, with the Secretary-General responsible for administrative, financial and organisational matters (like recruitment) while Mégret dealt with ideology, training and the Front's international relations. Today, while the potential for rivalry between the Secrétariat Général and the Délégation Général still exists, it should not be over-played. There is a limited overlap of membership between the two bodies: certain individuals, like Jean-Yves Le Gallou, sit on both. And Lang and Mégret's personal relationship seems to have none of the rancour of that between Mégret and Stirbois.

If Stirbois had erected the framework of the National Front edifice, then Lang and Mégret set about furnishing the Party with all the requirements of a modern political machine. Lang asserts that there was still much to do in 1988 when he took over as Secretary-General. He remembers that:

> At that time many commentators were saying that the Front was in a spiral of decline. We had lost our group in the National Assembly, and they believed we were on the way to disappearing. To ensure the survival of the Party we had to re-construct it from the bottom up. It must be remembered that the Front was established around the personality of Jean-Marie Le Pen, from the top downwards, and it was necessary to decentralise the organisation, to give it roots, to provide it with the true structure of a political movement with national dimensions.[46]

As we shall see, the Front is far from being a 'decentralised' formation. But Lang did have an important organisational task on his hands. The Party needed to find additional candidates, to attract new members and to train and mobilise its existing supporters. If the national electoral system made it very difficult for the Party to win parliamentary seats, then Lang believed it would have to capitalise on its ability to win local office, par-ticularly at the municipal level. Accordingly, he placed a consider-able emphasis on efforts to adapt the Party's rhetoric and message to meet local concerns, to find local echoes of its national themes of immigration, criminality, taxation and so on.

Expanding the Party's membership has also been an important goal, not least for financial reasons. Like so much of the Front's internal life, it is very difficult to get behind the public facade to obtain a comprehensive picture of its internal workings. The Party claimed to have about ten thou-sand members in 1983.[47] Some ten years later, Carl Lang insisted that the figure had grown to somewhere between seventy and eighty thousand. This meant, he said, that:

The Front was not a mass party, but a party of activists. In addition to the members who pay their subscriptions, there are around three hundred thousand people who at one moment or another have either been members of the National Front, or who have given it money. Today, we are probably the only activist [*militant*] political force on the Right, that is to say the only popular activist force, since the RPR has largely lost its popular activist base.[48]

Lang argues that the National Front and the Communists are now the only *militant* parties in France. The others are simply groupings of local office-holders and notables, or else have lost their activist base by becoming, as he puts it, parties of Government. The Front's own claims for its membership should be treated with caution. Academic experts suggest a significantly lower figure of some forty to fifty thousand.[49]

A discussion of membership figures leads on to the vexed question of money. Not surprisingly, this aspect of the Front's affairs is shrouded in almost total secrecy. Party leaders insist that theirs is one of the poorest parties in France. It is certainly the only party that charges for admission to its meetings. Yann Piat notes how, during her first months in the Landes Federation, she had to pay the Paris headquarters for election posters bearing Jean-Marie Le Pen's photo, leading her to comment that 'in the National Front nothing is free'.[50]

According to the accounts of those who have left the Party, Le Pen himself retains a resolute grip on its financial affairs, which are highly centralised.[51] While membership dues and donations are clearly an important source of revenue, much depends upon the personal wealth of Le Pen himself. Similarly the financial resources of many of the provincial Federations depend upon the means of a few wealthy local leaders.[52] To obtain a good position on the party list, National Front candidates are expected to pay for the privilege of representing the Party, and once elected must donate up to half their official salaries to the Paris headquarters.[53] (This practice, similar to the procedures of the Communist Party, has been a frequent source of tension within the Party and failure to pay up has often been used as a reason for an individual's exclusion.) The Front has also sought donations from sympathetic businessmen, and here the role of parallel bodies like the cercles d'Entreprise moderne et liberté, whose job is to promote the Party's message in the world of business and commerce, is important.[54]

The shadowy world of the Front's finances throws up some bizarre connections. In her biography, Yann Piat refers to another important source of revenue, the Unification Church of Reverend Moon, and the important role played by Pierre Ceyrac as the intermediary between Le Pen and the cult's leader.[55] Ceyrac, who once sat on the Front's Central Committee, headed a political organisation in France that was closely linked with the Reverend Moon's church. The initial go-between was Le Pen's hagiographer Jean Marcilly, who subsequently fell out of favour after running off with Le Pen's first wife. Ceyrac then took over the task of developing the contacts between the Front and the Unification Church that had begun some months before the European elections of June 1984. At this ballot Gustav Pordea, a former Romanian diplomat now living in France, secured the fourth place on the National Front list. Despite some press speculation that he was working for the Romanian security services, it seems clear that he owed his position to some sort of deal between Le Pen and the 'Moonies'.[56] Pordea was a supporter of the Unification Church. According to Marcilly, Moon was eager to infiltrate the European Parliament and in return Le Pen received some four million Francs. Le Pen himself denies any financial links betwen the two organisations; but it is clear that the Unification Church was attracted to the Front's strident anti-communism, and there are several reports of Le Pen having visited the United States to meet Unification Church officials, and even of a trip to South Korea to see Moon himself.[57]

One aspect of the Front's finances that is, in contrast, entirely open, is the funding it receives from the French Government. Following legislation passed during the late 1980s political parties have received some financial assistance from the state. In 1991, the Front was granted a mere 295 000 Francs.[58] (Given that the amount was related to the number of seats a party held in the Assembly and Senate, this was a relatively trifling sum – the Socialist Party received nearly 94 million Francs.) This figure rose dramatically, to some 28 719 350 Francs in 1993, after the rules were altered to take into account the number of votes a Party received at the last general election. As the fourth largest party in terms of its share of the popular vote, the Front now receives the fourth largest sum from the state.[59] According to Carl Lang, this amount was 'ten times more than the Front was generally used to managing', and it would, he argued, have a significant impact on the Party's activities in 1994.[60]

Money and members may be the basic building blocks of political formations but Mégret was also eager to reinforce the Party's ideological apparatus. In 1989 a Scientific Council – a sort of intellectual think-tank – was established, made up of sympathetic academics and experts. A parallel body, actually based in the Front's national headquarters, the Centre d'Etudes et d'Argumentaires, was also set up to flesh-out the Front's policy proposals and to feed ideas into its programme. A wide range of booklets have been published under its auspices on matters such as immigration, education policy and defence. An intellectual magazine, *Identité*, was launched (subtitled a *revue d'études nationales*) under the directorship of Mégret himself. This provides an important means of spreading the ideas of the Front's principal thinkers. Each thematic issue, tackling subjects as diverse as religion, democracy, foreign policy or the collapse of Socialism, contains a preface by Le Pen and frequent contributions from figures like Mégret and Le Gallou. As well as assimilating themes from the *nouvelle droite* and the Front's longstanding emphasis on nationalism and the threat of immigration, *Identité* represents a broad church. A variety of views are reflected within its editorial team. There are also frequent references to earlier far-Right traditions. A typical issue contains an article by Mégret attacking the egalitarianism of the Left; a piece alleging that contemporary advertising is promoting what the Front sees as a highly negative 'cosmopolitan culture' (illustrated by Beneton posters and a Citroen advert bearing the black American singer Grace Jones); and an article by Le Pen's lawyer, Georges-Paul Wagner, eulogising the royalist, right-wing thinker, Charles Maurras, who helped found Action Française.[61] Indeed, the emergence of this new right-wing intelligentsia within the National Front's orbit, some fifty years after the demise of Action Française, is one of the more significant and novel features of Le Pen's movement.[62]

In September 1993, the Front took the weekly newspaper *National Hebdo* explicitly under its control. Concern had been expressed, not least by Bruno Mégret, that its populist and strident tone was causing the Party some embarrassment. Le Pen emphasised that *National Hebdo*'s editorial line had changed since its new editor had been appointed, and in the future, he hoped that it would become a mouthpiece for the National Front's official positions.[63]

The Front has also adopted new technology to spread its message. There is a recorded telephone information service, updated daily, dubbed 'Radio Le Pen'. The Party also operates a computerised information service, via the minitel system, a national computer network that subscribers can access via their own telephone terminal. This provides press releases, details of local Front offices and activities, and it even has an interactive dimension, where members can express their views on the major issues of the day.

The Party has also developed an impressive training operation, run by an organisation called the Institut de Formation Nationale. This body, established by Bruno Mégret in 1989, is headed by Bernard Antony. It organises a variety of activities, ranging from evening conferences, to one-day or weekend courses, and a full-scale summer school. The subjects range from aspects of the Front's ideology to electoral organisation and public speaking. These events are held at several locations throughout France – in 1993–94, the evening conferences, for example, were mounted in eight cities to give as many people as possible a chance to attend. (These cities were Paris, Lyons, Marseille, Aix-en-Provence, Bordeaux, Toulouse, Nice, Toulon; in other words, the Front was playing to its areas of strength.)

Carl Lang and the Sécretariat Général have also been closely involved in this training programme. They have produced a comprehensive, spiral-bound manual for activists, *Le Guide du Responsable*, which now runs to eight volumes. It deals with everything from organising a local branch meeting, to contacts with the press, the electoral law, and how to design and produce posters. Everything is covered; the fourth part, dealing with propaganda, even has the recipe for the paste needed to put up posters. At each stage there are pauses and checklists for activists to test their understanding of what has gone before. It is a remarkable publication, owing more to modern management methods than to the traditional tracts of the Far Right. In short, it is a manual of which any political party would be proud.

Front leaders insist that their organisational work is far from complete. Mégret, speaking in September 1993, argued that:

> The National Front is a very modern political movement. It is still under construction. You can't put down the roots of an entirely new political formation in just a few years; certainly not in ten years. It is something that can't just improvise itself, it is an organisation which has not yet reached its full maturity. It began as a faction and must become a force of government. I don't know if we are half-way or even two-thirds of the way there, but we're heading in the right direction.[64]

This reference to 'ten years' is interesting since Mégret is repeating a common tendency within the Front, a rhetorical device which almost writes off the decade of the 1970s, and dates the Party's real birth from the start of its electoral ascent in 1983. While this may have much to do with internal rivalries (Mégret himself clearly was not even a member during much of the Front's early existence), such statements also point to the Party's effective rebirth in the 1980s and emphasise the significant organisational progress made over the course of the past decade.

HIS MASTER'S VOICE

The National Front is very proud of its organisation and is eager to provide the interested observer with its official publications (such as the twice-monthly newsletter, *La lettre de Jean-Marie Le Pen*) to prove that it is just like any other political party. But, as so often in politics, appearances can be deceptive. The Front claims not just to have accepted parliamentary democracy, but to have created an entirely democratic party machine. But how seriously should one take its democratic pretensions? To what extent is internal debate encouraged? And most important of all, what latitude is afforded to dissenting voices?

According to the National Front itself, the real day-to-day decision-making body in the Party is the Bureau Politique, originally made up of between twenty and thirty members, but enlarged after the Front's Ninth Congress in 1994 to 40 members. In theory, this meets twice a month and its composition reflects all the principal 'currents' within the Party. Its members are proposed by Le Pen himself for approval by the Front's so-called 'parliament', its Central Committee. In fact none of Le Pen's candidates for the Bureau Politique have ever been rejected and since the Central Committee meets rarely, perhaps only once a year, several individuals have been simply co-opted on to the Bureau in the intervals between the Central Committee's meetings.

The Central Committee itself is made up of 120 members. One hundred of these are elected by delegates to the Party's Congress; the 20 remaining members are nominated by Le Pen. Until the Party's Eighth Congress, in Nice in 1990, these delegates were selected by their Regional or Departmental party machines. But from 1990 onwards, Congress delegates have been elected by National Front members attending local regional and departmental conferences.

Internal democracy within the Party is imperfect and infrequent at best. The Party's own publications claim that the Congress should be held every two to three years and that it represents a sort of 'general assembly' for the movement.[65] In fact, this scheme is rarely followed. The Party's Nice Congress, in March 1990, came five years after the preceding gathering and the next Congress was not held until February 1994. The role of the Party Congress is more symbolic than real. The 1990 Congress, for example, re-elected Jean-Marie Le Pen as President, though this was no suprise, since his was the only name put forward. The vote of the Congress delegates for the members of the Central Committee does provide some insight into the internal balance of forces within the Front. At the Ninth Congress in February 1994, of the 100 names selected, 21 were new to the Central Committee. And overall, about half of its members were seen as being supporters of Bruno Mégret.[66]

This tilt towards Mégret was something that Le Pen clearly wanted to contain. And in a series of moves in the wake of the 1994 Congress, the

National Front President sought to dilute the Délégué general's influence. His actions demonstrated the strong personal grip he maintains on the Party's structures and indeed the marked limitations of the Front's internal democracy. In addition to his ability to top-up the Central Committeee with twenty nominees, Le Pen had also gained approval for the *bureau politique* to be expanded to a 40-strong body, again with its members nominated by Le Pen. Even more significantly Le Pen sought, in a two-stage process, to expand the Front's Executive Bureau, the small committee gathered around Le Pen himself, which is the Party's real decision-making body.

Until February 1994, the Executive Bureau was made up of the President, the Party's vice-President Dominique Chaboche (an administrative title, not Le Pen's successor), Bruno Mégret, and Carl Lang. At the Ninth Congress Le Pen brought one of the rising stars of the Party – Bruno Gollnisch – on to the Executive Bureau as vice-President for international issues. Gollnisch, a university professor, Regional Counsellor and Member of the European Parliament, has been described as 'a representative of the traditional extreme Right which doesn't have a negative view of the Vichy years and which displays a certain understanding or sympathy for the revisionist view of the Nazi holocaust'.[67] A few weeks later, Le Pen nominated one of his strongest supporters, Martine Lehideux, as a third vice-President.[68] To this small group must be added the name of Jean-Marie Le Chevallier, the Director of Le Pen's private office, his chief confidant, and a man who has an important influence over the Party's day-to-day activities.

Thus, in practice, the Front is a highly centralised machine with a strong, pyramid-like organisation. Power is held at the top and Le Pen dominates its internal life. The essential function of the party machine is not so far removed from the traditional Communist model, which, in organisational terms it mirrors closely: the party serves to transmit policy downwards to the foot-soldiers who actually put up the posters and staff the Front's local operations. Nonetheless, the Front's organisational edifice also performs an additional dual role, affording the Party its own 'democratic' credentials and giving its officials and members a clear sense of purpose within its hierarchy.

During the course of the Party's development Le Pen has made sure that no alternative power centres have been established. (The two posts held by Mégret and Lang as, respectively, political and organisational heads of the Party's machine bear out Le Pen's desire to avoid nominating a clearly designated successor who might challenge his leadership.) But Le Pen's pre-eminence is also due to the fact that a relatively small group of people (largely his own longstanding followers) have shared out whatever posts were on offer.[69] Even the National Front's deputies were unable to develop any real autonomy. After the 1986 general election, Le Pen and his henchmen dominated the Party's parliamentary group, imposing iron discipline and enforcing a political line of obstructionism and outright hostility to the Government of Jacques Chirac, which upset at least some of the more moderate Front deputies.[70] Le Pen's interpretation of the role of the Deputy is interesting. He seems to have seen the Party's elected office-holders as simply its mouthpieces in the National Assembly. When, for example, Yann Piat became the Party's only parliamentary representative in 1988, she claims that she was subjected to growing pressure to simply mouth the Party line, and this attitude reached its *reductio ad absurdum* with Mégret publicly announcing in advance (and with no consultation) how she would vote at an important division.[71]

It was this sort of attitude and her growing disillusion with Le Pen himself that prompted Piat to consider leaving the Party. In fact, she was expelled before she could take any action of her own. She joined the ranks of a growing body in French politics – the former members of the National Front. For the course of the Party's brief history has been punctuated with expulsions and resignations at both national and local level. In general terms, Le Pen and his lieutenants take an unsympathetic view of any divergence from the Party line. Yvon Briant, for example, was thrown out of the Front's parliamentary group in 1986 for failing to give his support to Le Pen for the forthcoming Presidential election of 1988. Briant, who had remained an official in the CNIP party, had fallen foul of Stirbois because of his far from negative attitude towards the mainstream conservative government of Jacques Chirac. Briant also hoped to bolster the voice of what he termed 'conservatives and liberals' among the Front's deputies against the hardliners like Stirbois.[72] Piat gives a dramatic description of the meeting at which Briant presented himself before Le Pen, the National Front President acting as both judge and jury.[73]

However, while internal discipline is harsh, dissent does not always bring expulsion. Much depends upon what the offending member has to offer the Party and what weight they represent within the Front's byzantine internal life. In the case of Pierre Ceyrac, the answer was clearly money. In 1987, in the wake of Le Pen's characterisation of the Nazi gaschambers as 'a point of detail of history', Ceyrac used an interview in *Le Point* to issue a thinly veiled public warning to those within the Party who saw it as a vehicle for racist politics.[74] More recently Ceyrac, a European Deputy and regional councillor for the Nord-Pas-de-Calais, again used the mainstream press, this time *Le Figaro*, to launch an implicit attack on Mégret, and the publication of a document entitled 'Fifty Measures on

Immigration', which Ceyrac believed gave too much emphasis to the issue and had cost the Party votes.[75] Le Pen was forced to discipline this dissident voice, giving him, in the National Front leader's own words, 'a fatherly reprimand' because, it seems, he detected 'no malice' in Ceyrac's criticisms.[76] Ceyrac retained his posts and remained on the Front's Central Committee. Le Pen's indulgence was perhaps an indication of the degree of financial support given to the Front by the Unification Church. Ceyrac finally quit the National Front in 1994. He claimed to be increasingly at odds with what he saw as Le Pen's drift towards racism and anti-semitism, though the real reason for his departure was probably political. The Unification Church had viewed the Front as a potential bulwark against Communism. And Front sources suggested that as this threat receded, so did the Unification Church's interest in the Party. [77]

In 1990, the political heirs of Stirbois sought to restore their influence in the National Front and to rescue it from what they saw as the sinister clutches of what they called 'the pontifical zouaves of ayatollah Romain Marie [Bernard Anthony] and the technocrats and hyper-conservatives of the Club de l'Horloge'.[78] The campaign is interesting in that it was launched from the margins of the Party by one of Stirbois' old political companions, Michel Schneider. He had been critical of the Front's direction for some time, prior to the Nice Congress of 1990, condemning the lack of democracy within the Party – not something, it should be added, that would have worried his mentor, Stirbois. The real issue was the Party's strategy and the declining influence of the old *solidariste* current in elaborating that strategy. Schneider had already left the Party, but his goal was to boost the potential leadership challenge of Stirbois' widow, Marie-France Stirbois. She was now the Front's only deputy and Schneider insisted that she should take over the organisation from Carl Lang. However, Marie-France was quick to distance herself from Schneider, and proclaim her continuing loyalty to Le Pen.[79] Even though Marie-France remained a potential standard-bearer for her husband's supporters, her public disavowal of Schneider was enough to keep her within the fold.

The case of Pierre Sergent is another interesting example of the toleration of dissent, though in his case it was not because of his potential power within the Party, but more because of what he represented. Sergent, a member of the Front's Bureau Politique, was a former resistance fighter, and the military head in metropolitan France of the OAS – the terrorist movement that fought against what it saw as de Gaulle's betrayal of French Algeria. After many years on the run, Sergent emerged to take part in mainstream political life. He joined the CNIP in 1983 and the National Front two years later. How comfortable he ever was in Le Pen's Party is far from clear. Nonetheless Sergent's career made him something of a hero in far-Right circles, and his longstanding position as a maverick figure gave him some measure of ideological leeway.

When three former National Front candidates in the Doubs Department left the Party in protest at the electoral impact of the presence on their list of Roland Gaucher, Sergent showed some understanding of their complaint. Gaucher, a former collaborator during the Vichy years, sits on the Front's *bureau politique* and was the director of the newspaper *National Hebdo*. (Indeed, it was the influence of Gaucher and his cronies over the weekly that had caused much of the Party leadership's embarrassment at its content.) Interviewed by *Libération*, Sergent, while deploring the resignation of the candidates, noted that more and more people in the Party were opposed to the attempts to justify collaboration, by those he described as '*nostalgiques de Vichy*'.[80]

Some two years earlier, Sergent had mounted a strong attack against the National Front President's position on the Gulf War to liberate Kuwait. Sergent was clearly appalled at the damage that Le Pen's seemingly pro-Iraqi tilt might do to the Party's electoral image.[81] However, he was prevailed upon to tone down his criticisms, to the extent that he gave a seemingly contradictory interview to *Le Monde*, insisting that there were no basic differences between himself and the Front's leader, while backing President Mitterrand's decision to mobilise French forces.[82] Sergent's backtracking was enough, in Le Pen's eyes, to square the circle. He remained inside the Party and received Le Pen's fulsome praise following his death in 1992.

These three examples, Ceyrac, Stirbois and Sergent, demonstrate the limits of dissent within the National Front. Le Pen rules with a rod of iron and it is this discipline, together with a widespread perception that political success depends upon at least the appearance of unity, that keeps the intolerant components of the Party together. Many more leading figures have either been thrown out of the organisation or have simply left, among them former Front deputies like Pascal Arrighi, François Bachelot, Guy Le Jaouen, and Yann Piat. Most of those leaving the Party claim to have had a sudden revelation as to its true nature. Arrighi and Bachelot, for example, departed after Le Pen's crude anti-semitic jibe against a Government minister – Michel Durafour – in 1988. Though in fairness it is clear that Arrighi, for one, was uneasy at the 'point of detail' remark some time earlier. However, it is hard to believe that those on the inside did not obtain a very good idea of the Front's real character and the darker side to Le Pen's own outlook much earlier. It was more a question of how much they could stomach.

For those who continue to carry the National Front's banner at elections, obedience to the Party hierarchy is seen as essential. Le Gallou told a gathering of Front regional councillors that unity had to be preserved at any price, and no sign of disagreement should be shown in public. Le Pen himself reinforced the message, noting that it was not acceptable to have diverging views within the National Front in any council debate.[83] And if anyone had any doubts as to what discipline inside the Party meant, in October 1993 Jean-Marie Le Chevallier, one of Le Pen's closest colleagues, spelt it out in simple terms. Writing to a dissident councillor who had left the Front, he noted that 'if you disagree with the Party that got you elected, you either shut up, or resign your seat'.[84]

The National Front has been forged into a well-organised and highly effective Party. From outside, its publications, congresses and structure look very much like any other French political formation. But its democratic credentials are paper-thin. It is a highly autocratic operation. Nonetheless, one man cannot control the detailed workings of such a large national organisation. Within the National Front there are clearly differing currents and viewpoints. And to an extent Le Pen must tolerate these to isolate effectively any potential rivals. But the essence of his approach is simple: he is the boss; and if anyone seeks to openly challenge his authority or to build a power-base for the future, they will either be marginalised, or Le Pen will use the considerable battery of organisational levers at his disposal to seek to dilute their influence.

The personal role of Le Pen in the rise of the National Front cannot be overestimated. He has been the Far Right's equivalent of de Gaulle; at one and the same time federator, saviour and Presidential hopeful. He is certainly no newcomer to the French political scene, having a long, and not always glorious, political career behind him. But he and the Front's propagandists have been able to draw on this record to create an almost idealised *curriculum vitae*. In the process they have succeeded in re-packaging Le Pen, enabling him to pose as the leader of a new force in French politics. Le Pen's strategy was also skilfully adapted to the Presidential system of the Fifth Republic. Le Pen cast himself as a future occupant of the *Elysée*, though he has clearly never had any chance of winning a Presidential election. Nonetheless, this 'pseudo-Presidential' approach played to his strengths; Le Pen was a highly effective political operator and he had at his disposal a highly personalised party machine. But this 'pseudo-Presidentialism' also afforded the National Front perhaps its only chance of political influence. It could not win the Presidency, but if it did well enough at elections, it could hope to bring pressure to bear on the parties of the mainstream Right.

3 The Electoral Rise of the National Front

Under the strong conservative Presidential regime of the Fifth Republic, the Far Right struggled for over two decades to make any electoral impact at all. In the Presidential election of 1965 Jean-Louis Tixier-Vignancour, a former minister in the Vichy government and longstanding Far-Right *notable*, capitalised on rancour at the granting of independence to Algeria to obtain 5.3 per cent of the vote. However, the extreme right-wing surge came and went. The Far Right, a heterogeneous collection of groups, fragments and individuals, seemed to have been entirely marginalised by the dominance of the mainstream Right: first the Gaullists, and then the duopoly of the RPR and the coalition of liberal and centrist parties, the UDF.

At the 1974 Presidential election, two years after the creation of the National Front, Jean-Marie Le Pen himself was only able to scrape together a derisory 0.76 per cent of the vote. In 1981 he was unable to even gather the required number of signatures to be declared a candidate. The National Front spent its first ten years crossing the electoral desert, unable to make any significant impact on the political scene. However, by the start of the 1980s the Party had been substantially renovated and re-organised, and when an opportunity came, it was at last able to make its presence felt.

The National Front's first breakthrough came in the 1983 Municipal elections. During the course of the Fifth Republic, local electoral contests have become increasingly politicised, assuming a national significance, and affording the voters an opportunity both to punish the government as well as to demonstrate a local preference. Here the Municipal elections of March 1983 were no exception. The Left had been carried to national office in 1981. But subsequent by-election defeats and the results of the Cantonal elections in March 1982 reflected a growing disillusionment with the new Socialist Government. The optimism of the early months of the Mitterrand presidency, the so-called 'state of grace', had given way to more mundane yet essential preoccupations with economic indicators, foreign debts and the strength of the franc.

The mainstream opposition parties, the Gaullist RPR and the Giscardien UDF, mounted a vigorous campaign, stressing the national significance of the Municipal contest. They hoped to use the municipal elections as a springboard back to national office. A disquieting feature of the Opposition campaign was its use of the immigration question to gather votes – an attempt to capitalise upon a vein of popular racism that equated the ills of unemployment and urban violence with the presence of large immigrant communities in many French towns. Immigration was discussed in immoderate terms by many RPR and UDF candidates. The UDF mayor of Toulon, for example, referring to the immigration question, said that France refused to become 'the dustbin of Europe'.[1]

The mainstream Right was seeking to mobilise support around an issue which Jean-Marie Le Pen had already made his own. Buoyed up by the evidence that his themes were now attracting a wider resonance, the National Front leader was further encouraged by the changes to the voting system brought in by the Mauroy government. These changes applied in all but the smallest towns; and while retaining the 'majoritarian' principle and party lists, they introduced an element of proportional representation, allowing local opposition parties to win seats on municipal councils. Here then was an opportunity for the National Front. The last time these municipal council seats were in contention was in 1977, when the National Front only presented candidates in Paris. This time it chose to fight only seven of the twenty *arrondissements* in the capital, but also to run its own lists of candidates in Nice and Montpellier. Elsewhere it sought to get its candidates on to either RPR lists or those of local conservative dignitaries. National Front supporters ran on such lists in three *départements*, Alpes-Maritimes, Indre-et-Loire, Isère and in the Ile-de-France region. In the town of Dreux, some 80 kilometres west of Paris, nine National Front members were given places on the RPR list, including the party's Secretary-General Jean-Pierre Stirbois. He secured the number-two position. RPR officials in the town were well aware that in the local elections of the previous year Stirbois had obtained over 12 per cent of the vote, and they were clearly worried that an independent National Front list could lose them the contest. The joint list went into battle with the call to 'reverse the flow of immigrants' coming into the town.

Le Pen waded into the first-round campaign with enthusiasm. He was running for a seat on the Paris council representing the twentieth *arrondissement*, a working-class area of high unemployment and with a significant immigrant population. The National Front's message was starkly simple: 'Two million unemployed is two million immigrants too many. France and the French first'. National Front posters proclaimed that a vote for their list, 'Paris aux Parisiens', was a vote against immigration, insecurity, unemployment, higher taxation and a government that was simply letting things slide.

Jean-Marie Le Pen won 11.26 per cent at the first ballot in Paris, though he claimed that his tally was up to 18 per cent in the most working-class wards. His explanation for his success was simple:

> I say out loud what people here are thinking inside – that uncontrolled immigration leads to disorder and insecurity. In the streets where foreigners sometimes represent 40 per cent of the population, French people have the impression of being submerged and excluded.[2]

Le Pen's vote derived as much from his own ebullient personality as from the social problems in this part of the capital. In the other six *arrondissements* where the National Front fought under its own colours, it achieved an average vote of just under 3 per cent. The Gaullist leader and Mayor of Paris Jacques Chirac steadfastly refused to countenance the inclusion of Le Pen and his supporters on the UDF/RPR list for the second ballot. Thus the National Front leader went into the second round alone, this time securing 8.5 per cent, failing to gain a seat as a municipal councillor, and having to accept the lesser political prize of local ward councillor.

In Dreux the right-wing list was narrowly defeated by the Socialists by a margin of only eight votes. The election was subsequently annulled following irregularities in the counting of the ballot papers, and a re-run was scheduled for September. This time the National Front and the mainstream opposition parties fielded two separate lists. That headed by Jean-Pierre Stirbois obtained a respectable 16.7 per cent of the first-ballot votes. Negotiations between the local National Front and the mainstream opposition parties followed, with national UDF and RPR figures taking a keen interest. A joint second-ballot list was agreed, with Jean-Pierre Stirbois accorded fifth place. On 11 September after a bitter and sometimes violent campaign, the opposition took control of Dreux with four representatives of the National Front gaining seats on the town council. Jean-Pierre Stirbois became assistant to the Mayor on matters relating to civil defence, with two other National Front sympathisers taking similar posts involving social affairs and culture.

The result at Dreux was the product of intensive local work by Stirbois and his supporters who had been active in the constituency since 1978. Between the mid-1950s and the mid-1970s Dreux's population had grown rapidly, many immigrant workers being drawn to the town by the expansion of local industries. However, by the early 1980s Dreux was suffering from all the familiar ills of unemployment and rising crime. Up to 24 per cent of the town's population of some 35 000 people were immigrants – ideal territory for the Front's simplistic anti-immigrant message. The question was whether this represented the start of a Far-Right revival or whether Dreux, or Le Pen's score in Paris for that matter, were merely isolated results, dependent upon the presence of forceful personalities.[3]

One month later a second Municipal by-election was held, this time in the Communist-controlled Paris suburb of Aulnay-sous-Bois. Here again the themes of immigration, unemployment and insecurity dominated the campaign, with the National Front eager to prove that, as in Dreux, its support was vital to the mainstream Right if they were to have any hope of defeating the Left. The National Front list obtained 9.3 per cent of the first-ballot vote, falling just short of the 10 per cent needed to continue through to the second round. This, to some extent, relieved the pressure on the mainstream Right who insisted that there would be no deals with Le Pen's supporters. The National Front leader condemned what he termed the 'ostracism' of his supporters by the mainstream Right, though he failed to call on them to abstain at the second ballot, preferring to urge the creation of a barrier against the Communists. In the event, the list headed by the Gaullist, Jean-Claude Abrioux, emerged victorious from the second ballot, the bulk of National Front voters transferring their support to the mainstream Right.[4]

With his sights now firmly set on the European Parliament elections of June 1984, Le Pen himself decided to stand in the December 1983 Legislative by-election at Morbihan in his native Brittany. He hoped to capitalise upon his local roots to keep the National Front in the headlines as the European election campaign got underway. Le Pen probably had no illusions. Whatever support his local origins might encourage, the two-ballot voting system used in legislative contests left small formations like the National Front at a huge disadvantage. The second round inevitably tended towards a great simplifying duel between Left and Right, with smaller formations (even if they did cross the theshold into the second round) only able to play a spoiling role. In Morbihan Le Pen won just over 12 per cent of the vote, not enough to go through to the second ballot. However, the result was interesting in that Morbihan, unlike Dreux and Aulnay-sous-Bois, was essentially a rural area, its economy resting upon agriculture and the sea, far removed from the problems of immigration and urban decay. Le Pen stressed the themes of moral laxity, unemployment and high taxation. If his message could create an echo in rural Brittany, then perhaps the National Front was on the way to developing a national audience.

Le Pen was certainly becoming a national political figure. On 13 February 1984 he was invited to appear on the programme *l'heure de verité* on France's second television channel. The format is a popular one, with a notable political figure being quizzed by a panel of political journalists. If the alliance between the mainstream Right and the National Front at Dreux had helped to legitimise the National Front's ideas, Le Pen's appearance on *l'heure de verité* marked yet another stage in the Party's acceptance as a political force that was much like any other, and certainly one that was no worse than the Communists. A SOFRES opinion poll conducted in May showed 65 per cent of those asked expressing little or no sympathy for the National Front leader. But some 18 per cent said they had a reasonable degree of sympathy with Le Pen, and just over 20 per cent of those polled agreed with the proposition that Le Pen was as much a part of the legitimate opposition as the leaders of the RPR and UDF.[5]

But what about the National Front voters themselves? Who were they? And how different were they from the electorate of the mainstream Right? Opinion poll data enabled the first tentative analysis.[6] For a start, the Far-Right electorate contained a significant number of working-class voters: some 29 per cent of its supporters were working-class as compared with 19 per cent for the Right-wing opposition as a whole. It was a more youthful electorate: some 41 per cent of its voters were under 35, as against 30 per cent for the opposition as a whole. In the opposition as a whole, voters were split almost equally between men and women. Not so on the Far Right, where men were a significant majority: 56 per cent to 44 per cent. Practising Catholics were more strongly represented in the electorate of the opposition as a whole than they were among the supporters of the Far Right.

In some senses the character of this younger, more masculine and more popular electorate seemed to echo the political sociology of at least part of the Left. No wonder, then, that 18 per cent of the sample claimed to have voted for Mitterrand at the first round of the 1981 Presidential election. Only 50 per cent of Far-Right sympathisers actually chose to describe themselves with this label. In terms of their position on the Left–Right axis, 27 per cent classed themselves as 'Right' and 15 per cent as coming from the 'Centre'. It was not so much that the extreme Right was expanding; it was more that the National Front was broadening its appeal beyond the Far Right's traditional boundaries. Jerome Jaffré, SOFRES' Director of political studies, concluded from the polling evidence that National Front voters (in many cases) knew little of their Party's ideological roots; they were simply the footsoldiers or *fantassins* of the electoral battle, unaware or uninterested in Le Pen's deeper ideological motivation or ultimate goals.

Given the difficulties posed by the two-ballot majority voting system for any new party trying to break into the mainstream of French politics, the Front was eager to capitalise on any chance to fight out a campaign using a proportional system. The European Parliament elections of June 1984 provided just such an opportunity. For Le Pen, the European contest had several advantages. For a start, proportional voting enabled the Front to escape from what Le Pen himself described as 'the permanent trap of the *vote utile*'. Secondly, the elections had little domestic significance: national office was not at stake, thus giving the Front ample opportunity to attract disillusioned or disgruntled voters from the other parties. Thirdly, the mainstream opposition went into battle with a joint list headed by Simone Veil. Enthusiasm for the European Community was not equally shared by RPR and UDF supporters and this, together with the prominent position afforded to Simone Veil, probably made elements of the potential RPR electorate uneasy. Veil, as one of Giscard d'Estaing's ministers, was responsible for the legalisation of abortion and was probably far too liberal a figure for many right-wing Gaullists to support. The fact that she was also Jewish enabled Le Pen to capitalise on a latent strand of right-wing anti-semitism in France. Thus, a political space was opened up on the flank of the mainstream Right, which the National Front sought to occupy.

Le Pen embarked upon a strident campaign warning that Europe was in danger of falling under either Soviet or Third World domination. His meetings were accompanied by a considerable degree of violence – Front supporters frequently clashing with left-wing demonstrators – and in Toulon a bomb ripped apart a hall in which the National Front leader was due to speak. On 14 June at the Front's last major rally in Paris, there was a public reconciliation between Le Pen and his old political mentor, Jean-Louis Tixier-Vignancour with whom he had fallen out after the failure of efforts to construct an extreme-Right list for the previous European elections in 1979.

On 17 June the list headed by Jean-Marie Le Pen won just over 11 per cent of the votes cast in metropolitan France – a percentage equivalent to more than two million ballot papers. It was the highest electoral total for the Far Right since 1945 and the National Front sent 10 deputies to the European Parliament. The vote for the National Front was highest in the eastern half of France, notably in the Ile-de-France (14.5 per cent) and the regions of Alsace (13.8 per cent), Languedoc-Roussillon (13.2 per cent), Provence-Côte d'Azur (19 per cent) and Corsica (13.2 per cent). Support for the National Front was largely confined to urban areas and was often linked to the presence of a large immigrant population, and was strongest in areas where former colonists from Algeria had been resettled. The small town of Carmoux in the Bouches-du-Rhône had the national distinction of having the largest proportion of *pieds-noirs* in its population. Here 32.8 per cent of people voted for Le Pen's list. However, links with areas that once supported *Algérie française* should not be overdone. Certainly the Front's best scores came in its natural bastion, the *départements* of the Mediterranean littoral, Alpes-Maritimes, Var and Bouches-du-Rhône, where it won 21.4 per cent, 20 per cent and 19.5 per cent respectively. Nonetheless, Le Pen also drew considerable support from urban areas in eastern and south-eastern France and in the belt of satellite towns around Paris: 15.9 per cent in the Rhône, nearly 14 per cent in the Haut-Rhin, 14.4 per cent in Yvelines and nearly 16 per cent in Seine-Saint-Denis. In the view of one analyst, the results demonstrated that the extreme-right vote no longer represented the cry of a backward-looking France, as it had in the 1950s and 1960s. Rather it was now the expression of the fears of an urban and modern France beset by economic crisis.[7]

It was tempting to compare the rapid electoral rise of the National Front with the superficially similar electoral eruption of Poujadism in 1956, when the protest movement of small shopkeepers, artisans and an assortment of extreme right-wing figures – among them Le Pen himself – won 11.4 per cent of the vote at the legislative election. However, the electoral geography was very different. The movement of Pierre Poujade obtained its best results in rural areas in central and south-western France where Le Pen's scores were well below its 11 per cent national total.[8]

The Poujadist wave receded almost as quickly as it had arisen. In the legislative elections of 1958, Poujade's supporters garnered a meagre 1.4 per cent of the poll. During the Fifth Republic similar electoral surges have also quickly drained away. The extreme Right's Presidential candidate Tixier-Vignancour's 5.3 per cent of December 1965 collapsed to 0.5 per cent for the extreme Right in the Legislative elections less than two years later. The question facing the National Front was whether it too would follow a similar path back to obscurity.

1985–87: LOCAL CONFIRMATION AND NATIONAL BREAK-THROUGH

The Cantonal elections of March 1985 were to prove a significant test. What the National Front lacked was a strong local base – essential in France – if it was to survive and prosper. In March 1982 it had only been able to field 65 candidates. Three years later, it contested more than three-quarters of the cantons at issue, with 1521 candidates in all, a significant indication of its developing local resources. It won 8.7 per cent of the vote – a record for the extreme Right in this type of contest. This was probably equivalent to a national level of support of around 10 per cent, taking into account those cantons where it did not field candidates. Once again it fared best in urban areas, around Paris and in the regions of Provence-Côte d'Azur and Languedoc-Roussillon in south-eastern France. In four of the Marseilles cantons the Front's score was over 22 per cent, and in one district of the city its candidate won just over 30 per cent of the votes cast.

Le Pen, angered by the mainstream opposition's failure to deal with him during the campaign, insisted that National Front candidates would stand again at the second ballot, wherever possible, performing a spoiling role against the mainstream Right and especially the RPR, for whose leader, Jacques Chirac, Le Pen seemed to harbour a particular bitterness. However, Le Pen seemed to change his mind within a matter of days, the Front's Bureau Politique demanding the withdrawal of any of its candidates whose presence in the second round might let in a candidate of the Left. Le Pen had clearly hoped for a higher score. The National Front gained only a single seat on a Departmental Council – these elections proving once again the problems posed by the two-ballot majority voting system for a party that had no political allies. Nonetheless, the National Front had demonstrated that it had started to put down local roots. An article in *Le Monde*, commenting on the outcome of the first ballot, noted that Le Pen had now become an established part of the French political landscape.[9]

President François Mitterrand's decision to introduce a proportional voting system for the legislative elections of March 1986 enabled the National Front to liberate itself from the tyranny of the *vote utile*. It fought the campaign as an autonomous political force, attracting more than two-and-a-half million votes and some 9.8 per cent of the electorate. Its score was marginally better than that of the Communist Party. The National Front won 35 parliamentary seats, the same number as the ailing Communists, and this enabled the Front to constitute its own parliamentary group. The National Front's entry into the Palais Bourbon and Jean-Marie Le Pen's triumphalism masked the fact that support for the Party had in fact declined somewhat since 1984. Le Pen had boasted that he would obtain 15 per cent and between fifty and one hundred seats. Its bastions lay once again in the south-east, along the Mediterranean coast, and in the large urban centres where its themes of immigration and insecurity received a significant resonance. In the Bouches-du-Rhône the Front won 22.5 per cent, out-distancing the list headed by the president of the UDF group in the National Assembly, Jean-Claude Gaudin. In Marseilles the Front received over 24 per cent (up nearly three points on its 1984 score) and it made similar advances in Pyrénées-Orientales and Vaucluse. It also made some progress in the former Socialist bastions of the Nord with 7.8 per cent of the vote (up 1 per cent) and in the Pas-de-Calais with

11.4 per cent of the vote (up just under 1 per cent). Almost two-thirds of the Front's deputies, 20 out of 35, were drawn from just three regions: Provence-Côte d'Azur (8); Ile-de-France (8); and Rhône-Alpes (4). None-theless, in the Paris region and in many rural areas the Front actually lost support. This was a result of two trends: first, a section of the mainstream Right's electorate that had opted for Le Pen in 1984 seemed to have returned to the fold in 1986; and secondly, in areas where the Front was already weak – in agricultural constituencies, for example – this very weakness encouraged voters to opt for one of the other opposition candidates.[10]

The mainstream opposition's success in the legislative elections ushered in the novel constitutional experiment of '*cohabitation*': a Socialist President having to co-exist with a Prime Minister and government of the Right. However, Jacques Chirac did not need the votes of the National Front deputies to secure his parliamentary majority. It was clear that the main-stream Right was eager to see a return to the old style of voting system, a step that would almost inevitably marginalise Le Pen's supporters.

The results of the regional elections, held on the same day as the legisla-tive ballot, were possibly of greater long-term significance. These too involved a proportional voting system; the National Front emerged with 137 Regional Council seats. If the National Front deputies in parliament could be largely ignored by the new government, its supporters in the regional assemblies were not so fortunate. The support of National Front councillors was crucial in enabling the mainstream Right to take or retain control of at least five regions: Languedoc-Roussillon, Haute-Normandie, Picardie, Franche-Comté, and Aquitaine. A variety of deals and arrange-ments were struck, and in each of the first three regions the National Front obtained one of the vice-presidencies of the council. In Provence-Alpes-Côte d'Azur, the President of the regional council, Jean-Claude Gaudin, granted local National Front leaders two vice-presidential posts, though he had no strict need of the Front's council votes to be re-elected.

The National Front's by-now firm anchorage in the political system was illustrated by a SOFRES opinion poll conducted in May 1987. Le Pen's audience was certainly not growing: 67 per cent of those questioned dis-agreed with his political ideas, the same figure as in a similar poll in October 1985, but 10 per cent more than when the question was posed in November the previous year. During the same period those expressing some measure of agreement with his views dropped by two percentage points to 24 per cent. Some 54 per cent of those polled disapproved of Le Pen's policy on immigration. However, 31 per cent did approve of Le Pen's strident anti-immigrant message – considerably more people than were prepared to vote for him – and it was clear from the polling data that support for Le Pen's ideas came from across the political spectrum, with 14 per cent of Socialist sympathisers, 17 per cent of communist sympathisers, 26 per cent of UDF supporters and 39 per cent of RPR supporters agreeing with his outlook.[11]

The significant vein of sympathy within their own ranks for Le Pen's ideas complicated the strategic calculations of the UDF and RPR leaders in the run-up to the Presidential campaign of 1988. The fear was that Le Pen's vote could hold the key to the election. His share of the vote would clearly influence the outcome of the 'primary' contest between Jacques Chirac and Raymond Barre. At the second round, his advice to his supporters as to how they should cast their ballots – and indeed the discipline with which they chose to follow his advice – could determine if François Mitterrand would remain in the Elysée. Even if some two-thirds of the electorate expressed a firm 'No' towards Le Pen and all his works, his views on immigration, at least, appealed to about one-third.

However, towards the end of the year there seemed to be good news for the mainstream opposition parties. A further opinion poll taken after Le Pen's characterisation of the Nazi gas-chambers as 'a point of detail of history', and violent scenes in the National Assembly after a policy of obstructionism mounted by the National Front deputies, indicated a clear drop in his popularity. Some 78 per cent of those questioned now expressed themselves as opposed to Le Pen's ideas, as against 18 per cent in favour. Some 65 per cent now described Le Pen and his party as a danger to democracy, 10 per cent more than in May, six months earlier.[12] However, the collapse in Le Pen's image and the apparent undoing of much of the respectability he had acquired after entering the National Assembly seemed to have had less of an impact on his hard-core electorate with some 8 per cent still indicating they would vote for him. Nonetheless, a Cantonal by-election in Marseilles in November 1987 left the Front with a little over 18 per cent of the vote, 2.4 per cent down on its poll in 1986. Although their candidate had to withdraw, the National Front voters were left as the arbiters of the contest, with Le Pen calling for their abstention at the second round. In the event a significant proportion of them failed to follow his advice, and therefore helped secure the victory of the mainstream opposition candidate.[13]

1988–89: THE GROUND TREMBLES

As the Presidential election of 1988 approached it seemed that Le Pen had managed to recover his position with some 11 or 12 per cent of those

Source: *Le Monde* 26 April 1988

polled saying they would vote for him.[14] Such a score would enable the Front to emerge as the leading candidate of the Right in many of its bastions – an encouraging outcome with the Municipal elections of 1989 less than a year away. At the first round of voting on 24 April, Jean-Marie Le Pen secured a remarkable 14.6 per cent of the vote in metropolitan France, a record for the extreme Right in the postwar period. Le Pen himself spoke of a political earthquake. He was barely two percentage points behind Raymond Barre and only 5 per cent behind Jacques Chirac. Le Pen emerged as the leading candidate of the Right in nine *départements*.

The Presidential contest marked a nationalisation of the extreme Right's appeal. The Front advanced in its now traditional bastions in the southeast, in the Nord-Pas-de-Calais, in the Rhône, in the capital itself and in the Paris region. Certainly the overall shape of the Front's implantation followed the pattern established at the European election in 1984 and the Legislative contest in 1986. In the aftermath of the Presidential contest, *Le Monde* summed up the Front's performance as a 'reflection of an urbanised France hard hit by the economic crisis and linked to the presence of a large immigrant population'.[15] Le Pen's advance, however, was much more than this, as the paper recognised, for 'the novelty of the result of the 24 April was that the National Front gained ground everywhere, extending its appeal well beyond the boundaries of its natural constituency'. Le Pen progressed in many rural *départements*, like Lot-et-Garonne and Haute-Loire, where his strong nationalism and anti-taxation message appeared attractive to farmers and shopkeepers alarmed by the consequences of the single European market. If the overall character of Le Pen's support was markedly different from that of the traditional Far Right, then here, at least, there was perhaps an echo of the message of *poujadisme*.

Indeed, the construction of Europe figured near the bottom of the list of concerns of Le Pen voters. They placed the triad of immigration, insecurity and unemployment among their principal motivations. Analysis confirmed once again that the Front's support came less from the traditional extreme Right, than from an electorate that, at least sociologically, seemed to stand somewhere between Left and Right. Apart from exhibiting a much stronger appeal to male rather than female voters, the National Front's support seemed to reflect the diversity of French society. The Party had sunk roots into all social groups, but it had made particular progress in attracting the young, owners of businesses, employees and workers and those who classed themselves as non-practising Catholics. The diversity of the Le Pen electorate was demonstrated by the fact that at the second ballot, of every 100 Le Pen voters who turned out, 26 voted for François Mitterrand and 74 for Jacques Chirac.[16] Since the early 1980s Le Pen has drawn on the support of three distinct, but by no means equal, groups. About half his votes in 1988 came from radicalised and disillusioned voters of the mainstream Right. It is clear that Le Pen had been robbing the Right, especially the RPR, of its popular base. Almost one-third of Le Pen's support came from new voters or those who had in the past abstained. The remainder were former voters of the Left. And here, despite an apparent and simplistic correlation (chronological if nothing else) between the decline of the Communist Party and the rise of the National Front, it seems that more of these former Left-wing voters came from among Socialist, rather than Communist ranks.[17]

Le Pen's score, though remarkable for an outsider in a Presidential contest, was very much a vote for an individual in a highly personalised campaign. It remained to be seen how far it would stand up in the subsequent Legislative elections. Le Pen insisted that the National Front should now be regarded by the UDF and RPR as the third legitimate component of the Right. He threatened that if the mainstream Right did not accord him this position, then he would run as many candidates as possible at the second round in a grand spoiling operation. When the RPR and UDF announced in May that they would fight under the joint banner of the URC (Union du Rassemblement et du Centre), support only one candidate in each constituency, and reject any deal with the Front, Le Pen rose from his hospital bed (he had suffered a mild heart-attack) to denounce what he called the union of 'patching things up and compromising principles'.

At the first round the National Front obtained 9.8 per cent of the vote. Le Pen himself won nearly 33 per cent in one of the Marseilles constituencies, and in nine constituencies in the Provence-Côte-d'Azur region his supporters topped the poll on the Right. Once again the question of local deals between the mainstream Right and the National Front was raised. The local UDF in the Bouches-du-Rhône agreed to stand down in eight constituencies where the mainstream Right had been defeated by Le Pen's legions. In the event, the National Front candidates, including Le Pen and most of his chief lieutenants, were unable to capitalise on their legitimation as the sole candidate of the Right: they did not carry any seats. Only in the neighbouring department of Var did the Front have any success: Yann Piat was re-elected and she became the Party's single representative in the National Assembly. She too was the only candidate of the Right at the second round and she benefited from the transfer of a significant proportion of the mainstream Right's vote. Le Pen might claim that she would make as much noise in the Assembly as a whole parliamentary group, but the results overall were a serious set-back, demonstrating once again the tyranny of the two-ballot system.

During the latter part of 1988 the National Front suffered several blows: it lost its foot-hold in the National Assembly in October when Yann Piat was expelled from the Party; and in November Jean-Pierre Stirbois, the National Front Secretary-General whose skills had done much to set the Party on its electoral rise, was killed in a car-crash. The National Front's public image seemed to be deteriorating: an opinion poll indicated that only 16 per cent of those questioned agreed with Le Pen's ideas, as against 80 per cent who rejected them. This marked a low point for the influence of the National Front leader's ideas.[18] The poll came only weeks after his latest anti-semitic comment when he condemned a Jewish centrist minister in the Government, Michel Durafour, as '*monsieur Durafour-crématoire*' – a reference to the Nazi gas-chambers. A series of Cantonal by-elections in the Front's bastion of Marseilles showed its support 10 per cent down on Le Pen's score in the Presidential first ballot. True, the abstention rate was high, but an analysis of the vote, canton by canton, suggested that in areas of Communist strength some National Front voters were returning to their PCF roots; and in areas of UDF and RPR strength, Front voters were shifting towards the mainstream opposition parties.[19] The Front's declining performance was confirmed in two legislative by-elections in January of the following year.[20]

It was an inauspicious start to the Municipal election campaign. Carl Lang, the new Secretary-General of the Party, stressed that the Front was going into battle under its own colours, but that it would not be held responsible for divisions within the Right between the ballots. The door was open to cooperation with the mainstream parties at the second round, though they would have to stop their ostracism of the National Front. The Municipal contest, with its element of proportionality, offered an opportunity to the Front but this type of election also required considerable local resources which the Party's organisation still struggled to muster. The Front was only able to put together lists in 214 of the 390 towns with more than 20 000 inhabitants. Nonetheless, this was a significant advance on 1983, justifying Lang's comment on the eve of the first ballot that whatever the result, it would be a success.

At the first ballot Le Pen's supporters won seats in 90 communes and obtained the necessary 10 per cent of the poll to remain in contention in 52 towns.[21] This was further evidence of the success of the Party's efforts to put down local roots, though its results overall were disappointing. Taking into account the many municipalities in which it did not present candidates, the Front's score probably represented little more than 7 per cent of the national vote.[22] The result was very much in line with the gloomy news coming from opinion polls and by-elections during the previous few months.

The mainstream Right's insistence on keeping the National Front at arm's length ensured that in contrast to previous elections (the 1985 Cantonals, the 1988 Presidential and the1988 Legislatives), where Le Pen had more or less urged his supporters to rally against the Left at the second ballot, the Front this time ran as many lists as possible at the second round. The trial of strength between the mainstream Right and Le Pen's supporters indicated the resilience of the National Front vote. In several cases this resulted in the defeat of the list of a well-placed mainstream candidate. In contrast, in those municipalities where the Front was unable to stand and where Le Pen had called for his followers to scorn the appeal of UDF or RPR candidates, large numbers of Far-Right voters opted for the mainstream lists.

While denouncing the exclusion to which the National Front had fallen victim – in large part, according to Le Pen, due to a secret deal between Chirac and the head of the principal Jewish representative body in France – the National Front President characterised the Municipal outcome as providing a suitable trampoline for the European election of June. At the outset of the campaign he expressed his hope that the National Front would double its representation in the European Parliament and gain twenty seats. As time went on Le Pen reined in his aspirations, ultimately hoping for no fewer votes than he obtained at the last European election in 1984. Here at least, he was not disappointed. The National Front won an 11.7 per cent share of the vote, its second-best performance since 1983 and once again sent 10 parliamentary members to Strasbourg.[23] In the six years since 1983, French voters had been to the polls some ten times and the National Front had become anchored in the political system at a consistent level of around 10 per cent.

Without proportional representation at legislative contests, however, it seemed that the Front would generally be unable to capitalise on its increasingly solid implantation. Without a change in the parliamentary voting system three conditions appeared essential for the National Front to prosper: it had to have good local roots; the climate of public opinion had to favour its principal themes of immigration and insecurity; and it had to be able to conclude some sort of electoral pact with the parties of the mainstream Right. At the Legislative by-election in Dreux in November 1989 two of these elements were undoubtedly present.

In Marie-France Stirbois, the widow of its former Secretary-General, the Front had an effective and well-known candidate. The controversy that erupted in October over the right of Muslim girls to wear the headscarf at school, caused deep divisions among the ruling Socialist Party and played straight into the hands of the National Front. Immigration and the 'threat to the French way of life' were at the forefront of peoples' minds. But at Dreux the third condition, a deal with the mainstream Right, was unnecessary. Marie-France Stirbois emerged from the first ballot with nearly 42.5 per cent of the vote, her nearest rival, the RPR candidate, obtaining only 24.6 per cent. Stirbois did especially well in neighbourhoods which had in the past shown strong left-wing traditions.[24] At a by-election in Marseilles, held on the same day, the National Front candidate also made spectacular gains, securing 33 per cent of the vote. The novelty of these two contests was that in each case the second round was a run-off between the National Front and the mainstream opposition candidate, in one case RPR, in the other UDF. Furthermore, they were contests that the National Front had a good chance of winning.

Despite some somewhat nuanced pleas from both Left and Right for their supporters to rally behind the mainstream candidates, Marie-France Stirbois cruised home to victory in Dreux taking 61 per cent of the vote.[25] Dreux, with its significant immigrant population and urban ills, had become a veritable political laboratory for the National Front. However, this image is partly misleading: much of the constituency consists of rolling farmland, with neither an immigrant's face nor a high-rise HLM to be seen. A detailed analysis of the result is interesting since it shows that Marie-France Stirbois polled well in rural areas as well as attracting urban discontent.[26]

In Marseilles the National Front was defeated by the UDF candidate by a margin of some 5 per cent. Nonetheless the Front did win a cantonal by-election in the Bouches-du-Rhône, in a seat that the Socialist Party had held for the past fifty years. In all cases it was clear that significant numbers of mainstream voters on the Right were willing to give their support to the National Front. The salience of the immigration issue was an important factor, since opinion polls have consistently shown that Le Pen's views on immigration have a strong resonance among a relatively wide audience.

1991–94: PROGRESS AND ISOLATION

The victory in Dreux, once again, gave the National Front a presence in the National Assembly. The Party's political fortunes were clearly improving. Le Pen's curious position during the Gulf conflict and his apparent sympathy for Saddam Hussein, while causing some short-term problems, did not seem to have any lasting effect. Opinion surveys showed the Front's ideas gaining ground. A poll published in October 1991 showed one person in three expressing some measure of support for Le Pen's ideas.[27] This was a record level and 38 per cent of those questioned approved of his views on immigration. The majority might regard Le Pen's ideas as racist and his party as a threat to democracy, but his appeal clearly extended to a potential audience that was much larger than just his core voters.

The opinion polls encouraged National Front leaders to hope for great things from the Regional and Cantonal elections of 1992. Bruno Mégret believed that Le Pen's supporters could move into the 15–20 per cent bracket in the Regional contest, leaving behind the 10–15 per cent zone that had characterised the Party's best scores during the 1980s. He hoped for considerably more Regional Council seats than the 137 obtained in 1986. Indeed its actual tally had declined to less than one hundred after a series of defections in the wake of Le Pen's anti-semitic comments. In contrast to the local *notables* who had rallied to National Front lists in 1986, its candidates in 1992 were largely drawn from among Party *cadres* and members. In the Front's bastion of Provence-Côte-d'Azur, Le Pen was convinced that his formation would emerge as the largest political force.

At the national level, the Socialist Prime Minister, Edith Cresson, at times seemed intent on using Le Pen and his Party as the principal plank in her campaign against the mainstream Right. However, this exposure only provided the Front with a mitigated victory. The Regional elections saw the Party consolidate its position as a significant political force, though the results in the crucible of the south-east were less good than the Front and indeed many of the analysts had predicted. In personal terms the results were a disappointment for the Front's leading figures.[28] Bruno Mégret came third in the Bouches-du-Rhône, while Le Pen himself had to make do with second place in Alpes-Maritimes. Nonetheless, in the Provence-Alpes-Côte-d'Azur region as a whole the Front came in second place with 34 out of the 123 regional assembly seats. Overall, the Front obtained second place in France's three largest regions; it won a significant position in at least five more and achieved a respectable regional power-base. Its score of nearly 14 per cent should be compared with just under 10 per cent at the regional contest in 1986.

Once again the National Front's success had been facilitated by the pro-portional voting system. The Socialist Party had been routed in the regional contest and its defeat was confirmed in the cantonal voting. Here the election was fought out using a two-ballot majority voting system, over successive weekends. The National Front, with some 12.5 per cent, achieved its highest score in a cantonal contest, but failed to pick up more than an isolated council seat. While the National Front vote exhibited its familiar contours, it also enlarged its social base, attracting more votes from women, from people with a university education and from practising Catholics.[29] If one treats the two ecological lists as separate parties, then the National Front was the leading formation in attracting the votes of the 18–24 age-group.

Overall the Front's performance was positive, though deceptive. It was unable to cash in its gains for any significant political influence. Its voice was not decisive in the election of regional council presidents. By running candidates at the second ballot of the cantonal contest it was only able to prevent the election of RPR or UDF candidates in a relatively small number of cases. Its nuisance value was significantly circumscribed; the simple fact was that the Left was far too weak to give the Front a decisive role. The Maastricht Treaty referendum in September 1992 was similarly a disappointment for the National Front. Le Pen had hoped to be the standard-bearer for the 'No' campaign; instead, he found this position and his best lines stolen by the dissident Gaullist campaign run by Philip Séguin and Charles Pasqua.

The political isolation of the Front gave its campaign for the Legislative elections of 1993 an increasingly bitter tone. Carl Lang com-pared the Front to the fabled tortoise, confident that it would ultimately catch the electoral hares – a strategy presumably for the long term. Nonetheless, Le Pen hoped to capitalise on the series of scandals that sur-rounded the Socialist Government; his campaign slogan, '*mains propres et tête haute*' (clean hands and head held high), seemed particularly appropriate. Towards the mainstream Right there would be no compro-mise. Le Pen, who stood for election in Nice, stressed that as many National Front candidates as possible would go through to the second round. He argued that the Right was just as bad as the Left and that there was no reason why he should favour those who had voted 'Yes' to Maastricht and who were noted for their hostility towards the National Front. On 21 March, the National Front won 12.4 per cent, its best-ever percentage in a Legislative contest. It had clearly established itself as the fourth political formation in France. However, even the redoubtable Marie-France Stirbois was unable to hold her seat at Dreux. The mainstream Right swept through the doors of the National Assembly, achieving the largest parliamentary majority ever. The National Front was marginalised. Even in its south-eastern bastions, neither Le Pen nor any of his chief lieutenants was able to secure victory.[30]

However, in many cases it was a close-run thing. At Dreux Marie-France Stirbois gathered 49.8 per cent of the second-ballot vote. Bruno Mégret in Marignane took 49.5 per cent, Marie-Claude Roussel in Marseilles took 45.2 per cent and Le Pen himself in Nice, 42 per cent. The National Front was consolidating its position. It seemed quite capable of attracting a significant proportion of mainstream Right voters at second ballots where its candidates were in a duel with the Left. And in triangular contests it was generally able to hold on to its voters – a fact which once again underlines the specific nature of the National Front vote.[31]

Once again the diversity of the National Front's electorate was displayed. However, there were changes: the margin between its male and female supporters was narrowing; its appeal was strongest amongst the young; and its popular character was becoming accentuated. Whatever the diverse origins of its support, National Front voters were united in the salience they afforded to issues like immigration and insecurity. The Front was also quite capable of attracting support in more rural areas, where issues like European agricultural policy and the GATT trade round created disquiet, and where the regional press helped to spread the sense of urban alienation and unease prompted by a changing world. Opinion polls show consistently that the National Front's voters are the most pessimistic, the most uncertain about their future, and the most critical of existing parties and politicians of all the electorate. A vote for the National Front is at least as much a vote 'against' the existing system as it is a positive affirmation of support for Le Pen's ideas.

However, during the early 1990s, opinion-poll evidence suggested that support for Le Pen's ideas was generally waning. As the Front gathered for its Ninth Congress in February 1994, a SOFRES study indicated that 73 per cent of those questioned – more people than ever – believed that the Front represented a danger to democracy.[32] The proportion of people declaring themselves in agreement with the ideas defended by Le Pen and the National Front had slumped to 19 per cent – from 32 per cent in October 1991. Among conservative voters, over the same period, the proportion backing the Front's ideas had almost halved. Le Pen's strident anti-immigrant message, his defence of traditional values, and his emphasis on combating crime and delinquency still attracted support. But overall the poll provided a sombre message for the Front. Cantonal elections were only a few weeks away, and the next European, and ultimately, the next Presidential elections, beckoned.

The cantonal elections in March 1994 involved seats that were last fought over in 1988. Le Pen's target was to take some 10 per cent of the first-ballot vote, effectively doubling his share compared with 1988. In practice the Front won 9.67 per cent; a result hailed by Le Pen as a 'triumphal success'. Virtually all of the Front's 93 candidates who were eligible to go through to the second ballot did so.[33] National Front spokesmen insisted that Le Pen's formation would stand alone against all the other parties at the second ballot, which they did, to little avail. Overall some eighteen hundred Front candidates had stood in the Cantonal contest; only three of its candidates were ultimately elected.[34] While Bruno Mégret railed against what he called 'the republican front' that had sought to block his party's advance, Le Pen condemned the lack of media attention given on election night to what he described as 'the only political movement that was clearly increasing its vote in comparison to the results of 1988'.[35] But whatever the National Front President's upbeat assertions, the results – just as in 1992 – indicated the Front's increasingly marginal role. The Party's standard-bearer in Nice – Jacques Peyrat – warned that the Front had to break out of its isolation by pursuing a line that was more open towards other formations. He argued that if the Front didn't respond quickly to this challenge it would be condemned to return to the political ghetto. And looking ahead to the next municipal contest in 1995, he emphasised that there was no other way for Le Pen to capture the town hall in Nice than 'to put his National Front credentials in his pocket'.[36]

The European elections in June 1994 provided further bad news for Le Pen. The National Front's vote was down on its previous showing in 1989. Le Pen's 10.5 per cent of the ballot was well short of his self-declared target of 15 per cent. Worse still, the Front was outdistanced, not just by the right-wing anti-Maastricht list of Philippe de Villiers, but also by the left-wing populist list headed by Bernard Tapie. The results presented a mixed picture. The National Front's vote went down significantly in a number of *départements* where it had achieved its best scores in 1989. In contrast, in over twenty, it actually increased its share of the vote, but only by a small amount. *Le Monde*'s headline said it all: 'The National Front marks time'.[37]

Indeed, the European results in many ways illustrated the limits of Le Pen's appeal. Bruno Mégret tried to encourage party activists by insisting that although the Front's own vote had largely reflected the 'solidity' of the Party's electorate, the results still indicated a 'spectacular increase in the audience for Le Pen's ideas'.[38] He deduced this by claiming that since de Villiers' proposals were, in his view, little more than a slice of the National Front's own programme, the two lists' totals could simply be added together. By this reckoning Le Pen's ideas were supported by some 25 per cent of the electorate, which Mégret suitably inflated to a potential audience of some 30 per cent. In fact quite the opposite case could be argued. Evidence from opinion polls suggests that Le Pen's and de Villiers' electorates are not to be equated in this way: Le Pen held on to the bulk of his traditional electorate; and while the l'Autre Europe list of de Villiers did attract some National Front voters, the majority of its support seems to have come from the mainstream Right.[39]

De Villiers' departure from the Parti Républicain (one of the constituents of the UDF) prompted some lively polemics. The Party's Secretary-General, José Rossi, insisted that there was only 'the thickness of a cigarette paper' between de Villiers and Le Pen.[40] But for all his ultra-conservatism, de Villiers' movement – Combat pour les Valeurs – is not quite the same as the Front. For one thing, de Villiers has not given immigration policy such a central place in his rhetoric. It is clear that de Villiers provides a more respectable home for the mainstream Right's anti-European, more traditionalist, voters. Some of these people may have voted for Le Pen in the past, but for most, Le Pen's image and rhetoric put him beyond the political pale.[41] Viewed in this light, de Villiers' success raises fundamental questions about the Front's own ability to broaden its appeal.

However, the electoral rise of the National Front has been dramatic. In the space of ten years it had established a highly professional machine and had put down local roots. It had developed a loyal following and, despite fluctuations, it had achieved a fairly consistent level of support. However, the mechanics of the electoral system have prevented it from capitalising on its position. In the Cantonal elections of 1992, for example it obtained only one seat; and in 1994 only three. At the Legislative elections of 1988 it sent only a single Deputy to the Palais Bourbon, and in the Legislative election of 1993 it was denied any parliamentary representation at all.

Nonetheless, wherever there is an element of proportional representation, as at the 1986 Legislative contest, or in Regional or Municipal elections, the Front has been able to make its mark. President Mitterrand has been much criticised for introducing the voting system that let the National Front into parliament in 1986, though the subsequent election saw nearly all of the National Front deputies turned out of office. In retrospect, it was probably the introduction of the principle of proportionality at the Regional and Municipal levels which did more to help Le Pen's supporters establish themselves. But whatever its own representation, the National Front's political influence still depends, in large part, upon the pressure it can exert on the mainstream Right. And this in turn, is closely related to the overall correlation of forces between Left and Right. A comparison of the 1986 and 1992 regional elections illustrates this point.

But quite apart from the institutional constraints on the National Front, its advance remains limited due to its negative image among much of the electorate. In 1991, some 80 per cent of voters regarded it as a racist and sectarian party; 76 per cent believed that it did not have the capability to govern. This net rejection of the Front and its themes must be qualified, however, by the fact that under the right conditions (so far displayed only in specific local contexts as in Dreux), the Front can indeed overcome the institutional hurdles and beat all comers. Central to the Front's electoral appeal is the importance which it gives in both its rhetoric and policy to the issue of immigration.

4 Immigration as a Political Issue

During the course of the 1980s, immigration became one of the central issues in French political life. As we have already seen, it was a potent factor in many constituencies during the municipal elections of 1983, which marked the National Front's first significant electoral breakthrough. The perceived problem of immigration was also at the forefront of campaigning in the European elections of 1984, in the 1986 Legislative contest, and in the Presidential election of 1988.

The issue was seized upon by elements of the media with evident relish and turned into a debate about the very future of France itself. In October 1985, the conservative *Figaro-Magazine* published what it described as an 'explosive dossier' devoted to immigration, including the results of a demographic analysis of a kind, which, it claimed, had never been published before.[1] The tone of the article was well summed-up by the magazine's cover: a bust of Marianne (the symbol of the Republic) shrouded in a Muslim veil, with the caption 'Will we still be French in thirty years time?' It was, perhaps, no surprise that *Figaro-Magazine*, which had long been a vehicle for the ideas of the *nouvelle droite*, should have presented the immigration theme in such apocalyptic terms. The left-leaning daily *Le Matin* roundly condemned the article as nothing more than 'racism on glossy paper'; and its editor, Max Gallo, claimed that the piece well illustrated what he called the 'collaboration' of the mainstream Right with the ideas of Jean-Marie Le Pen.[2] While the *Figaro-Magazine* article certainly encapsulated the emotional tone of much of the public debate surrounding immigration, mainstream politicians of both Left and Right displayed a remarkable ambivalence towards the whole issue, which did much to lend credence to Le Pen's simplistic assumptions.

The rise of the National Front, with its xenophobic, anti-immigrant message, did much to keep the issue of immigration at the forefront of the political agenda, and, of equal importance, to define the terms in which it was discussed. Immigration, in this populist view, was presented as a rising tide of mainly North African and Muslim faces. Immigration was linked to unemployment, to urban crime and delinquency, indeed to all of France's urban ills. Few, if any, mainstream political leaders were willing or indeed able to challenge these connections successfully. The response of mainstream politicians of both Left and Right to the strident anti-immigrant rhetoric of Le Pen was neatly demonstrated by the then Socialist Prime Minister, Laurent Fabius, who, in a television interview in September 1984, acknowledged that Le Pen was asking the right questions, even though he was providing the wrong answers.[3]

Since the early 1980s, Governments of both Left and Right have struggled to demonstrate to voters that they are tough on immigration. For the Socialist Party this has proved especially difficult. Immigration is an issue where the tone and volume of a Party's pronouncements often seem to count more than the actual content of its policy. Here, the Party's ideological portmanteau of liberal assumptions and good intentions has proved a major burden. The Socialists have indeed been tough on immigration, but they have always sought to present this policy as going hand-in-hand with a humane and enlightened attempt to integrate those immigrants already in France. In the highly charged atmosphere engendered by the rise of Le Pen, this dual approach has left them open to charges of weakness and a lack of resolution from both the mainstream Right, and from the National Front in particular

But the parties of the mainstream Right have had just as many problems as those of the Left in grappling with this issue. They see the immigration issue as one they can use to win back voters from the National Front. Such votes could be crucial in any 'primary' battle between conservative candidates at the first round of a Presidential contest. But this is not just an internal political battle within the right-wing camp. For in a future battle for the Elysée, the candidate of the mainstream Right, at the second ballot, might well need the backing of National Front voters in a close-run electoral race against the Left. This intense competition for a section of the right-wing electorate has provoked mainstream political figures like the Gaullist leader Jacques Chirac, and the former President Valéry Giscard d'Estaing into harsh words on immigration; at times they have spoken of immigrants in terms that echo the rhetoric of Jean-Marie Le Pen. Indeed, the pervasive influence of the Front's agenda is remarkable. Even though immigration was not prominent in the 1993 National Assembly election campaign – immigration controls, identity checks, and a reform of the rules governing the acquisition of French nationality nonetheless became a prominent and early element in the victorious Balladur Government's legislative programme.

The creation of this continuing debate on immigration is Le Pen's greatest and most abiding achievement. It is a paradoxical one, because immigration in his terms – a flood of foreigners sweeping over the frontiers – has long ceased. The inflow of immigrant workers, for so long a feature of the French economy, was largely halted in 1974 soon after President

Valéry Giscard d'Estaing took office. Since then the number of immigrants, as a proportion of the total population, has remained remarkably stable. Only specific categories of people have been allowed entry: workers with essential skills, the families of those already present in France, and refugees obtaining political asylum.

French immigration statistics are often confusing, with different government agencies and departments providing a variety of different calculations. The 1982 census, for example, gave a figure of some 3.7 million foreigners out of an overall population of some 55 million, while the following year the Ministry of the Interior came up with a figure of 4.47 million – a considerable difference. None of the official statistics makes any allowance for illegal immigrants, where estimates range wildly from three hundred thousand up to one million. The census returns are accepted as underestimating the immigrant population; many immigrant families are unwilling to provide accurate information to an official figure who knocks at their door. Conversely, the Ministry's figures are a significant overestimation, taking into account applicants for residence permits whose requests are being processed, and excluding deaths, naturalisations and those immigrants returning to their country of origin. In a field where perceptions are often more important than facts, definitional problems abound. Many people regard the second-generation of North African immigrants born in France – the so-called *'beurs'* – as immigrants, though for all legal purposes most of them are actually French.[4]

This apparent statistical uncertainty has proved a boon to the National Front, with Le Pen alleging that the real number of immigrants was more like six million, though quite how he calculated this figure is unclear.[5] In establishing the Higher Council for Integration in the spring of 1990, the then Prime Minister, Michel Rocard, pointed to the damaging impact of these apparently contradictory official statistics, noting that the new organisation's task was to get rid of the spectres which surround the presence of foreigners in France, by 'substituting as exact an understanding as possible of the facts relating to the flow of immigrants, for the incomplete, incoherent, and sometimes inaccurate information currently available'.[6]

However contradictory the official statistics may be, the overall picture of immigration that they provide is clear. It is a picture of remarkable stability since the mid-1970s. Some 70 per cent of the foreign population in France has been resident there for more than ten years. In a briefing paper prepared for the National Assembly debate on immigration in June 1985, the then Socialist Government attempted to set out a sober assessment of the statistics. Basing its evidence on the 1982 census returns, it quoted the figure cited above of some 3.7 million foreigners. (In 1990 the figure was actually closer to 3.6 million.)[7] This represented about 6.8 per cent of the French population, a small increase on the 1975 figure of 6.5 per cent and not so very different from the proportion of foreigners in 1931 of 6.6 per cent.[8] Between 1975 and 1982 the number of foreigners resident in France had increased by some 240 000. In fact some 735 000 people had entered the country, but this figure was off-set by those returning home and those who became naturalised French citizens.

While the overall proportion of immigrants in France has not increased dramatically, there has been a significant change in their origins. In 1982, Algerians made up the largest group, followed by Portuguese, Moroccans and Italians.[9] Less than half the foreigners resident in France were European, compared with some 75 per cent in 1962, and over 40 per cent of the immigrants were of African origin, compared with only 20 per cent two decades earlier.[10]

The Government briefing paper also pointed to the uneven distribution of immigrants within France. More than half the foreign population was concentrated in just three regions: Ile-de-France (36 per cent); Rhône-Alpes (12.5 per cent); and Provence-Alpes-Côte-d'Azur (nearly 9 per cent). Not surprisingly, immigration was largely an urban phenomenon, these figures corresponding to the three great cities of Paris, Lyons and Marseilles. More generally, the statistics indicated that two foreigners in every three lived in a town of more than 100 000 inhabitants.

If the proportion of immigrants in the French population has remained relatively stable, the changing nature of the immigrant communities – less European, more identifiably 'foreign' – has undoubtedly helped to create the unease on which the Le Pen phenomenon thrives. Le Pen has skilfully picked up and manipulated the issue of immigration, using it as a focus for the Front's appeal. The immigrant has been resurrected as the traditional scapegoat for all of France's ills. The fact that immigration proper is controlled and regulated makes little difference to the terms of the debate. Leaving aside the struggle against illegal immigration, which has taken on a political importance far beyond its practical significance, the debate is actually not about immigration at all. Immigration has become a sort of shorthand for a complex pattern of concerns – the fear of unemployment, of housing problems, rising crime, AIDS, drug abuse, and uncertainties about France's place in the world and the meaning of what it is to be French. In pointing to the perceived threat from immigrant communities (and especially North African Muslim immigrants) already living in France, Le Pen has raised the spectre of the enemy within. And, in large part, the issue of immigration really turns on the place in French society of this large, seemingly permanent, and increasingly non-European minority population. Inevitably, then, the political debate has broadened to include not just measures to stamp out the flow of illegal immigrants, but to touch on the whole question of French nationality and citizenship, and the extent to which people from quite different cultures are free to practise their religious traditions and lifestyles within the French system. The debate has raised questions about France's traditional tolerance towards newcomers, and has led to a growing discussion about the emergence of a new tide of racism and anti-semitism.

IMMIGRATION: DEFINING THE ISSUE

While the National Front has been the principal beneficiary of the political debate on immigration, it was not actually Le Pen's party that first brought the issue on to the political agenda. It was in fact the Communists, who at the start of the1980s, launched a campaign against what they saw as the over-concentration of immigrants in Communist-run municipalities, especially in the Paris region.[11]

On Christmas Eve 1980, a group of PCF sympathisers, led by the Communist Mayor of Vitry, used a bulldozer to destroy the power supplies and staircases of a hostel used by immigrant workers. This local action was subsequently backed by the Party's national leadership. The PCF General Secretary, Georges Marchais, sent an open letter to the Rector of the Paris Mosque justifying the Mayor's actions.[12] Marchais noted that he approved of the Mayor's 'refusal to allow the already high number of immigrant workers in his commune to increase'. The General Secretary insisted that the Communists were no racists, but that immigration was one of the evils created by capitalism. And in an argument which received a clear echo in later National Front propaganda, he claimed that the current immigration policy was 'as much against the interests of the immigrant workers and of most of their home countries as against the interests of French workers and of France'.

Marchais insisted that there were simply too many immigrants in Communist-run areas, the threshold of toleration had been passed, and that the pressure on social resources was unbearable. 'When the concentration [of immigrants] becomes very great', he argued,

The housing crisis gets worse; council housing is cruelly deficient and numerous French families cannot have access to it. The costs of the social services necessary for immigrant families plunged into misery, becomes impossible for the budgets of communes peopled by workers to bear. Schooling is not able to support the situation and school backwardness increases amongst children, as much immigrant as French. The health expenses [also] increase.[13]

Marchais called for an equitable distribution of immigrants between different areas, and for a halt to all further immigration, both legal and clandestine. The Communists' enthusiasm for direct action against immigrants was again in evidence a few weeks later, when the Communist Mayor of Montigny-les-Cormeilles helped to organise a demonstration outside the home of an immigrant family accused of drug-dealing.

The Communist Party's emphasis upon the link between immigration and urban deprivation is of central importance. As one American expert has noted, 'the political issues of immigration were nurtured and defined in an urban context, particularly in cities governed by the Left'.[14] Marchais' comments reflected longstanding Communist concerns dating back to the late 1960s. In 1969 the Communist Mayors of the Paris region had protested against what they saw as the inequitable distribution of immigrant workers. During the 1970s such concerns manifested themselves in practical terms: in many towns and cities non-European immigrants were excluded from new municipal housing projects on the basis of the need to maintain immigration below a putative 'threshold of tolerance'. In truth, the Communist Party's attitude was not so very different from that of the other parties, though its position is important because so many immigrants were concentrated in Communist-run towns. (By 1977, immigrants made up more than 10 per cent of the population in 55 per cent of Communist-run towns of over 30 000 inhabitants.)

The political problem of immigration thus came to be seen as one of competition for scarce resources: for housing, welfare services and ultimately, in the National Front's view, for jobs. When the issue re-emerged on to the electoral agenda at the 1983 Municipal contest it took an especially strident form. Three factors were at work here. The tone of the debate was fundamentally influenced by the National Front's excessive and exclusionist rhetoric, which, on several occasions was readily adopted by politicians of the mainstream Right.[15] The growing economic crisis and opposition to the Socialist Government's austerity programme gave the immigration issue a sharper edge. And in the longer term a third factor also played its part: the infiltration into the political system of a new system of ideas – those of the so-called *nouvelle droite* – which, as we have already seen, helped to provide a new vocabulary and ideological justification for anti-immigrant views.

When the Left came to power in 1981, the Government sought to give immigration policy a more humane and liberal dimension. Many expulsions were suspended and the rights of family members to join breadwinners already in France were reaffirmed. Rules relating to immigrants' rights of association were relaxed, enabling them to form their own self-help and lobbying groups. The whole process of expulsion, which had been a largely administrative matter under the previous administration, was brought under the jurisdiction of the courts, in theory safeguarding immigrants' rights. The system of providing state aid for immigrant workers who wished to return home – instituted in 1977 – was abandoned. And in an attempt at a fresh start, all those illegal immigrants who had entered France before 1 January 1981, and who had stable employment, were given proper papers. (Some 130 000 people benefited from this measure.)

The Socialists began with the best of intentions. But it quickly became clear that the real motor behind policy in this area was not so much the objective problems posed by immigration, but the public perception of these problems. During the early 1980s, immigrants were becoming much more visible in French society, not just as a topic of debate, but as actors in their own right. There was a series of damaging strikes in the car industry – an important employer of immigrant workers – many of whom were now losing their jobs as the recession bit harder. There was also a series of violent disturbances in inner-city areas, culminating in the 'long hot summer' of 1983 with several attacks on immigrants, involving firearms, one of which resulted in the death of a 10-year-old Algerian boy who was letting off fireworks in a Paris suburb to celebrate the ending of Ramadan.

The Mayor of Paris, the RPR leader Jacques Chirac, decided to launch his own immigration clampdown. He said that 'France no longer had the means to support a crowd of foreigners who abused her hospitality'.[16] According to Chirac, 'the threshold of tolerance had been passed in many areas, and this risked provoking a racist reaction'. The checking of immigrants' papers would henceforth be much more rigorous, and Mr Chirac insisted that municipal services, schooling, welfare and so on would only go to legal immigrants. While arguing that immigrants should be spread more evenly throughout the city's *arrondissements*, Mr Chirac also supported the idea of grouping immigrants of the same nationality into a given area – he did not use the word ghetto – claiming that the Moroccan and Tunisian ambassadors in Paris had both expressed their backing for such a scheme.

The strong showing of the National Front in Dreux in September 1983, together with Mr Chirac's offensive, provided strong evidence that the Government risked being outflanked on the issue of immigration. They had already decided to shift their ground. While the generosity of the initial Socialist policies should not be overstated, the summer of 1983 marked a new emphasis in the Government's thinking.[17] The Secretary of State responsible for immigrant workers, Georgina Dufoix, insisted that the new tougher line was not a break with the generosity of 1981.[18] Once again the principal target was clandestine or illegal immigrants. She argued that only if illegal immigration were halted, would it be possible to improve social conditions for immigrants already in France. She attempted to refute the Front's linking of immigration with unemployment. She argued that since 1974 the number of immigrants in the workforce had remained relatively stable, while unemployment had more than quadrupled.

But if the Government's policy was still founded upon two elements – assistance for the integration of those legally in France, and stringent controls on those trying to enter the country illegally – it was clear from her remarks that the presentational emphasis was very much on the latter. Indeed, according to Dufoix, the very success of integration depended on the efficiency of entry controls.[19] The procedures for expelling illegal immigrants were speeded up, and in 1984 steps were taken to reintroduce state-aid for voluntary repatriation (though the scheme was given a new name). The new measure prompted *L'Express* magazine to publish a 17-page *dossier* under the headline 'Immigrants: Is a Return Possible?'; though, while the Socialist measures included more cash than the previous conservative Government's scheme, it was far from clear why it should have been any more successful.[20] In addition there was a tightening up of the rules governing the entry of immigrant workers' families.

In October 1984 a new actor joined the immigration debate in the form of the anti-racist movement, SOS-Racisme. This organisation, headed by Harlem Désir, was strongly backed by President Mitterrand himself, and was launched to spread the anti-racist message, especially among the young, through marches, pop concerts and other local events. Paradoxically, its activities, along with the pronouncements of Le Pen and his lieutenants, did much to keep the immigration issue in the public eye.

Immigration figured prominently in the 1986 general election campaign. Its outcome – a victory for the mainstream Right, with the National Front gaining its first parliamentary seats – meant that the subject would remain a staple of the day-to-day political debate. A series of terrorist attacks in Paris, of Middle Eastern origin, added an additional element to this debate, with immigration controls now closely linked with law and order, and internal security.

The centrepiece of the new Government's immigration policy was the so-called *loi Pasqua*, named after Interior Minister Charles Pasqua, dealing with the entry and stay of foreigners in France. This required anyone entering the country to prove they had adequate means of support.

Henceforth it would be much more difficult for individuals to obtain or renew the ten-year residence permits introduced by the preceding Socialist administration. The legislation also significantly widened the categories of people who could be expelled or refused entry on the grounds that they represented a threat to public order. Expulsions were taken out of the hands of the judiciary, and could now be carried out on the orders of the local Prefect.

The Chirac Government had already taken rapid steps to bolster police powers to carry out identity-checks in public places. Indeed, the intensity of police operations was a clear indication that the new Interior Minister desired to present a tougher policy. The Government did not delay in using its new powers. In mid-October 1986 police rounded up a large number of Malians from immigrant hostels on the outskirts of Paris. Those without permits were arrested, served with expulsion orders, and within days just over one hundred were put on board a chartered jet bound for Bamako.

This episode prompted considerable disquiet among human rights groups, Church leaders and opposition politicians. The police initially argued that the Malians were drug-pushers, though it emerged that only a handful had been convicted of such offences. The rest were simply illegal immigrants, who, it seemed, had been summarily expelled without being afforded any right of appeal. The whole manner in which the operation was carried out shocked many people, including some within the Government's own ranks. In response to Pasqua's insistence that 'the law was the law', Claude Malhuret, a UDF politician and Secretary of State for Human Rights, noted that while the law had to be respected, this 'policy of charter-flights risked leading the most xenophobic elements of French public opinion to believe that the Government did not strongly condemn racism'.[21]

Nonetheless, despite the controversy engendered by the *loi Pasqua* and the police operations and expulsions that it sanctioned, at least one analyst believed that, by the late 1980s, an 'ambiguous consensus' had developed between the mainstream parties on the subject of immigration.[22] All effectively supported an immigration policy based on four elements: strict frontier controls; firmness in dealing with illegal immigrants; measures to help the integration of foreigners already in France; and State aid for those who wished to return to their country of origin.[23] What differences there were related to the content of particular legislation (the *loi Pasqua*, for example), and to disagreements over the best means of achieving the integration of immigrants. (Should they, for example, be afforded the vote in local elections?)[24] Another analyst spoke of 'a camouflaged consensus', where politicians of both Left and Right, given the highly charged nature of the debate, insisted on emphasising their differences, rather than the broad areas of agreement between them.[25]

But apart from the increasingly sterile debate about who was tougher on immigration (a debate repeated in similar terms in both 1988 and 1993), the arrival of the Chirac government introduced a new battleground, proposing a reform of the Nationality Code, to make the conditions governing the acquisition of French nationality more restrictive. Le Pen had long argued for such a measure, and while Chirac's thinking did not go as far as the Front would have wanted, the Prime Minister was determined to cut the ground from beneath Le Pen's feet by making this issue his own.

FOREIGNERS AND FRENCHMEN

Forced by circumstances to co-exist with a President of the Left and with the race for the Elysée Palace only some two years away, the new Prime Minister was eager to win over National Front voters. He determined that the best way to do this was to try to capture some of Le Pen's burgeoning support on the issue of immigration. The joint UDF and RPR election platform had insisted on the need to 'reinforce national identity'. Accordingly, the new Chirac Government set out to reform French Nationality Law, one of Le Pen's longstanding demands.

The proposed reform fell far short of the National Front's ambitious agenda. The main thrust of the legislation presented to the Cabinet by the Justice Minister, Albin Chalandon, was to end the automatic right to citizenship of children born in France to foreign parents. Under the existing Nationality Code, anyone born of immigrant parents, who had been resident in France for five years or more, automatically received citizenship at the age of 18. In future, this automatic provision was to be abandoned. Instead there was to be a so-called voluntary element; individuals would have to make a formal application for French citizenship, lodged between the ages of 16 and 23. Those who had committed crimes punishable by a prison sentence of six months or more would not be eligible to obtain citizenship under the new scheme. In an attempt to stamp out marriages of convenience, the proposed legislation challenged the right of a spouse to obtain French citizenship through marriage to a French national. This right was now to depend upon a probationary period during which the authorities could check if the couple were actually living together as man and wife.

The Government insisted that the reforms represented a modest proposal and in practice, while representing a marked break with tradition, it is far from clear that the number of people obtaining citizenship each year would have been markedly different. In March 1987, as opposition to the proposal increased, the Minister responsible, Albin Chalandon, argued that 'the differences between [the] existing law and our Bill is not in the text but in peoples' heads'.[26]

But by now the Chirac Government was already on the defensive. Its foray into the emotional area of nationality law was condemned by the Left and fundamentally opposed by the President himself. Mitterrand feared that the new measures would divide French people and increase the alienation of the children of immigrants already torn betwen two cultures. The Government also had problems elsewhere. Assailed by student and industrial unrest, it had little stomach for the fight to push through its Nationality proposal. Chalandon spoke of the danger of proceeding with the Bill in 'a climate of ideological confrontation'.[27] The Government had already begun a series of consultations with anti-racist groups and other interested parties. In March 1987 there was a huge demonstration against the Nationality Bill in Paris involving some two hundred organisations. Many critics believed that, whatever the details of the text, the Government was allowing the National Front to set its agenda.

The Prime Minister, Jacques Chirac, was looking for an honourable way out. The creation of a 16-strong 'Commission of Wise Men' under the vice-president of the Conseil d'Etat, Marceau Long, to study the whole issue was one way of postponing a decision on presenting the new Bill to parliament. But by the autumn of 1987 it was increasingly clear that there were growing divisions within the Government's own ranks – differences both within the RPR, as well as opposition from leading UDF politicians.[28] Furthermore, Chirac came under simultaneous criticism from the National Front, for whom the measures did not go far enough, and from the telegenic Harlem Désir and SOS-Racisme who were implacably opposed to the new Code. He also had to contend with the unease of the Presidential-hopeful and former Prime Minister, Raymond Barre, together with leading centrist figures in the UDF like Pierre Méhaignerie. In early September 1987, Chirac bowed to the inevitable, effectively acknowledging that there would be no reform of the Nationality Code before the Presidential election, unless it could be proved that there was a consensus on the issue.

The expert commission published its report in January 1988. Many of its hearings had been broadcast on television, enabling the French public to follow the complex legal and moral issues involved. The report accepted that there was a need to change and simplify the the existing legislation. For children born in France to foreign parents it backed the principle that there should be some form of voluntary demand for citizenship on the part of the individual concerned. This could take various forms and citizenship could be granted at the age of 16. If the request came between 16 and 18 years of age, a criminal record would not be a barrier to the acquisition of citizenship, and over 18 the range of convictions that might prevent the granting of French nationality would be much reduced (largely relating to terrorist or drug-related offences). The delay before the spouses of French nationals could acquire citizenship would be doubled from six months to a year, but here too the regulations would be much simplified.

For all practical purposes the report was a more liberal document than the Government had perhaps envisaged. The Commission's President, Marceau Long, noted that the 'wise men' did not set out to reduce the number of people obtaining French nationality each year. On the contrary, if their recommendations were followed, he accepted that the numbers would actually go up.[29] It was clear that Long saw one of the commission's most important tasks as the adaptation of the nationality code in order to facilitate the integration of young people born in France, whatever their ethnic origins.

The report received a predictably negative reaction from Jean-Marie Le Pen. But while welcomed by Socialist experts on the immigration problem (like Gérard Fuchs) and liberal members of the RPR (like Michel Hannoun), it represented a disappointment to the Government. The document was quietly put to one side. Chirac's efforts to seize the immigration issue from the hands of Le Pen had resulted in a spectacular failure. The National Front accused the Government of capitulating to the pro-immigrant lobby. Hardliners, like Charles Pasqua, who believed that only a muscular policy could counter the rise of Le Pen, were deeply disappointed. Chirac went into the Presidential race with a vague commitment to submit the reform of the Nationality Code to a referendum, but the election outcome, and especially Le Pen's strong showing, indicated that there was considerable mileage in the immigration issue for a Party that had no scruples and was willing to present an explicitly racist policy.

With the return of the Socialists to power in 1988, the focus of the debate moved away from the acquisition of citizenship and returned to the area of immigration controls. President Mitterrand made it clear that he wanted the controversial *loi Pasqua* to be abrogated.[30] There was a significant difference of opinion between the President and his new Government. The Interior Minister, Pierre Joxe, wanted the Pasqua legislation amended rather than abandoned altogether. Joxe was concerned that the Right might try to capitalise on the Left's reforms, accusing the new Government of laxity in dealing with illegal immigration.

Nonetheless, the President had his way. The new Socialist legislation – the *loi Joxe* – gave those facing expulsion a 24 hour stay of execution so that they could appeal to a tribunal. It re-established the rules of 1984 surrounding the granting of ten-year residence permits (an attempt to give foreigners legally in France a greater sense of security), and while retaining some elements of the Pasqua measures, it gave them a more liberal cast. However, the timing of the new law was singularly unfortunate. It was submitted for parliamentary debate only weeks before the European elections in the summer of 1989. The opposition tabled scores of amendments, there were rancorous exchanges, but little serious discussion. Immigration policy again came to the forefront of the political debate, in stark, adversarial terms; and a newspaper headline noted that immigrants were once more the hostages of the ballot box.[31]

The Socialists had learnt from their experience of government in the early 1980s. There were to be no pendulum-like swings of policy between generosity and firmness. But just as in the post-1984 period, Socialist efforts to promote the integration of immigrants seemed to co-exist uneasily with the demands to present a tough policy towards illegal immigration. The whole issue of chartered transport to carry those expelled from France, anathema to the Socialists when enacted by Charles Pasqua, haunted the Socialist Prime Minister Edith Cresson, who took office in May 1991. In an attempt to display a 'no nonsense' approach to illegal immigration, she insisted that scheduled airlines could not be expected to carry groups of often emotional people back to their countries of origin. Thus other means would have to be found. And she rejected the use of the word 'charter' insisting that these were cheap-rate flights for holidaymakers – those expelled were travelling free of charge.[32]

If the reform of the Nationality Code had been shelved by the Socialist Government, the place of immigrants in France and their ability to participate in French political life were again raised by the debate about according them the right to vote in local elections. This was a longstanding element of Socialist policy. It had been in Mitterrand's programme in 1981. Indeed, after the Left's victory the then Foreign Minister, Claude Cheysson, on a visit to Algeria in the summer of 1981, told his hosts that legislation granting immigrants the vote would soon be put before the National Assembly. Within days, this was flatly denied by another Government spokesman, who argued that such a move would be premature: legislation would not come before the 1983 Municipal elections, and would not serve the immigrants' best interests.[33]

This issue had seemed less problematic during the 1970s. In 1979, Jacques Chirac had backed the idea of a municipal vote for immigrants who had lived in an area for at least five years.[34] But with the growing prominence of the immigration debate and the rise of the National Front, voting rights for immigrants became a highly contentious issue, for which there was little public support. When Mitterrand reopened the whole question in 1985, the mainstream opposition reacted with horror. However, even the President's comments were guarded and provisional. Speaking at the conference of one of France's oldest human rights groups, the Ligue des Droits de l'Homme, he noted that the participation of immigrants in local government was 'a fundamental demand that will have to be satisfied.' But he stressed that the Government would have to gain popular support for such a measure. It could not act contrary to the public mood.[35]

Whatever the sincerity of the President's personal commitment, his message was clear: for the moment, the issue of immigrants' rights to vote was best left on the back-burner. In his 'Letter to the French People' prior to the 1988 election, Mitterrand acknowledged that the vast majority of the French population was hostile to such a change and he regretted that the current state of morality prevented immigrants being given the vote. Jacques Chirac had already reversed his policy. His Presidential platform in 1988 unequivocally restricted the vote to French citizens. By the end of the following year, he was urging people to demand a referendum before voting rights could be granted to immigrants; and in 1990 the RPR launched a national petition against immigrants' voting rights.

In May 1990, despite considerable differences within the Socialist Party's own ranks, the Government abandoned any idea of affording immigrants a local vote, at least for the immediate future. Prime Minister Michel Rocard had launched an attempt to reach a consensus with the mainstream opposition on the vexed question of immigration, through a series of 'round table' meetings; and the RPR and the Parti Républicain insisted that they would not attend the second session unless the right of immigrants to vote was publicly dropped from the political agenda.[36]

However, the outcome of this search for compromise, for a de-politicisation of the immigration issue, was unimpressive. Both Government and opposition suspected the other of political manoeuvres and of seeking to use the 'round table' talks for their own ends. While the dangers and emotions associated with the immigration issue made the search for common ground a reasonable goal, both Left and Right were deeply divided, and maintaining a consensus within each camp was difficult enough. For Chirac and the other leaders of the mainstream Right, the essential problem posed by Le Pen remained; and, however distasteful the Le Pen phenomenon, it was evident that the route to future electoral success did not lie in a consensus with the Left.

The issue of immigration was as highly charged as ever, and the eviction of nearly all the National Front deputies from the National Assembly in 1988 offered little respite. The so-called 'Headscarves Affair', which erupted in October 1989, was heavily exploited by Le Pen to focus attention on what he saw as the threat posed by an alien, Muslim minority, unwilling to subscribe to French norms.

The 'Affair' began when three teenage schoolgirls in the town of Creil, in northern France, were refused permission to wear the Muslim headscarf in lessons. The girls were sent home, the Principal insisting that school was not the place for what he described as an 'excessive external display of religious or cultural ties'.[37] The Government, the Socialist Party and anti-racist and human rights groups were all deeply divided. While SOS-racisme, for example, backed the girls' right to wear the veil and insisted that they be accepted back at their school, the long-established anti-racist organisation, LICRA, strongly opposed the wearing of the headscarf in state schools.[38] The episode raised a variety of complex issues, not least religious freedom and the boundaries of tolerance, complicated by a peculiarly French dimension – the longstanding and strongly defended Republican tradition that separates religion from secular state education.

While the French debate on immigration may have turned more upon fear than actual facts, it has sometimes displayed a remarkable amalgam of high moral principle and base political expediency. This was particularly true during the so-called 'Headscarves Affair'. For while the National Front was quick to seize upon the episode in crude terms – to highlight what it saw as a threat to the French way of life – for many other politicians and intellectuals, the debate was posed in no less stark terms. It was about the nature and specificity of France itself. In this view France had long been *une terre d'accueil* (a welcoming land), for successive waves of immigrants. During the nineteenth century, a whole range of demographic and economic factors meant that France accepted huge numbers of immigrants, while most European countries were actually losing citizens to the colonies and the United States of America.[39] But France's welcome to the 'huddled masses' of southern and eastern Europe was linked to a specifically French model of integration, or, one might rather say, assimilation. The American 'melting pot' – what French analysts like to describe as 'Anglo-Saxon multiculturalism' – was not to be the French way. Immigrants were to be turned into Frenchmen, and the State educational system was to be the focus of this effort. Thus, State schools were non-confessional; their task was not to highlight diversity but to instil French Republican values, whatever the pupils' origins or outlook. The demand by a minority of Muslim students to wear headscarves thus challenged a longstanding French tradition and system of beliefs.

While the National Front attempted to make political capital out of the 'Affair', mainstream politicians of both Left and Right called for calm, while insisting that the French tradition of secular education should be defended. Leading Socialist figures, like Pierre Mauroy (a former Prime Minister), and Jean-Pierre Chevènement (Minister of Defence and a former Education Minister), rallied to defend this traditional view, while Prime Minister Michel Rocard issued conciliatory-sounding statements which did little to hide his deep embarrassment and unease.

Similar incidents had occurred elsewhere in France but the episode in Creil threw the whole isssue of integration into stark relief. 'Should we allow Islam into our schools?' ran the headline in the weekly news magazine *Le Point*, while other newspapers were quick to oppose the problems of *intégrisme* (fundamentalism) and *intégration*.[40] Such a juxtaposition ran easily off the tongue, but the 'Affair' risked being blown out of all proportion. In Montpellier, for example, a small number of students had been wearing headscarves during lessons without incurring the hostility of the school authorities, or the attention of the national media.[41] The issue was whether the headscarf constituted a form of religious propaganda; there was no consistency – in some places it apparently did, and in others it did not.

The Government's statements seemed to compound its problems. The Education Minister, Lionel Jospin, asked schools, in the last resort, to accept girls wearing the headscarf, even in the classroom.[42] This drew immediate criticism from the Right and from the Communists, and further divided his own Socialist supporters, many of whom believed he was being too conciliatory. Within the Socialist Party there seemed to be two interpretations of the secular position. One, the more traditional view – which was defended by a significant proportion of the Party's established leadership, and which was based on principles going back to the Third Republic – saw the state school system as a training ground for future citizens. In their view its purpose was to assimilate people from different backgrounds, irrespective of their religious, regional or different cultural origins. A second view championed a 'new secularism', allowing each individual in a school to express their differences as they saw fit. This 'new secularism' was supported by those like Julien Dray, who were close to SOS-Racisme, and by some of the Education Minister's own political circle, though this was perhaps seen as the thin end of the wedge for militant secularists.[43]

With its own supporters divided and uncertain of the way ahead, the Government determined to call upon the advice of the Conseil d'Etat (the country's highest judicial authority). It was asked to rule on whether the wearing of religious symbols like the headscarf was compatible with the secular educational system. This was one method of extricating the Government from a difficult position, or at least of postponing the agony, but the Council of State's Solomon-like judgement hardly resolved the matter. It determined that individual schools could authorise or deny the wearing of headscarves as they saw fit. And the Minister of Education would lay down guidelines to assist schools in drawing up their own regimes.[44]

By any standards the 'Headscarves' Affair' had been poorly handled by the Government. It was a bonus for Jean-Marie Le Pen who insisted that France was being colonised by Islamic fundamentalists. The controversy raged during the run-up to the parliamentary by-election in Dreux, won by the National Front. The episode did little to further the cause of integration. An opinion poll published at the end of November, showed that French people had an overwhelmingly negative view of their Muslim neighbours. Some 71 per cent saw the word 'fanaticism' as best summing up their image of Islam, 66 per cent were against non-European immigrants having the vote at local elections, and 75 per cent were opposed to the wearing of headscarves in state schools.[45]

Islam is now France's second largest religion and it is clear that its adherents pose particular problems for the French model of assimilation. It is not enough to insist simply, as one junior Socialist Minister did, that 'Islam must accept the Republican pact. That is to say, accept the separation of Church and State, renounce polygamy, the low status of women and the wearing of headscarves in school.'[46] French Governments have already begun to explore ways of helping to accommodate Islam within French society. Pierre Joxe, while Interior Minister, established a study group composed of some 15 leading figures in the Muslim community to discuss such issues. In time, Joxe hoped for the development of a French-style Islam. As he put it: 'Muslim religious practices will assume on our soil a specific aspect, and will colour themselves with the traditions that they [the Muslims] find in the country that has received them.'[47] Again, such a development is very much in the future. Nonetheless, France's Islamic community remains relatively moderate in the expression of its faith. There were few incidents, for example, during the Gulf War, when it was feared fundamentalists might whip up support for the Iraqi leader, Saddam Hussein. However, the fundamentalist temptation remains something that French Governments will have to contend with. It could still become an attractive option for unemployed, second-generation youngsters, uncertain of their roots, who feel themselves rejected by France.

However, while the controversy surrounding the wearing of headscarves soon provoked fewer headlines, the Conseil d'Etat's judgement and the Education Ministry circular that stemmed from it, by no means resolved the matter. The issue continued to dog even the centre-Right Government of Eduard Balladur elected in 1993. In at least one school, teachers went on strike to protest against the wearing of headscarves by a small group of students.[48] And a visiting Turkish Imam or Muslim religious leader was expelled for stating that the law of Allah had to take precedence over the law of France.[49] The Education Minister, François Bayrou, came under a stiff attack from RPR Deputies in the National Assembly, who insisted that the existing legislation was inadequate and that while the Conseil d'Etat might interpret what was on the statute book, it was up to Parliament to change it.

In September 1994, just a few weeks after the start of the new school term, the Education Minister chose to issue a new circular to schools, toughening the Government's position. While not mentioning the headscarf by name, it banned 'any outwardly ostentatious symbols whose precise effect is to separate certain children from the general rules of school-life'.[50] While making a distinction between 'ostentatious' and 'discreet' symbols – the latter tolerated because they reflected only an individual's personal conviction – Bayrou's new text did little to clarify the situation. How, for example, might the courts interpret the term 'ostentatious'?

The Minister was taking a serious risk in placing this issue back into the media spotlight. It was no coincidence that he published the new circular against a background of growing violence and intolerance in Algeria. And he may also have had an eye on the electoral calendar: a firmer position against the headscarf would certainly go down well among the Government's more conservative supporters. But if his aim was to establish clear ground-rules to stem any tendency towards Islamic fundamentalism in schools, the Minister may have missed his mark. As one commentator noted, the real debate was not about whether the headscarf should be allowed, rather what constituted the best means of discouraging it.[51] And the Government's approach inevitably prompted a confrontation between the school authorities on the one hand and Muslim parents on the other. Indeed, while the wearing of the headscarf is seen as an indication of the radicalisation of at least some French Muslims, opinion poll evidence suggests that this community is, by and large, relatively moderate in its outlook and strongly oppposed to the intolerance of the Islamic fundamentalists in Algeria.[52]

Some months prior to the reopening of the 'Headscarves Affair', the Balladur Government was already deeply embroiled on another front. In some senses this was a repeat of the situation during the first period of *cohabitation* in 1986. Once more the Right's legislative programme was influenced by the prospect of a Presidential election and the need to re-assure right-wing voters. The Government launched a three-pronged assault to prove it was tough on immigration: the Nationality Code was to be reformed; the regulations relating to the entry and stay of foreigners were to be tightened; and measures to enable the police to check identity papers were to be be reinforced.[53]

Indeed, the Nationality legislation was the first important bill to be put before the new National Assembly. This was in large part inspired by the findings of the Marceau Long Report, and based upon a text already passed by the conservative-controlled Senate, some three years earlier. Once again, powerful emotions were raised by the idea of making citizen-ship for those born of foreign parents something that had to be requested between the ages of 16 and 21 rather than an automatic entitlement as pre-viously. Parents would no longer be able to apply for French nationality on behalf of their under-age children. This tampering with the so-called *droit du sol* (the idea that anyone born on French territory was French) prompted one Communist politician, Jean-Claude Gayssot, to declare that 'only one previous regime had tried to restrict this right, that of Vichy'.[54] Indeed for the Government's critics, the new legislation relating to identity checks also conjured up visions of the Vichy years – an excessive parallel, perhaps, but one which did nothing to calm the political mood.

Balladur's Interior Minister, Charles Pasqua, made it clear that his objective was 'zero immigration'; an unattainable goal, though a useful rhetorical device.[55] More realistically, a former Socialist adviser now on Pasqua's staff, Jean-Claude Barreau, claimed that there were some 150 000 immigrants each year (the usual figure given is around 100 000) and that a figure of some 60 000 would be more appropriate given France's economic climate.[56]

The Government was determined to put the problems of the 1986–88 period behind it. Prime Minister Balladur believed that his huge majority and evident popularity would help him get the legislation through. The Socialist Party's ability to influence the public debate was virtually elim-inated by its crushing defeat. The Government's immigration legislation was toughened by RPR deputies during its passage through the National Assembly, something that caused considerable unease among centrist Catholics within the UDF. And when one RPR Deputy, Alain Marsaud, was criticised during the debate for having tabled an amendment to give mayors greater power to prevent marriages of convenience, he rounded on his detractors, saying that 'We are in France in 1993, not Vichy in 1942.'[57]

In reality, however, the Governments problems were more constitu-tional than party-political. The Constitutional Council objected to several elements of the Government's immigration legislation. Charles Pasqua, intent on proving that he would do anything to get his tough legislation through, took issue with the Constitutional Council's decision. The whole issue risked a dangerous rift between President Mitterrand and the Balladur Government. In the end, the Balladur Government prevailed on Parliament to amend the Constitution so as to restrict the right of foreigners to seek asylum in France. (The Constitutional Council had asserted that this right was guaranteed by the preamble of the 1946 Constitution, later incorporated into the Constitution of 1958.) These changes to the rules regarding the handling of political asylum cases prompted anguished cries from human rights organisations who feared that France's traditional openness towards political refugees would be called into question. Henceforth, an asylum-seeker refused permission to stay in another European Community country would not be allowed to make a second asylum application to France. Pasqua's law had carried the day.

A RISING TIDE OF RACISM?

Given the salience of issues such as immigration and nationality, there have been growing concerns that France is experiencing a rising tide of racism, prompted by the influence of Le Pen on the national political debate. However, to measure the levels of prejudice and intolerance is no easy matter. Is France today a more racist society than in the past? Or is it simply the case that an ever present undercurrent is now more visible in French political life? In the view of many of those involved in combating racism, the answers to both questions should be in the affirmative. As Pierre Aidenbaum, President of LICRA, notes:

> What we have witnessed in France over the past twelve years is what we would call a normalisation of racist rhetoric. Since the rise of the National Front and the arrival of Jean-Marie Le Pen on the political scene, there have been statements and writings from this party which say that the problems of French society, especially unemployment and rising crime are due to the fact that we have too many foreigners in France. Hence immigration equals unemployment; immigration equals rising crime. We had hoped at that time for a massive response from the mainstream parties; this didn't happen. And beyond that, taking into account the relatively important poll of the National Front in certain French towns, there was on the part of the political class, and especially on the part of the Right, a move to take up this rhetoric, for fear of

losing votes or giving ground to the National Front. This led to a discourse which, albeit in more elegant terms, echoed the rhetoric of the National Front.[58]

But the comments of mainstream politicians have not always been couched in more 'elegant' vocabulary. In 1985, for example, Charles Pasqua asserted in forthright terms that immigrants were not in their own homes in France, but in somebody else's, and should behave accordingly (*Les immigrés ne sont pas ici chez eux. Ils sont chez nous.*)[59] Only a few weeks earlier, the UDF parliamentary leader Jean-Claude Gaudin, referring in a radio interview to Marseilles, commented that 'when you arrive there and see this population you have the impression you have entered Algiers. But we are in France. We are in Marseilles. We cannot tolerate this immigration, especially as these immigrants want to keep their cultural identities.'[60]

The rhetorical excesses of conservative politicians reached new heights in 1991 when the former Interior Minister, Michel Poniatowski, asserted in an interview with *Le Figaro* that there was a clear link between immigration and unemployment, and that 'the immigrant population, principally North Africans and Blacks, had a high propensity to commit crimes'. Poniatowski, something of a maverick, had been responsible for handling immigration matters up to 1977 during Giscard d'Estaing's presidency. Asked if he shared Le Pen's political outlook, Poniatowski said that on immigration the National Front had some sensible proposals, and that on this issue, he would go further than Le Pen.[61]

If Poniatowski was expressing the views of a hardline fringe of the mainstream Right, then Jacques Chirac could hardly be considered an extremist. However, the rise of Le Pen seems, on occasion, to have affected even his political balance. The Mayor of Paris, like the other potential Presidential candidates on the Right, was eager to scoop up votes that might otherwise go to other contenders. Speaking before an RPR gathering in Orléans (the day before Poniatowski's interview appeared), Chirac claimed that France was suffering from 'an overdose of foreigners'. He told his audience an anecdote about a typical French worker living in the poor, working-class district of Paris known as the Goutte d'Or:

who sees his next-door neighbours – a family where there's one father, three or four wives and twenty-odd kids, getting fifty thousand francs in social security payments without going to work; add to that the noise and the smell and it drives the French worker crazy. It's not racist to say that we can no longer afford to re-unite families.[62]

The Socialist government of the day immediately denounced his comments, while Jean-Marie Le Pen noted wryly that he was surprised to see that more and more people were rallying to the ideas of the National Front, while at the same time continuing to try to put it beyond the pale.[63]

It seems in retrospect that Chirac's calculation of the welfare payments that his 'typical' immigrant family would receive were as erroneous as Le Pen's frequently touted immigration statistics.[64] But the tone of the immigration debate in France derives more from fear and emotions, rather than from facts and reasoned argument. Not to be out-done in this rising tide of rhetoric, the former President, Valéry Giscard d'Estaing, also waded into the fray. In an article calling for a fundamental reform of the nationality law, he warned that the problem of immigration was fast becoming one of 'invasion'.[65]

Prejudicial rhetoric of this kind may have had some cynical electoral justification, but it did little to harm Le Pen's prospects. Indeed, it probably reinforced his message, indicating that much of the French mainstream Right seemed to be asking very much the same questions as Le Pen, and finding broadly similar answers. If the 'Headscarves Affair' had prompted an emotionally charged debate centred on the problems of integration, then the desecration of a Jewish cemetery at Carpentras in May 1990 provoked a torrent of condemnation that did much to focus discussion on the twin issues of racism and anti-semitism.

The desecration, in which over thirty graves were damaged and a body was exhumed and tampered with, took on a symbolic importance: a tangible example of a rising tide of anti-semitism in France. In part, this was due to the nature of the incident and the horror at the attempt to impale the exhumed body of an 80-year-old man on an umbrella pole. But the gravity of the incident did not explain the scale of the response.

Carpentras was indeed the site of one of the oldest Jewish communities in France, and its cemetery symbolised the continuity of the Jewish presence in the country. But the real answer to the scale of the so-called 'Carpentras syndrome' lies elsewhere. The episode was seized upon by both politicians and sections of the media in an attempt to isolate Le Pen and his followers.[66] In the days after the desecration, a wave of protest swept France, culminating in a demonstration in Paris which drew some 200 000 people, including the President of the Republic. The perpetrators of the attack were never identified. But for many people the culprits were all too obvious: the Carpentras desecration and other similar acts were blamed on Le Pen, and the rising level of intolerance for which he was held responsible. The initial comments of the Interior Minister, Pierre Joxe, were typical: 'There is no need for a police investigation to know who the criminals are.... The criminals have a name. They are called racism, anti-semitism, intolerance.'[67]

Initially Le Pen seemed on the defensive. For a time, the furore made it difficult for the National Front to find halls for many of its local meetings. Its legitimacy was called into question. But paradoxically, the media hyperbole did much to assist Le Pen in turning around the argument. He saw a conspiracy on the part of the authorities to stigmatise the National Front, aided and abetted by a hostile press.[68] And the Party faithful knew that the media could not be trusted. On the eve of the discovery of the desecration, Le Pen had stressed what he saw as the weight of Jewish influence over the French press.[69] However large the wave of spontaneous anti-racist feeling provoked by the Carpentras attack, Le Pen emerged from the affair insisting that he and the National Front were its real victims.

Despite Le Pen's posturing, it was clear that Carpentras had dealt a severe blow to the French Jewish community's self-confidence. Such attacks, however, were by no means a rarity. So to what extent is Carpentras to be seen as a sign of a growing atmosphere of intolerance and anti-semitism? During the early 1980s some observers were actually writing in reassuring (albeit cautious) terms about a decline of popular anti-semitism in France.[70] However, by the late 1980s, several factors – not least the rise of Le Pen, the growing availability of anti-semitic and revisionist material, and episodes like Carpentras – encouraged a much less optimistic view.[71]

If there is a growing perception of racism and anti-semitism, to what extent are things actually getting worse? This is a complex and difficult area, but since 1990 a government-sponsored body, the National Consultative Commission on the Rights of Man, has published a detailed annual analysis of the climate of intolerance based upon opinion polls and evidence taken from interested organisations and experts.

The opinion-poll data on French attitudes is illuminating. The Commission's reports over successive years, with the same questions being asked, yield some evidence of the French perception of racism during the recent past.[72] Nine out of ten people in the survey believe that racism is widespread and that North Africans, and youngsters born in France of North African origin, are its principal victims. At one level the surveys indicate some positive signs, suggesting that roughly 50 per cent of French people would be prepared to sign a petition against racism and that some 25 per cent would be prepared to demonstrate against racist acts. But in November 1992, some 41 per cent of those surveyed expressed their clear antipathy to France's North African population and an overwhelming 65 per cent thought there were too many Arabs in France, with

22 per cent thinking there were too many Jews. (The figures in February 1990 were higher, 76 per cent and 24 per cent respectively.)

These last figures may suggest signs of a modest shift in public attitudes, but the evidence is contradictory. In November 1992, 63 per cent of those surveyed believed that immigrant workers were a burden on the French economy, as opposed to 54 per cent two years earlier. And some 40 per cent of those questioned have consistently admitted to having at least some racist attitudes.

The data produced by these surveys has been used to produce a typology of French attitudes to racism and anti-racism. This yielded six categories of French citizen, ranging from confirmed racists, through to militant anti-racists.[73] Just over 21 per cent fall into this former category, exhibiting outright hostility towards North Africans, *les beurs*, and Jews. By far the largest group (nearly 34 per cent) fell into the category of those tempted by racism, in this case displaying essentially anti-Arab attitudes, though without the virulence of the confirmed racists. The survey demonstrates once again the receptive audience for Le Pen's 'witches brew' of intolerance. Indeed in some senses it is a growing audience, since the proportion of confirmed racists has increased from 14.8 per cent in February 1990 to 21.4 per cent in November 1992.[74]

Over the past decade, all of the mainstream parties have become increasingly aware of the problem of racism. Even the first '*cohabitation*' Government of Jacques Chirac, between 1986 and 1988, felt compelled to take on the issue for fear of leaving the ground open for the Left. In large part this was a response to the campaigning of SOS-Racisme and its media-friendly leader, Harlem Désir, whose appearance on the television programme *L'heure de vérité* in August 1987 created almost as much interest as Le Pen's own appearance some three years earlier. The conservative neo-Gaullist Government did not want the fight against racism to be exclusively linked with Désir, whom they regarded as sympathetic to the Socialist opposition. The need to act was given added urgency by a series of unpleasant, racially-motivated attacks during the summer of 1987, during which at least two immigrant workers were murdered.

The Chirac Government determined to launch an anti-racist effort of its own. It decided to establish a national mediation service to study the problem and intervene locally when racist incidents erupted. Legislation would also be amended to enable the Minister of the Interior to ban the sale of material inciting racial hatred to minors. Indeed, Charles Pasqua even hosted a meeting of over twenty Jewish and anti-racist groups for an exchange of views.[75] As a centrepiece for the Government's efforts, the Secretary of State for the Rights of Man, Claude Malhuret, asked the RPR Deputy, Michel Hannoun, to produce a report on discrimination in France and how to tackle it.

The Hannoun report was published in November 1987. It concluded that people with racist views were no more numerous in France than in the past, but their racism was more intense. The greatest risk, in Hannoun's view, was the danger of contagion – that racist ideas would pass into a larger section of the population. It was this larger group, the 'potential racists', who were the focus of the Report's proposals.[76] In essence Hannoun advocated a threefold strategy, involving education, sanction and integration. Anti-racist legislation would be strengthened, educational provision for immigrants improved and greater attention paid to issues such as racism, the rights of man and historical revisionism in school and university courses. Hannoun also advocated the creation of a new, better-coordinated body to represent France's Muslim community.

While anti-racist groups, like SOS-Racisme, welcomed the Hannoun report, the Interior Minister cautioned that while it would serve as a starting point for the Government's thinking, that was not to say that all of Hannoun's thoughts would become legislation.[77] Indeed, the report ran into increasing opposition within Hannoun's own RPR party, with one spokesman, Franck Borotra, insisting that it was wrong to see all the difficulties of integration as being due to racism. It was, in his view, a two-sided problem, and immigrants themselves had a duty to adapt to French life and patterns of behaviour.[78] Hannoun appeared to have gone further than the Chirac Government had wanted, and his report was quietly dropped.

The mainstream Right's ambivalence on how best to tackle racism was again seen in 1990, when the Socialist Government of Michel Rocard invited all the leaders of the major parties to a 'round-table' on racism at the hôtel Matignon. Although both Chirac and Giscard d'Estaing refused to attend, they sent their principal lieutenants. What the Right had clearly feared would be a political manoeuvre on the part of the Prime Minister appeared to have been a limited success. All sides emerged from the Matignon meeting insisting that there had been a useful exchange of views and several points of agreement.[79] A bizarre note was struck by Yvon Briant, the leader of the small right-wing party, the CNI, who complained that Jean-Marie Le Pen himself should have been invited. Whatever the limited success of the round-table meeting, the whole exercise fell far short of what was required to combat the climate of racism – a clear,

unambiguous consensus on the part of all the mainstream parties to reject
the vocabulary of intolerance, and to stress their fundamental agreement
on the broad strategy for dealing with immigration, rather than playing on
the issues which divided them.

That the problem of anti-racism was every bit as divisive as immigration, was shown a few weeks later with the adoption of legislation, sponsored by the Communist Party, toughening the penalties that could be
given to those convicted of racist or anti-semitic acts, including a prohibi-
tion on standing for elected office for five years. A new offence was
created, the crime of 'revisionism', the denial of the Nazi Holocaust
against the Jews. However, these reforms, in large part directed against Le
Pen, were strongly opposed by the mainstream Right.

During the course of the 1980s and into the 1990s, immigration and the
related issues of integration and racism have assumed a prominent and
seemingly permanent place in the French national debate. There is a
widely-held perception that immigration is a problem, and it is a perception that Governments of both Left and Right have done little to dispel.
The constant changes to the statute book underline the problem. While
successive Governments struggled with the issues, the mere fact of adding
to the statute book reinforced the idea that there was indeed an immigration problem – if not, then why legislate at all? Indeed, the legislative
importance given to immigration and nationality reforms by the Balladur
Government – after an election in which immigration did not, for once,
figure prominently – was an indication of the giant shadow that the
National Front leader still cast over the French political system.

Nobody successfully challenged the National Front's analysis of the ills
afflicting French society. It was not enough, in Laurent Fabius' unfortunate turn of phrase, to assert that the Far Right was offering the wrong
answers to the right questions. Inevitably immigrants became the conve-
nient scapegoats for all of the country's problems. The fact that France's
relationship with its North African immigrants was underscored by a long
history of colonialism and a savage war for Algerian independence (which
the French effectively lost) only compounded the problem. Immigration
has thus become identified in many people's minds with unemployment
and rising crime. And the actions of successive Governments served to
reinforce such connections. In late 1993, for example, the publicity given
to Government attempts to clamp down on Islamic fundamentalist terror-
ists, hostile to the Algerian regime, risked establishing yet another nega-

tive equation – that of immigration and fundamentalism. This was again the case in the summer of 1994 when Charles Pasqua launched a massive security sweep against alleged Islamic militants in the wake of the murder of three French *gendarmes* and two members of the French Embassy staff in Algiers.[80]

Such simplistic equations can all be challenged. Nonetheless the onset of the economic crisis, rising crime, urban decay, and a variety of other factors – not least, a deeply-felt political malaise and concern about France's future role in the European Union – have created a climate of unease and insecurity. Immigration was increasingly perceived to be a problem; for many people, the problem. And while the mainstream parties struggled to cope, Le Pen skilfully manipulated the issue. Their failings left him conductor of the orchestra; Le Pen set the agenda, and henceforth everyone would dance to his tune.

5 The National Front's Programme and Ideology

The National Front's emphasis upon the fight against immigration has led some people to ask whether it should be seen as effectively a single-issue party.[1] However, part of the Front's novelty on the Far Right is that it presents a comprehensive set of policies covering almost every area of political concern. Nonetheless, these policies are often simplistic and incoherent. Some of the greatest inconsistencies appear, for example, in its economic programme. The Front is clearly much better at identifying problems and enunciating catchy slogans than it is at proposing effective and difficult remedies for France's economic and social ills.

But since it has no chance of coming to power, the conceptual integrity of its programme is not really at issue. Its policy statements are merely there as a campaigning tool, enabling the Front to claim the rhetorical high ground and to argue that it alone has new ideas to cope with the current crisis. In fact there is little that is new or indeed exceptional in the Front's amalgam of proposals. All parties might arguably claim to be against corruption, in favour of reducing unemployment, or eager to maintain France's standing in the world. But behind this banal facade lurks a package of rather darker assumptions. Le Pen's sloganising and strident rhetoric are directed not only at establishing his own patriotic credentials; they are intended to deny those of the other political formations.

The Front's espousal of democracy can be seen in a similar light. It is able to portray itself as the victim of undemocratic forces – an electoral system, for example, that works in favour of the 'gang of four' established parties. Le Pen is clearly willing to use the democratic system for his own ends. His desire to introduce a strong element of plebiscitary democracy through the use of referenda provides him with a populist appeal over the heads of the other parties, who, in his view, are eager to restrict the fruits of democracy to themselves. Again, the debate is shifted on to ground where Le Pen's own simplistic remedies can be marshalled against the opposition.

Nonetheless, the place that immigration occupies in the Front's programme is clearly exceptional. In its 1993 manifesto – *Three Hundred Measures for the Rebirth of France* – the problem of immigration and the Front's proposals on how to deal with it, were covered in the very first of its eighteen chapters.[2] Immigration is an omnibus-issue for Le Pen, encompassing family policy, health, the Front's attitude towards law and order, and French identity. Its pre-eminence both helps to mark out the Front from other formations, and also provides a sort of 'ideological aspic' in which the Front's other policies can be suspended.

LE PEN'S WORLD VIEW

For Jean-Marie Le Pen, politics is nothing less than a Manichean struggle for the survival of the French nation and French identity. Le Pen inhabits a Hobbesian world, where every small country is the potential prey of those who are more powerful. 'Since the start of time,' Le Pen proclaims, 'the earth has been shaken by struggles for influence between conquerors and those who have submitted to their will. Nations and whole civilisations have disappeared because they no longer fulfilled the necessary conditions for their survival.'[3]

The threat, however, is not just external; there is always the enemy within. And in Le Pen's view, a nation's internal strength is closely linked to its ethnic, religious, social and economic homogeneity. 'The more homogeneous a country', he writes, 'the more it possesses an historic density, the more it develops an energy which is proportional to the size of its population.'[4] Thus the expansion of the French population is one of the central elements in Le Pen's thinking. He believes that a falling birth-rate is at the root of Europe's decline, and that a reversal of present demographic trends will be the motor for its resurgence.

In Le Pen's outlook the threat to French existence comes from two principal directions: to the east, there is (or at least was) the threat of Soviet-style communism; and from the south there is the Islamic threat – a burgeoning demographic force beating at the gates of Europe as in the Middle Ages. Both of these enemies already have their fifth columns in place, sapping French strength. No matter that the Soviet Union has collapsed; for Le Pen, French communism continues to orchestrate its insidious campaign against French values. It is seen as being at the centre of the anti-racist movement; and as the motivating force behind the 'cosmopolitan intelligentsia' that wages 'intellectual terrorism' against the defenders of French values.[5]

For Le Pen, the political struggle is a simple confrontation of opposites: good ranged against evil, order against disorder, national identity favoured over internationalism (what Le Pen calls *mondialisme*), and civilisation over barbarism. In this struggle the National Front puts itself clearly on the side of the angels, for, as Le Pen notes, even if there are agnostics and atheists in his camp, 'the Right ....is philosophically attached to the natural order and the Christian message'.[6]

The natural world provides many metaphors in Le Pen's thinking. His outlook is influenced by a strong dose of social Darwinism – individual men and peoples must obey the same laws as the rest of the natural world – where only the fittest will survive and prosper.[7] And in Le Pen's mind there is no doubt as to who is the best: 'We believe in the superiority of western civilisation', he writes, and 'in the necessity of its authority in the world, tempered with Christian charity and European humanism.'[8]

Le Pen is against what he sees as the factors which have caused France's decline, denouncing at one and the same time the former Soviet Union, moral collapse, the weakening of both the social and religious order and the family. However, his strongest condemnation is reserved for what he calls the 'mortal threats of a falling birth-rate and immigration'.[9] His ideology is a confection of traditional values and simplistic socio-biology. In many ways it is an echo of longstanding concerns on the Far Right of the French political spectrum: the rejection of an increasingly cosmopolitan world, the obsession with falling birth-rates and the demographic struggle, the cry of 'the nation in danger', and the search for an all-purpose scapegoat. In Le Pen's world, the North African immigrant has taken on the traditional place of the Jew in the frontline of the Far Right's demonology.[10]

However, it would be wrong to see the National Front as simply a resurgence of a longstanding current in French politics, running back through the collaborators of Vichy, to the fascist leagues of the 1930s, the strident patriotism of the anti-Dreyfusards, and the muscular appeal of demagogues like General Boulanger. What distinguishes Le Pen, quite apart from his ability to build and maintain a cohesive and well-rooted political party on the Far Right, is his self-proclaimed acceptance of not just the electoral path to power, but of the parliamentary system itself. Le Pen describes himself as a 'Churchillian democrat', mis-quoting the wartime British Prime Minister, to the effect that 'democracy is without doubt a very bad system, but I don't know of any other'.[11]

To this end, Le Pen has accepted the heritage of the French Revolution, in an attempt to place himself within the Republican mainstream. In an article written in 1985, calling for 'a true French revolution' that would return real power to the people, the National Front President notes:

Everyone in the political class is getting ready to celebrate the bicentenary of the revolution of 1789. Why not? France is four thousand years of European culture, twenty centuries of Christianity, forty kings and two centuries of the Republic. The National Front accepts all of France's past.[12]

Le Pen's acceptance of the French Revolution is ambiguous at best. He has strenuously sought to reconcile the Revolutionary trinity of 'Liberty, Equality and Fraternity' with the traditional values of 'Work, Family and Country' championed by Marshal Pétain during the Vichy regime. Rearranging the order of the words that appeared on countless posters throughout Vichy France during the 1940s, Le Pen notes that 'the love of liberty, equality and fraternity doesn't stop anyone, quite the contrary, from loving their family, their country or work that is well done'.[13]

In fact the National Front has consistently expressed its opposition to the ideas that stemmed from the Revolution – notably the Declaration of the Rights of Man – ideas which it believes continue to undermine France to this day. Hence for the National Front it is not 1789, but 1793, the Vendéean rebellion against the revolutionary authorities in Paris, that should be celebrated: a rebellion that was suppressed by the blue-coated revolutionary armies with appalling brutality. As Bruno Mégret, the National Front's délégué général, explains:

> The French Revolution was not as positive an event as people say and we don't believe that the history of France began in 1789. [We believe] that this revolution was a rupture which was damaging to France and that the ideas which flowed from it are not part of our outlook. Above all, the way they are currently put into practice, with what we call the 'ideology of the rights of man', is something that is very negative. Therefore we reject the rupture of 1789 ... and we reject the totalitarianism of the ideology called 'the rights of man' which it has generated today.[14]

This seemingly contradictory reference to 'totalitarianism' is an interesting example of the Front's ability to turn the ideas of its opponents on their head. Mégret, one of the Front's principal ideological thinkers, asserts that the doctrine of the Rights of Man is now used by the Left as a sort of ideological showcase to hide its real aims, to defend the primacy of individual rights over those of the collective and to elevate the rights of immigrants over those of Frenchmen. The doctrine of the Rights of Man has become, in his words, 'a war machine against the nation'.[15]

This emphasis on the importance of national and collective rights is fundamental to the Front's political ideology. Le Pen has stated that he believes in 'the sacred rights of the individual with regard to the state, but that he also believes in the sacred rights of the collective with regard to its continuity'.[16] And it is clear that in achieving a balance between 'authority and liberty' it is the higher interest of the group that must prevail.[17] For Le Pen, politics is not about abstract equality, but justice. He notes:

> The egalitarian movement which involves the levelling of age-groups, the sexes and peoples, is in my opinion to be criticised because it hides reality, which is fundamentally unequal, that is to say there are some inequalities which are just and some equalities which are unjust. We are for justice and not for equality. The theme of equality seems to us to be decadent.[18]

Le Pen abhors the welfare state, describing it variously as a deadly trap and as a milch-cow which has progressively destroyed the notion of individual responsibility.[19] The National Front proposes a much more limited view of the State's function, 'to defend the nation and its people, to maintain order and to dispense justice'.[20] Of course the principal task of any National Front government would be to map out the path to national renewal. And a clear indication of the Party's priorities is given by the ministerial portfolios they demanded in 1987 as the price for their cooperation in any future broadly-based right-wing government. Bruno Mégret noted that there were two priorities: the Front would insist on the creation of a Ministry of Population, taking responsibility for family matters, demography and immigration (everything pertaining to French identity), and a Ministry of Development, charged with all the economic and social aspects of the national revival. In addition, not one to hide the Party's soaring ambitions, Mégret noted that the National Front would also like to hold a re-named Education portfolio, the 'Ministry of Public Instruction', the Justice Ministry, and a newly established Ministry for Civil Defence.[21]

THE CENTRAL PLACE OF IMMIGRATION

Looking at the National Front's ideology and sampling its rhetoric, it would be easy to dismiss it as essentially a single-issue party, mobilising on the theme of immigration, and seeing the expulsion of immigrants as a panacea for all France's ills. However, this would be a mistake. Since the early 1980s the National Front has developed into a sophisticated political party with policy proposals on a wide range of issues. Nonetheless, opposition to immigration and the defence of French identity remain its dominant themes, with the Front capitalising on concern at urban crime, delinquency, and the general disillusionment with politics and politicians. The anti-immigrant message enshrined in a wide-ranging programme of 'national preference' is a fundamental element of the National Front's economic doctrine. 'National preference' means putting French citizens first in their own country. They would have first call on scarce state provision like health-care, housing, and welfare benefits. In short, the concept of 'national preference' conditions the Front's whole political outlook.

Opposition to immigration is the central mobilising tenet of Le Pen's movement, occupying a similar position to the role performed by 'the class struggle' in an orthodox Marxist party. In addition, as discussed in Chapter 2, the strident anti-immigrant message works both as an ideological solvent and glue, helping to subdue political differences between the various factions in the Party's leadership and bind them together.

For Le Pen himself, the campaign against immigration is merely the latest stage in a centuries-old struggle that has pitted European civilisation against successive waves of invaders. In his view, the National Front defends France against the immigrant-tide just as the Greeks stood firm against the Persians at Marathon, the Franks defeated the Saracens at Poitiers, and Christian forces fought the Turks at Lepanto and at the gates of Vienna. Never one to miss the force of historical analogy, Le Pen once told an audience to rapturous applause, that at Poitiers, France had defeated the 'great-great-great-grandfathers of the then-Algerian President Boumedienne'.[22]

Borrowing a meteorological metaphor, Le Pen insists that between areas of low demographic pressure – such as Europe where birth-rates are low – and areas of high demographic pressure – like North Africa where despite poor living standards, population growth is rapid – there will inevitably be sociological storms and almost irresistible currents of migration.[23] The declining birth-rate in western Europe is leaving a void. And Le Pen – once more drawing on a simplified socio-biology – warns that nature abhors a vacuum; thus indigenous European populations will rapidly be replaced and submerged by foreign populations.[24]

Le Pen has no hesitation in recognising ethnic diversity and racial differences:

> In this world where different races, different ethnic groups and different cultures exist, I take note of this diversity and this variety, but I establish a distinction between individuals and peoples or nations. I cannot say that Switzerland is as large as the United States. I cannot say that the Bantus have the same ethnic aptitude as the Californians, because this is simply contrary to reality.[25]

Citizens may be equal under the law, in Le Pen's view, but men are not. And for Le Pen it is entirely natural to prefer to live among one's own kind. As he regularly says, 'I prefer my daughters to my cousins, my cousins to my neighbours, my neighbours to those I don't know, and those I don't know to my enemies'.[26]

Le Pen insists that a plurality of cultures and peoples must be preserved, but clearly not in France. He rejects the 'Anglo-Saxon' and American models of integration – 'multiculturalism' and the politics of the 'melting-pot' – which seek to mix up peoples, as unrealistic and dangerous options. Le Pen believes that all peoples have a role to play 'which is adapted to the geographical environment in which they were born, live and die. They are the products of an historical evolution and, just like individuals, they have a past, they have origins, their own characters and a singular destiny.'[27]

A recognition of difference thus implies a belief that everyone has a place in the world where they feel most at home. Le Pen notes that there is an intangible relationship between a living individual and his land. Just as an animal feels sheltered in its biological space and seeks to mark out its territory, so human beings need a homeland.[28] It follows that for the National Front, the French homeland cannot be open to immigrants, except under the most exceptional circumstances. Where foreign workers are admitted, they can, at best, only have the status of provisional immigrants or temporary workers. And if French interests dictate that they should return from whence they came, then the Government should have every right to force them to leave.[29]

The National Front's programme of 1985 contained a series of measures to deal with immigration: proposals to restrict access to French nationality and to provide financial assistance for the repatriation of immigrant workers. However, the Party's anti-immigration proposals were presented in their most extensive form in November 1991, with a document setting out 'fifty measures for resolving the problem of immigration'. It was no coincidence that these measures were unveiled at a time when anti-immigrant feeling was growing. In October 1991 more than a third of people questioned by the pollsters claimed to support Le Pen's ideas on immigration. Leaders of the mainstream Right had sought to give voice to the unease, Jacques Chirac speaking of the 'odour' of the immigrant areas and Valéry Giscard d'Estaing warning of the dangers of an invasion.[30] The National Front's consistent response to the mainstream Right's attempt to ape its muscular rhetoric on immigration has been to insist that voters have no need of the mainstream Right's pale imitation of its policies when they can have the real thing.

The 'Fifty Measures' – the Front's comprehensive answer to what it saw as the dangers posed by the immigrant enemy within – were arranged in several broad categories.[31] To create the necessary conditions for tackling the whole question of immigration, a Ministry of Population would be established and state funding would no longer be provided for immigrant associations. The Nationality Law would be rewritten to rule out the automatic acquisition of French citizenship by children born in France to foreign parents. Naturalisation would be the only method of acquiring French nationality and the whole application process was to be made much more rigorous. Double-citizenship would also be abolished. Adopting an idea first raised by the Party's then Secretary-General Jean-Pierre Stirbois in 1985, the National Front made it clear that its legislation would be retrospective: all naturalisations since 1974 would be called into question. This raised clear parallels with the Vichy regime, which sought to deprive certain categories of people of their French nationality, even though their citizenship was obtained quite legally before the laws promulgated by the new regime.[32]

The National Front sought to protect French identity by instituting quotas for immigrants in schools. Ethnic ghettos were to be dismantled. Steps would be taken to impede the construction of mosques, and the opening of Islamic religious schools and centres would be tightly regulated. All new immigration would be halted. Existing immigrants would no longer be able to bring in their families. The rules for granting political asylum would be tightened up, frontier controls strengthened, and health-checks for potential carriers of the AIDS virus would be instituted at the border.

Underlining the all-embracing aspect of its anti-immigrant campaign, the 'Fifty Measures' included a series of steps in the economic sphere. Priority in employment would be given to French workers. Immigrants would be the first to be sacked and French nationals would have priority access to housing, family benefits and so on. A new label would be created for products designating that they had been 'made in France by French workers'. Steps would be taken to organise the return of immigrant workers to their countries of origin. Clandestine immigrants would be hunted down and expelled, as would delinquents, once they had served their prison sentences.

The National Front's 1993 Programme – *Three Hundred Measures for the Renaissance of France* – affords pride of place to immigration policy in a profusely illustrated and professionally produced glossy paperback book of more than four hundred pages. A brief introductory essay draws heavily on reports and booklets produced by the National Front's own think-tank and study groups, to argue that immigration has not been halted, that immigration and criminality are closely linked, that immigrants are a major factor in causing unemployment, and finally, that far from being an asset, immigrant workers are a financial drain on the French economy.[33] The Front's proposals largely follow the steps outlined in its 1991 document, though there is no mention of the controversial plan to make the new Nationality legislation retrospective.

Not surprisingly the National Front is as critical of the policies of the conservative Balladur government of 1993 as it was of the previous Socialist administrations. Interior Minister Charles Pasqua's attempts to tighten up the Nationality Law are seen as lacking coherence. Jean-Yves Le Gallou, the member of the Front's Délégation Général responsible for policy studies, characterises the two approaches to immigration policy that dominate French politics as being on the one hand, that of 'a France open to the winds' as against the policies proposed by the true defenders of national identity, the National Front.[34] Yvan Blot, another member of the Front's ruling circle with political roots on the *nouvelle droite*, has made it clear that, in his view, the immigration policies of all the mainstream parties, Left and Right, are based on the same premise. Only the National Front provides a real alternative.[35] This is an echo of Blot's dominant theme – that social democracy, described as 'an ideology of decadence' now dominates the world. The French mainstream Right, the United States Administration, even the former Communist Parties of Europe are all mesmerised by it, and the real political cleavage in France is no longer between Left and Right, but between the National Front and Social Democracy.[36]

The anti-racist movement that has developed in response to the emergence of the National Front is regularly vilified in the Far-Right press. For Yvan Blot, anti-racism is the 'gnosticism of our times'. Its is, he claims, 'based on a hatred of races which are seen as being obstacles to a perfect unity of mankind. It is founded on a rejection of Creation, of reality, of human diversity.'[37] The anti-racists, he believes, are creating an 'explosive ethnic mosaic' and France risks becoming another Lebanon, a Yugoslavia or Los Angeles. Le Pen himself believes that the place of anti-racism in the Socialist party's outlook is akin to that of anti-clericalism in the ideology of the Third Republic – a campaign to mask the questionable legitimacy of those in power.[38] For Le Pen the goal of anti-racism is nothing less than the destruction of the French and European heritage.

THE ECONOMY, TAXATION AND INDUSTRY

The National Front's economic outlook has an explicitly nationalistic emphasis. As Bruno Mégret writes: 'contrary to internationalist economists for whom the economy has no other function than that of assuring individual prosperity ..., we consider that the economy must also serve the national interest'.[39] Le Pen himself has been a longstanding supporter of denationalisation and the development of a form of popular capitalism through widespread shareownership.[40] Le Pen's own economic outlook seems to consist of various borrowings from the liberal economic orthodoxies that held sway in Britain and America during the early 1980s. Nonetheless, Le Pen claims that he was something of a forerunner in this field, noting that the Front's own liberal economic outlook has its origins in the pamphlet *Droite et démocratie économique*, published in 1978, some two years before President Reagan came to office and before the world had ever heard of 'Reaganomics'.[41]

The National Front's support for the liberal economy owes much to the influence of the French 'New Right'. Its 1985 proposals for instituting a programme of 'national preference' in employment, for example, drew heavily on the text of a report published by the Club de l'Horloge and written by Jean-Yves Le Gallou, then a member of the Parti républicain, now a member of the Front's Bureau Politique.[42] The National Front's programme to combat unemployment contained such proposals as fixed-term employment contracts and pay-scales (if necessary, below the level of the minimum wage) to give the young unemployed a job. Subsequently, however, the Front has rallied to the support of established social benefits, the minimum wage, the 39 hour week and five weeks of paid holiday.[43]

However, economic policy is an area where the different ideological traditions of the Party's leadership are most clearly evident. The strong dose of economic liberalism often sits uneasily with the overarching demands of a politics of 'national preference'. The Front's policy seems to be torn between two poles – a sort of francophone Reaganomics on the one hand, and nationalist corporatism or protectionism on the other. When questioned, National Front leaders insist that there is no inherent contradiction in their position, though Bruno Mégret, for example, insists that liberalism has its limits:

> We are for the free economy, for competition, the freedom of enterprises, the reduction of taxes, and of excessive state regulation. But the major question which is facing France today, and in my opinion, other European countries, is to determine over what territorial area this free economy will operate. For the internationalists and the ultra-liberals, who don't recognise any territorial limits, this free economy can extend from one side of the planet to another, putting into competition without any state barriers, businesses in Paris, London, Seoul and Singapore. For us, territory exists, the nation exists, and we consider that the principles

of the free economy must be applied within territorial limits, we believe, within the nation.[44]

Mégret accepts that the free market can be extended to the other nations of the European Community – what he calls 'a community preference' akin to the narower 'national preference' – on condition that the external barriers around its member states are sufficiently strong. This strident economic nationalism has become an ever more dominant theme in the National Front's discourse during the early 1990s. The whole concept of the global economy is seen as masking a huge transfer of power from Europe to other parts of the world. National Front leaders accept that a web of complex economic relationships ties nations together. But these lines of interdependence are not seen as being neutral; they are power relationships and all too often – and certainly in relation to the United States – they tend to be relationships where the stronger economic partner dominates.[45]

In June 1993 the National Front launched its campaign for 'a new protectionism', a veritable war against the whole concept of international free trade.[46] The Front called for the abandonment of the General Agreement on Tariffs and Trade (GATT), seen as the motor of free trade, and its replacement by a regime that would create legitimate rules to permit sensible competition with a level playing-field.[47]

For the domestic economy the National Front's programme, with its emphasis on reducing taxation and public spending, has almost a *poujadiste* vein – an attempt to relieve the burden on the little man, the small shopkeeper or businessman. The Front wants progressively to abandon income tax. It proposes a variety of measures to help small businesses, to ease their access to funding and to reduce the amount of State bureaucracy with which they have to deal.

As well as seeking to defend small and medium-sized companies, Le Pen's nationalist economics makes him a strident defender of French agriculture. Here too, he believes, there is little to choose between the policies of the mainstream parties of Left and Right. For example, France's decision in June 1993 to accept an agreement between the European Community and the United States on production levels of oil-rich crops like oil-seed rape, soya and sunflower, was seen by the Front as demonstrating that the Balladur government was solely intent on pursuing the disastrous agricultural policies of its Socialist predecessor.[48] Le Pen condemned the move as a capitulation to the American farming lobby. France, he said, was sacrificing its farmers to American economic imperialism.

In opposition both to the world trading order (GATT) and the bureaucracy of Brussels (the Common Agricultural Policy), the National Front proposes to change the whole style of French agriculture, moving from what it calls intensive farming, to an agriculture of balance and harmony. For the National Front, agriculture has a threefold mission: to ensure France's self-sufficiency in foodstuffs; to maintain the French landscape; and through the survival of rural life, help to preserve the roots of the French people.[49] Accordingly the Front proposes a series of measures to assist farmers: a moratorium on their debts, for example, and fair prices for their produce instead of subsidies. Fishing and forestry are to be promoted, and the Common Agricultural Policy would be revised to re-establish a preference for Community-grown goods.

Quite how the National Front would disengage France from the perils of the international economic order is far from clear. However, the coherence of its economic doctrines does not really matter. The Front's economic policy is there to mobilise its supporters – to capitalise on their discontent, and to emphasise the Party's distinction as the sole force that has ready answers to the difficult questions of the day.

The National Front has even been able to turn its thoughts to new political issues that have come on to the agenda, like ecology. Le Pen himself claims a longstanding interest in environmental matters. It is an aberration, he says, that the Left has become the champion of the ecological issue, which, in his view, is the natural territory of the political Right. Ecological awareness, he believes, is a conservative phenomenon. The Left's philosophical insistence on material progress cannot be reconciled with the needs of the environment.[50] The Front wants to step up research into environmental matters, impose heavier penalties on polluters and provide tax incentives for environmentally-useful investment. In a swipe at the French High-Speed Train, its 1993 programme promises to end the 'Jacobinism' of the French railway system – a reference, it seems, to the centralising tendencies and population shifts which (it claims) are created by a road and rail network radiating from Paris. Overall, though, there is little in its specific environmental proposals that would embarrass most of the other French political parties. Indeed, the National Front faces the same problems that they do, in adapting an essentially liberal economic outlook to the needs of the environment.

THE FAMILY, HEALTH AND WELFARE

For the National Front, the institution of the family is at the very centre of the battle for the survival of France. In Le Pen's view, 'it is the building block of the nation'. 'When the family is weak', he writes, 'the country is threatened.'[51] It follows that women have a key role to play in the nation's destiny. Le Pen may wax eloquent on the cult of the Virgin Mary and express his admiration for Joan of Arc, but in his view women have a fundamental mission – to give birth and to bring up children.[52] Exalting the role of motherhood, Le Pen notes that 'nothing is more beautiful and more useful for the nation as a whole and indeed for their personal happiness, than the construction of a healthy family'.[53] The family is the foundation of the nation and encouraging women to have more children is seen as the best way of stemming France's decline. The legalisation of abortion in 1975, in Le Pen's view, was nothing less than 'official anti-French genocide'.[54]

The family is the context in which the Front sets its whole approach to womens' issues. While the Party makes much of its leading women representatives, like Martine Lehideux, who, in July 1994, became the first female member of its Executive Bureau, its policies are strongly traditional, though often couched in quasi-feminist terms. For the former Deputy, Marie-France Stirbois, the Front's policy is all about creating choice for women.[55] But this is not the option of choice over her own fertility. The Front proposes to abolish abortion except under the most exceptional medical circumstances. Measures would be taken to enable childless couples to adopt the babies of women who might otherwise have sought abortions. Indeed, the legal preliminaries would be agreed even before the infant was born. The choice facing women, as far as the Front is concerned, is between working or staying at home. In reality, according to the Front's programme, many women are forced into work by the need to obtain a second wage for the family. Its policy is to encourage more women to stay at home to rear children. The Front proposes to create a so-called 'maternal' or 'parental' wage, which would be paid to the father.[56] And Front spokesmen frankly admit that the underlying aim of this policy is to take women out of the job market, a strategy which they hope will help to alleviate male unemployment.

Le Pen has argued that the ageing of the French population has inevitable political consequences. Older voters tend to opt for short-term measures favouring themselves rather than taking the longer view and backing policies that might favour the next generation.[57] Thus Le Pen has proposed measures to increase the voting powers of the young. The National Front wants to introduce a 'family vote' where parents would be able to have additional votes to cast on behalf of their children. The Front's 1993 programme is vague on the details of this proposition, while noting that it would give families and children their just weight in the decision-making process.

Just as French citizens must have priority in housing and social benefits, so too in health-care, where Le Pen insists that hospital beds must be reserved for the French people who paid for them.[58] The Front's health policy emphasises preventive medicine and stresses the need to find financial savings in the state-hospital system. Better management and greater administrative autonomy for individual hospitals should help to cut costs. And the Front believes that the number of beds can be cut by having more one-day surgery and by encouraging those who are able, to be hospitalised elsewhere, either at home or in some other sort of institution.

All parties are in favour of better, and where possible, cheaper health care. The Front, however, sought a distinctive appeal by representing immigrant workers as a threat to French peoples' health, capitalising on the fear of disease, specifically AIDS, to mobilise support. Le Pen has long argued that immigration has had a serious impact on the nation's health, not just in terms of the drain on resources but in terms of disease as well.[59] Thus the immigrant and disease are closely linked in Le Pen's world-view, and the Front seized on the threat of AIDS to launch a populist and highly misleading campaign which played up the danger of an epidemic disease sweeping the country.

Towards the end of 1986, one of the Front's members of parliament, François Bachelot, a cancer specialist by profession, called for the creation of so-called *sidatoriums* (the acronym for AIDS is SIDA in French) to isolate and look after AIDS sufferers.[60] According to Dr Bachelot systematic screening would have to be introduced, and people coming from high-risk countries would have to be stopped at the frontier and placed in quarantine. 'It is vital', he said, 'to halt the process of infection even if this means giving priority to the French population over the rights of certain individuals.'[61]

Le Pen coined the term '*sidaïque*' to describe AIDS sufferers, a deliberate choice of words evoking memories of a similar sounding term '*judaïque*' (literally 'judaics') used by the Vichy regime to describe the Jews. Le Pen claimed that AIDS was highly contagious and could be easily transmitted through contact with the tears or saliva of the sufferer, a view not shared by respectable scientific opinion. He claimed there were 250 000 AIDS sufferers, whom he likened to modern-day lepers.[62] Le Pen argued that it was the National Front's pressure that had galvanised the Chirac government into action. The Health Minister, Michèle Barzach, had already announced that an AIDS test would be made part of the standard prenuptial medical examination in France. Le Pen reserved particular scorn for Barzach who was on the more liberal wing of the RPR, and his choice of words may well have had something to do with her Jewish origins.

POLITICAL INSTITUTIONS AND LAW AND ORDER

The National Front claims to have accepted the parliamentary system, but it is far from happy with the current state of French democracy. Le Pen once castigated the mainstream parties for thinking themselves safe behind what he called 'the Maginot Line of majority voting'.[63] Apart from the brief introduction of a proportional voting system for the 1986 Legislative elections, the so-called Maginot Line has proved rather more formidable to the National Front's aspirations than did its real-life counterpart to the German mechanised divisions. The National Front has generally been denied any seats in the National Assembly, and clearly the introduction of proportional representation is high on the list of the Front's institutional reforms.

Whatever his democratic pretensions, Le Pen has clearly hinted that the National Front's political exclusion could lead it into seeking another path. Speaking in May 1990, just as the National Assembly was beginning to debate a Communist-sponsored bill to tighten up anti-racist legislation, Le Pen called on his supporters for vigilance and action, appealing to 'the national discipline of all our activists, who, if needs be, will carry out the orders which their leaders give them'.[64] Bruno Mégret, interviewed in 1993, noted that:

> Those in power, by preventing the Front's voters, but also those of the ecologists, from having their legitimate representation in the National Assembly, are artificially locking up the system. And I think this is very dangerous, not only are they locking it up, but in addition, according to [Prime Minister] Balladur's approach, they are sending the whole thing to sleep. And I think this could lead to a fairly rude awakening, not unlike what we experienced in France in 1968.[65]

National Front spokesmen are hinting that the Party's acceptance of democracy is conditional at best. And Le Pen's own democratic credentials sit uneasily with his stated support for the authoritarian regime of General Franco in Spain, and his more recent backing for the military regimes of General Pinochet in Chile and General Videla in Argentina.[66]

Le Pen believes that the existing political system is decadent and the political class, as a whole, corrupt. He is equally unflattering on the role of the National Assembly, describing it in 1986 as 'no longer an element of a parliamentary democracy, but a screen for a bureaucratic and technocratic system'.[67] 'It is necessary', he argued, 'to give France modern and efficient institutions to match its needs.' The National Front believes in so-called direct democracy, extending the use of the referendum to all the major issues of the day. It also wants to institute a system of popular initiatives along the lines of the Swiss model, where a sufficient number of signatures will enable a referendum to be held at either local or national level.[68] The Front believes that with such measures, political life would no longer be hostage to the internal dynamics of the political parties, peoples' civic spirit would be developed, and the media would be encouraged to treat issues with greater seriousness. Indeed Le Pen proposes to codify the powers of the media in the Constitution. The Front's sometimes unhappy relationship with journalists – in 1992 several correspondents were beaten up at the Fête Bleu-Blanc-Rouge – suggests that such constitutional provisions would actually hamper journalists in going about their business. The Front's 1993 programme places the emphasis on making the media more responsible, and tightening up legislation dealing with both the press and broadcasting.

National Front leaders insist that the media's support for anti-racism and successive Socialist Governments' influence over the judiciary, have led to a situation where the upholders of law and order are placed in the position of the accused.[69] Le Pen argues that immigrants are largely responsible for urban crime and the collapse of public order.[70] However, the Front also believes that the police have been both morally and materially disarmed. Accordingly, Le Pen proposes a series of measures to improve police pay and conditions, to improve their training and to give them additional manpower and resources. Expelling the foreign prisoners in French jails will, according to the Front, free a significant number of cells and secure savings that will enable money to be ploughed back into the prison system. Punishment, in general, would be made more severe and the death penalty would be restored, not just for murder, but for those involved in organised crime, in large-scale drug-trafficking, and for terrorist offences including hostage-taking. Along with its 'get tough' measures, the Front's proposals to deal with law and order require a full-scale moral renewal, with the family, schools and the media all having their part to play in re-establishing the distinction between good and evil.

EDUCATION, CULTURE AND THE ARTS

For Le Pen, the revival of France requires a 'major programme of national education ... with the aim not only of producing workers capable of producing goods against the best international competition, but also of giving them the means to bring up their families with dignity and to enable them to become free citizens in a free country'.[71] The existing educational curriculum is seen as being one of the chief causes of France's malaise. Jean-Yves Le Gallou, writing in the Front's intellectual magazine *Identité*, notes that, in his view, the history taught in French schools places the emphasis on only two episodes – the Revolution, and France's experience during the Second World War . He claims that this history teaches children that France has a shared responsibility for Nazi crimes and is to be execrated for its whole colonial experience. It is, he says, 'a mutilated history', and France must rediscover the whole of its past.[72] The National Front has denounced what it calls 'a Soviet-style education extending 'from the nursery to university', and calls on the French people to destroy the ideological 'Berlin Wall' that stands between them and a true national education.[73] The Education Ministry is described in the Front's 1993 Programme as 'the last of the bureacratic dinosaurs, now that the Red Army is no more'; and corresponding to this 'monster' is the main teaching union, the Fédération de l'Education Nationale, whose tentacles spread throughout the system.[74]

The Front proposes to increase parental choice in schooling, not just between state schools but also between state and private education. Families would be given a monthly cheque or voucher to enable them to choose where to send their children. There would be a greater emphasis on educational standards, with schools encouraged to provide academic prizes and league tables of results. The content of courses like philosophy and history would be reviewed to ensure that they were providing a balanced view of the subject. And any sign of bias among the teaching staff would be heavily punished.[75]

The Front's campaign against immigration is carried over into its education policy. No non-French teachers would be employed in primary or secondary schools; and in higher education foreign teachers would only be employed on fixed-term contracts. French culture would become one of the cornerstones of the educational system. The Front notes that: 'The teaching of history will favour knowledge of our national continuity, placing an emphasis on the glorious pages of our past.' It will also stress 'the most glittering periods in European history and the most noteworthy elements of the western tradition'.[76]

The National Front is opposed to the US domination of mass culture. Indeed, the travails of the Euro-Disney theme park are seen as exemplifying the problem. In the Front's view, it cannot attract sufficient visitors because it ignores French cultural specificity.[77] But the Party is also against what it sees as the highly centralised and elitist culture, currently funded by the state, which separates 'the cultivated few' from the 'mass of the public' and takes little account of regional cultural variations.[78]

The Front's campaign for a new protectionism includes a call for the protection of the cultural sphere. Once again 'the free market' is placed in opposition to 'national identity'. Bruno Mégret believes that there is a campaign by the free marketeers and internationalists to cut people off from their cultural roots, which stand in the way of the creation of a new world society.[79] But for Mégret, all is not lost. The cultural counterattack must begin with the young: better Astérix or (the adopted) Tintin, than Mickey Mouse; better the heroes of French history than Superman. In Mégret's view, the State has an essential role to play in preserving 'the national memory, encouraging the spread of French culture and guaranteeing the conditions for free artistic creation that is both popular and with national roots'.[80]

Quite what sort of art the National Front favours is difficult to say. However, Le Pen himself has expressed his fundamental dislike of contemporary styles, insisting that today artists are no longer interested in creating beauty, but are obsessed with originality. He regrets the abandonment of traditional sources of inspiration like mythology, the Bible and the Ancient Greeks.[81] If the views of Yvan Blot are anything to go by, then the Front's preferred style is the Baroque. Writing in *Identité*, he argues that while this was an international style, it was not cosmopolitan. It had a distinctively national emphasis in each of the countries of Europe, and Blot argues that the Baroque is a style with roots, glorifying tradition.[82] For Blot, a neo-Baroque style is singularly appropriate for today's conditions. The original Baroque arose out of a Europe that was just emerging from the Thirty Years War, ravaged by plague and disease, and still threatened by the Turks. Today, according to Blot, Europe is only just leaving behind the trauma of the Second World War, and with an AIDS epidemic looming on the horizon, the Turk of yesteryear has been replaced by Islamic fundamentalism.[83] In the cultural sphere Blot frequently betrays his *'nouvelle droite'* origins, arguing for example that there is no such thing as a 'Judeo-Christian civilisation'. It is absolutely false, he believes, to see Christianity as an outgrowth of Judaism, and European Christian civilisation as nothing more than a continuation of eastern civilisations.[84]

On a more practical level, cultural protectionism clearly has important implications for the GATT trade round, and the Front has been quick to support state-aid to the French film industry in its struggle against the monolith of Hollywood. In arguing for a preference to be given to French culture, the National Front's General Secretary, Carl Lang, reserves particular scorn for the English, who he says have accepted the US cultural invasion as a fact of life.[85]

The National Front's cultural programme is intended to defeat both the American onslaught and the 'Socialist counter-culture', which is described as being '*intello-marxiste* and cosmopolitan'.[86] State-funding for the Arts would be confined to works that 'respect national identity'. Museums would be revitalised and streets and squares renamed to glorify French heroes, artists and leaders, rather than Marxist ideologues and Communist fellow-travellers.[87] The French language would be encouraged, notably in the scientific sphere, by the creation of world-class journals where French research papers could be published in French. At least 60 per cent of the programmes broadcast on television would have to have been produced in France.

FOREIGN POLICY AND DEFENCE

The National Front's foreign policy is based on the idea that France has a unique mission in the world. Le Pen stresses both the need for a return to French independence and the primacy of French national interests. In many ways it evokes parallels with the strident tone of some of General de Gaulle's more emphatic pronouncements during the 1960s. But the National Front does not see itself as emulating the man who, in its view, abandoned French Algeria. France's whole foreign policy over the course of the twentieth century is condemned as contributing to the weakening of its international position.[88]

However, Le Pen recognises that the collapse of Communism and the ending of the Cold War has reshuffled the pack – the diplomatic game is not going to carry on as before. And he insists that elements of Gaullist foreign policy – the General's approach to the Arab world and his support for emerging democracies, for example – should be resurrected.[89] Mitterrand's France, he believes, sacrificed the first element during 'the calamitous war against Iraq and forgot the second in its dealings with eastern Europe'.[90] The new democracies in Poland, the Baltic States and what was then still Czechoslovakia, risk a return to Communism if the West does not help alleviate their economic problems.

As with economic and cultural policy, so too in the sphere of foreign relations. As far as the National Front is concerned, France has rallied to the 'New World Order', which is simply a vehicle to ensure American dominance. Le Pen believes that this has reduced France to a position where it simply hires out its elite troops to the United Nations – a United Nations, moreover, which is also dominated by the Americans.

Le Pen accepts that a 'France first' policy cannot mean that France will stand alone on the international stage. But France's diplomatic links must be organised according to their priority and subordinated to the country's real national interests. Pride of place clearly goes to ties with other European states. Though the National Front's view of Europe has little to do with either Maastricht or Brussels, Le Pen believes in a Europe of the nations. As he says: 'To be loyal to Europe, one must be loyal to one's own country. To love Europe, it is necessary to love one's own country.'[91] Le Pen advocates a much looser 'confederal' arrangement for Europe, and even this construction cannot be rushed.[92] For Le Pen, even that central motor of European unification – the Franco-German alliance – must be rethought. Writing after the crisis in the European currency system in the summer of 1993, he argued that Germany had lost interest in Europe, its attention was focused on the problems of financing its own unification. Hence the Paris–Bonn relationship should be recast to take account of this new reality.[93] Nonetheless, the Front's 1993 Programme insists that the special alliance between the two countries must be preserved.[94]

Indeed, despite the rhetoric, this document stresses that France will remain a loyal ally of the United States, even if it refuses to accept the *diktat* of the New World Order. As with Germany, it is a rebalancing of the Paris–Washington relationship that is required. The Front both admires and is unsettled by Japan's economic performance, insisting that political and cultural relations with Tokyo must be distinguished from the economic realm. The former should be intensified, while the latter would be seriously affected if trading imbalances continue into the long term.[95]

The Catholic strand in the Front's leadership gives it a strong sympathy for Catholic and Christian groups around the world who are seen to be under threat. Thus Le Pen is a strong supporter of the Maronite Christian community in Lebanon. (Certainly, sympathy for the Lebanese Christians is by no means confined to the Front, but its statements in their support are especially strident.) National Front demonstrations have condemned both 'Syrian atrocities in Lebanon and France's passivity' in speaking up for the Christians.[96] The reactionary Catholic ultra-nationalist organisation, Chrétienté-Solidarité, led by Bernard Antony (a member of the Front's Bureau Politique and one of the Front's Members of the European Parliament), has an important influence here, as does the daily newspaper *Présent*, which Antony helped to found. And while both Le Pen and Antony welcomed the peace accord between Israel and the Palestinians in September 1993, Antony stressed that this agreement did not end the suffering of the Christians of Lebanon, whose country remained a manoeuvring ground for the Israeli and Syrian armies as well as the Palestinian militia.[97]

Chrétienté-Solidarité and *Présent* also strongly support the Croat cause in Bosnia-Herzegovina. The organisation has even held its 'summer school' in Croatia and the newspaper organises regular trips to the front-lines in the former Yugoslavia. According to Antony, the National Front wholeheartedly supports the Croats, and *Présent* has repeatedly called for a western miiitary intervention against what it has consistently described as the *'serbo-communistes'*.[98] However, it is by no means clear that Antony's view is the dominant one within the National Front's leadership, which seems torn between solidarity with Catholic Croatia and a gener-alised policy of non-intervention where France's own vital interests are not at stake.[99]

Le Pen himself has consistently condemned the Socialist Government's deployment of troops to the United Nations peacekeeping and protection forces in Croatia and Bosnia. When Mitterrand decided to send an air-craft-carrier to back up French UN troops, Le Pen condemned what he called 'the Socialist Government's flashy humanitarianism that sold French soldiers' lives so cheaply'.[100] In a subsequent television interview he asserted that before attempting to stop rape in Bosnia, one should first eliminate rapes in the Paris region. And he was reluctant to single-out Serbian ethnic cleansing in Bosnia for special criticism, commenting that he condemned ethnic cleansing just as he condemned 'breast-cancer, hail-storms and road accidents'.[101] The Front's divisions on Yugoslavia are interesting in that they highlight some of the differing tendencies within the Party's leadership, and demonstrate that, despite Le Pen's iron grip, diverging views (at least on peripheral issues) are expressed, and appar-ently tolerated.

The National Front's foreign policy is also influenced by its domestic emphasis on the problem of immigration. Relations, for example, with Black African states are to be placed on a more 'realistic' footing, taking into account a variety of factors – notably the importance of French inter-ests and the number of French expatriates, the strategic significance of the country concerned and the extent to which the state participates in the resettlement of its own nationals currently living in France.[102] This last factor will be critical in determining France's relations with the countries of North Africa. The National Front proposes to tear up all existing agree-ments with Algeria which, in any case, it claims the Algerians have not respected. Bilateral ties will be renegotiated on a mutual basis, with both sides accepting the principal of non-intervention in the affairs of the other.

The Front's 1993 Programme notes that France has no reason to choose between what it calls the '*militaro-socialiste* dictatorship of the FLN' and the Islamic fundamentalists.[103]

In fact some elements within the National Front clearly believe that the success of the fundamentalists could work in their favour. Le Pen himself has in the past welcomed local electoral successes of the Algerian fundamentalists, on the basis that they would form a strong government and would call back their citizens who were living overseas.[104] More recently the far-Right press certainly rejoiced at the fundamentalists' success in the Algerian elections of December 1991.[105] *Minute-la France*, run by Serge Martinez (a key figure in the Paris federation of the National Front and a member of its Bureau Politique), welcomed what it called 'the victory of obscurantism and intolerance' in Algeria, heralding it as the triumph of the '*djellaba nationale*' over '*le jean cosmopolite*'.[106] When the Algerian military stepped in to deny the fundamentalists power, most French politicians were loath to criticise the coup. Only the former President Valéry Giscard d'Estaing and Le Pen condemned the Algerian military: Giscard on the grounds that democracy could not be placed in parentheses whatever the electoral outcome; and Le Pen because he saw a fundamentalist regime as the best way to halt future immigration and to get Algeria to take back its nationals currently resident in France. And clearly, as an editorial in *Le Monde* noted, it would be advantageous for the Front's own campaigns if it could play on the fear of an Islamic Algeria just on the other side of the Mediterranean.[107]

In defence matters Le Pen has consistently advocated a strengthening of France's armed forces. In his view its limited military role in the war against Iraq demonstrated the inadequacy of its existing weaponry and organisation.[108] Le Pen has long argued for a move away from conscription, to a fully professional army.[109] The ability of all three armed services to intervene to protect French interests or nationals overseas would be improved, and the Air Force's transport fleet would be modernised and upgraded to deploy a brigade-size force at a distance of up to five thousand kilometres within 24 hours. A volunteer National Guard would be established for home defence, to help maintain public order and to support the regular armed forces.[110]

On nuclear matters, Le Pen has long argued that France's deterrent was a sham, an illusory Maginot Line, given the absence of any comprehensive system of civil defence and nuclear shelters.[111] The ending of the Cold War means that the Front now gives this theme a lesser prominence, and its 1993 programme stresses the role that civil defence can play in dealing with natural disasters and accidents. The document argues that

France's nuclear deterrent must be adapted to the new strategic situation. The Front believes that it is still necessary to retain France's heavy nuclear force targeted against enemy cities (though quite whose cities is not specifically spelt out) as a sort of insurance policy if international circumstances change. However, a new generation of small, air-delivered nuclear weapons should be developed, capable of being used against enemy forces in the field. The National Front argues that less powerful and more accurate weapons will help to bolster deterrence, especially if the threat of their use is more credible.[112] Casting a watchful eye on the threat from 'the South', the Front proposes bolstering radar coverage and anti-aircraft defences on France's Mediterranean flank, and the establishment of an anti-ballistic missile system to protect the most vulnerable cities from attack.

While stressing that France alone must control its nuclear arsenal, Le Pen argues strongly in favour of a new European defensive alliance, in which France's nuclear weight would clearly be a factor.[113] This alliance would replace NATO, which the Front believes is now no longer relevant given the ending of East–West tensions.

As the leader of a Party which claims to defend strongly the interests of the French armed services, Le Pen's attitude towards the 1991 war to liberate Kuwait was surprising, to say the least. Baghdad had been a long-standing customer for French weaponry and technology, and governments of both Left and Right had sought to maintain cordial relations with the Iraqi ruler, Saddam Hussein. However, all the mainstream parties turned against Iraq following its invasion of Kuwait. While the Socialist Government was uneasy with the Bush Administration's seemingly belligerent attitude towards Iraq, preferring a more cautious approach, it nonetheless participated in the United States-led coalition of Western and Arab States that were ultimately to evict Saddam Hussein's forces from Kuwaiti territory.

Le Pen was virtually alone on the Right in opposing French military intervention. (Indeed only Jean-Pierre Chevènement, the Socialist Defence Minister, who was soon replaced, and the Communists expressed any significant misgivings.) It was, he argued, 'a poorly thought-out adventure'; the invasion was an inter-Arab problem and France's own interests were not at stake.[114] Le Pen claimed that the massive western response was an over-reaction and insisted that an attack upon Iraq would be seen as an assault by the West on the whole of the Arab world.[115] The National Front leader sought to develop his own diplomatic initiative. He finally met Saddam Hussein in Baghdad, which he visited as the head of a delegation of extreme-Right Members of the European Parliament in November

1990. While refusing to accept that French nationals held by the Iraqis were actually hostages, Le Pen sought to claim credit for their release, though the actual Iraqi decision came some weeks before Le Pen's own diplomatic gambit. In a National Assembly vote on the Gulf crisis, the Front's only Deputy, Marie-France Stirbois, voted against the Government.[116]

When the air campaign against Iraq was unleashed, Le Pen was initially silent; and it was some days before he expressed his support for French troops in the field, while still condemning the Government and describing the war as a 'mishap of history'.[117] Le Pen argued that even Iraq's nuclear programme did not justify the war – you couldn't take on everyone who was developing nuclear weaponry – and he accused 'the bellicose Socialist Party' of having started all of France's wars during the twentieth century.[118] Le Pen's own peace plan called for a negotiated settlement, which would leave Kuwait as a neutral state with merely an internal police force. Sovereignty would be shared between Iraq and the ruling Kuwaiti dynasty – the Al-Sabah clan. Not surprisingly, Le Pen's position earned him fulsome praise from Iraq's ambassador in Paris. [119]

As has already been discussed in Chapter 2, Le Pen's Gulf position caused some internal dissent within the National Front and indeed within the far-Right camp as a whole. The daily newspaper *Présent* seemed at first to be uncertain as to whether it should follow Le Pen's pro-Iraqi tilt.[120] And the far-Right press in general did not share Le Pen's appreciation of Israel's position, which he described as 'taking a sensible political stand' by remaining on the sidelines of the conflict.[121] For the weekly *Minute*, the financial muscle of the powerful pro-Israel lobby was at work on the press, pushing any line favourable to the Jewish state. For *Présent*, which now seemed to have resolved some of its uncertainties, Israel was at the very centre of the Gulf crisis.[122]

There was every indication from opinion polls that Le Pen's position was causing some unease amongst National Front voters, though reports suggested that most activists seemed content to follow their leader's line.[123] By mid-January 1991, just before the first allied air strikes, Jérome Jaffré of the polling organisation SOFRES, noted increasing opposition among the general public to French involvement in a war, with National Front supporters moving closer to Le Pen's view.[124] However, it became clear that once full-scale hostilities broke out, public opinion, including National Front voters, swung firmly behind the fight.[125]

Le Pen's prediction of the course of events proved wrong at almost every turn. If things had gone badly wrong for the Western allies then perhaps his idiosyncratic position might have attracted some support. But his stand only served to confuse his voters and although it is clear that this had little long-term impact on the National Front's electoral performance, Le Pen was, nonetheless, taking a major political risk.

It is difficult to be certain about his motives. But it is clear that there were probably several factors at work. Pascal Perrineau, head of the Paris-based Centre for the Study of French Political Life, believes that Le Pen was playing for high political stakes. He was hoping to carry off a political coup, by appearing to be the only real statesman, the man who had warned against catastrophe, who would be vindicated when the body-bags containing dead French soldiers were flown home from the Gulf. Le Pen clearly overestimated Iraq's military capabilities – but he was not alone in doing so – and if the casualties had mounted, his position would perhaps have been more tenable. Perrineau also points to other factors: the French Far Right's traditional anti-semitism – a belief that the only country that would prosper from the conflict would be Israel. And he also cites the Front's growing antipathy towards multinational organisations, which was becoming a more important element in its rhetoric at this time. There was, argues Perrineau, a certain affinity between French and Iraqi nationalists ranged against the polyglot army of the United States-led, United Nations-inspired coalition.[126] Another of France's leading experts on the Front's ideology, Pierre-André Taguieff, believes that Le Pen saw the Gulf conflict as a way of re-emphasising the Front's distinctive position. But he also argues that the pro-Iraqi tilt served an important internal function, helping to consolidate ideological elements on the Far Right who had long criticised Le Pen for his apparently pro-American and even pro-Israel views.[127]

Le Pen's attitude towards the Jewish state is certainly ambivalent. In his writings of the early 1980s there are at times approving references: for example, Israel is described as a modern and well-run state, in the same category as Switzerland, for the level of civil-defence protection it affords its citizens.[128] Maybe Le Pen felt some sympathy for the strongly national-ist, right-wing Likud elements in Israel's coalition. In the past, though shunned by leaders of the French Jewish community, Le Pen has sought out their counterparts in the United States, meeting in New York, in February 1987, with 24 representatives of American Jewish organisations, with whom he claims to have had 'positive and cordial' exchanges.[129] There were even overtures, through intermediaries, to the Israeli authorities, with Le Pen clearly eager to improve his image as a statesman by visiting Jerusalem. These too were shunned by the Government in Jerusalem.[130] However, the salience of anti-Jewish and anti-Israel rhetoric in the far-Right press, and the frequently hostile comments of Le Pen himself, suggest that, at heart, the National Front has a very different agenda.

THE MASK SLIPS

To the outside world and the average French voter, the National Front is a xenophobic, stridently nationalist party, with an overwhelming focus on the perils of immigration, especially from North Africa. If there are racist overtones, then they seem to be of an anti-Arab nature – an opposition to a group of relatively recent arrivals on the French scene. This is the visible face of the Party. But beneath its coded language and the references to 'internationalists', 'cosmopolitans' and 'lobbies', lurks a deeper and more traditional layer of antipathy.

In the columns of the far-Right press, much of it run by people with close ties to the National Front, there are frequent references to an alleged Jewish-inspired conspiracy. This is an echo of a much older pattern of thought on the French Far Right – the world of Edouard Drumont, Maurice Barrès, and Charles Maurras. For the *National-Hebdo* columnist François Brigneau, the Jewish vote, mobilised by the Israeli Government, was responsible for the victory of the 'Yes' camp in the 1992 Maastricht referendum – a vote mustered against France's true interests.[131] A headline in *Présent*, referring to the campaign to bring the one-time collaborator Paul Touvier to justice, proclaimed that the then Minister of Justice, Pierre Méhaignerie, was only hounding Touvier because of pressure from the Wiesenthal Centre in Jerusalem.[132]

Pressure from the leadership of the French Jewish community on the mainstream Right is seen as being directly responsible for the National Front's political isolation.[133] The Jewish organisation B'nai B'rith comes in for special condemnation in Brigneau's sardonic column. Its orders, he claims, have forced the major political parties to place the National Front in quarantine. The Chirac Government's decision in 1986 to return to majority two-ballot voting at general elections was once again due to pressure from what Brigneau describes as the *Grand Lobby*.[134]

An 'investigative' double-page spread in *National-Hebdo* the previous year claimed to reveal a significant overlap in membership between B'nai B'rith and American masonic organisations. (Freemasonry is seen by the Front as one of its principal international enemies.)[135] Even the French Church is depicted as falling under B'nai B'rith's influence, with the then Archbishop of Lyons, Cardinal Decourtray, the recipient of a B'nai B'rith humanitarian prize, coming in for particular criticism.[136]

For Le Pen, the far-Right press has the great advantage of deniability: National Front leaders consistently argue that such articles reflect no more than the personal views of their authors. Nonetheless, whatever their links with the Party, these authors are nearly all listed in the Front's 1993 organisational handbook. But what of Le Pen himself? In his earlier days he admits marketing records of Nazi songs; but he insists that the same label sold discs of Jewish folk music. It follows that, in his view, he cannot be an anti-semite.[137] Regarding the Jewish people, he waxes lyrical, noting that though 'dispersed to the four corners of the world', and 'one hundred times menaced with extinction, they not only preserved their originality, but their prodigious vitality, which led the oldest people in the world to create its youngest State'.[138]

However, while insisting that he is no anti-semite, Le Pen, by implication, is eager to stress that he sees no obligation to favour the Jews either. In his first appearance on the television programme *L'heure de vérité* in February 1984, he noted that he 'considered Jews just like any other citizen, but not as citizens with superior protection'.[139] And he saw no reason why he was obliged 'to like the Veil Law (on abortion), to admire the paintings of Chagall, or to approve the politics of Mendés-France'.[140] Of course all three of the individuals named were or are Jewish. The naming of Jews in this way is a common theme in the National Front's discourse. Yvan Blot, speaking at the Party's summer school in 1991, noted that Mr Bush's 'new world order' defended 'the interests of Madame Veil, Monsieur Jean-Jacques Servan-Schreiber and Madame Barzach … in short, you can see what I mean to say'.[141]

Le Pen has not shrunk from personal abuse of Jewish political figures. In 1988 there was his black-humoured word-play on the name of Government Minister Michel Durafour – 'Durafour-crématoire', a reference to the Nazi gas-ovens. The following year he confronted Lionel Stoléru, the Planning Minister, on a televison news bulletin, and demanded if as President of the Franco-Israel Chamber of Commerce, he had dual (French and Israeli) nationality. And when Stoléru later referred to police operations in the Sentier area of Paris – the garment district – against illegal workers, Le Pen commented that 'you could have a round-up', using the word *rafle*, the term used to describe the gathering of Jews by the Vichy militia and police.[142]

Of course Le Pen's most infamous comment came in 1987 when he was questioned on his attitude towards the so-called revisionist historians who deny that the Nazi Holocaust of the Jews ever took place. Le Pen replied that he couldn't say that the gas-chambers didn't exist, he hadn't been able to see them himself, but he characterised the whole matter as 'a point of detail in the history of the Second World War'.[143] In May 1990, a court condemned Le Pen and awarded symbolic damages to a coalition of civil rights groups and associations of those deported by the Nazis. The judges declared that the National Front leader's remarks 'called into question, minimised, or at the very least made less dramatic, the suffering inflicted on the deportees and especially the Jews and Gypsies at the hands of the Nazis'.[144]

Two years later, Le Pen did mildly criticise the film-maker, Claude Autant-Lara, a National Front Member of the European Parliament, who, in an interview with the monthly *Globe* magazine, referred to Simone Veil's imprisonment in a concentration camp, noting that while she played on her experiences, she nonetheless survived. 'When I speak of genocide,' he commented, 'I always say that in any case they missed mother Veil.'[145] Subsequently *National-Hebdo* published an article headlined 'Jews against Christians Enough' with a picture of a seven-branched candelabra, a symbol of the Jewish faith, burning a cross. Le Pen argued that Autant-Lara was wrong to say what he did, but minimised the importance of his words, saying the remarks didn't merit the fuss that they created. *Globe's* major sin, according to the National Front leader, was evidently to have published shocking comments that were made in private.[146]

Le Pen's own position on the Jews was made clear in an extended interview published in *Présent* in July 1989, where he spoke of 'a Jewish international (*sic*) which played more than a negligible role in creating the anti-national spirit'.[147] Le Pen was of course careful to note that this didn't imply that all Jews were involved. The culprits were those who claimed to speak on behalf of the community as a whole. This alleged distinction is a key element of the Front's method of arguing its case, part of an often-repeated litany which includes the racial innuendo directed against Jewish political figures.

Leading Front members, who have since left the Party, reveal a strong anti-semitic current. François Bachelot claims that revisionism – the theory which denies that the Nazi Holocaust against the Jews ever happened – was a regular topic of conversation within Le Pen's closest circles.[148] And another former Front member, Olivier d'Ormeson, announced that he had left the Front in 1987 following the 'point of detail' controversy, because he had realised that Le Pen actually believed that the Holocaust had never taken place and that Hitler should be pardoned.[149]

The verbal excesses of the National Front President have also been reflected by its supporters at a local level. In November 1992 in Strasburg, a National Front regional councillor and two other activists were found guilty on charges relating to their use of the name of a defunct local paper to publish a racist newsletter.[150] And the anti-semitic discourse of the Party's leadership is often reflected in a much cruder form in local party publications.[151]

In an attempt to prove that even some of Le Pen's best friends were Jewish, a satellite organisation – the French Jewish-Christian Friendship

Circle (Cercle d'Amitié Française Juive et Chrétienne, the CAFJC) – was founded by Fernand Teboul, an Algerian-born Jewish ex-serviceman, and a National Front Municipal Councillor in the Vaucluse. (The National Front itself already has a Cercle National des Juifs Français.) Bernard Antony agreed to become one of the organisation's joint-Presidents, which claims a national membership of about 100 Jews and many more non-Jews. Jewish community groups argue that these claims should be treated with considerable caution.[152] Nonetheless, the Circle's activities are interesting in that it displays another tactic of the Front and its associated organisations – the inversion of charges of racism.

In a so-called 'Carpentras Appeal' launched in January 1993, the CAFJC claimed that France was the object of a campaign of defamation without historical precedent, which placed it in the ranks of those nations where anti-semitism raged.[153] The appeal was named after the town of Carpentras, where a Jewish cemetery was desecrated in May 1990. This incident was generally seen as indicative of the growing climate of racial intolerance engendered by the National Front, though the National Front itself denied that any of its members had anything to do with the attack, the perpetrators of which were never found. Thus for the CAFJC, Carpentras, far from being an anti-semitic act, becomes a symbol of 'anti-French slander'. In a similar vein, Le Pen once rounded on those who would accuse the National Front of anti-semitism, claiming that it was the Front that was the real victim of a conspiracy that was branding it as the heir of the Nazis. In a reference to the yellow star worn by Jews in Nazi-occupied Europe, Le Pen ironised that Front members might one day be forced to wear a tricolour star.[154]

Such references to the Holocaust raise questions about the National Front's whole attitude to France's experience during the Second World War. It is clear that Le Pen's followers include both former members of the French Resistance and former collaborators. Indeed, for Bruno Mégret this is one of the remarkable features of the Front, for he claims that it is 'the only political movement which has turned the page and which has succeeded in gathering together both sides, and, to some extent, in reconciling the French people, fifty years later, after this tragic and terrible division'.[155] In May 1993 the Front's Scientific Council organised a conference entitled 'From One Resistance to Another: History in Question 1940 to 1993'. This sought to paint the National Front as the true heirs of the Resistance, waging a similar struggle albeit against the immigrant enemy. But while stressing the large number of *résistants* in the Front's ranks, Le Pen noted that during the four years of the Occupation Frenchmen who didn't make this choice were also motivated by honour and patriotism. He insisted that the task of national reconciliation was one of the Front's principal goals.[156]

The Front believes that the historical page should be turned and this is a consistent element in Le Pen's discourse when dealing with such matters as the culpability of Paul Touvier or the trial of Klaus Barbie. The National Front leader insists that politicians should forget this particular past and deal with the problems of the present. President Mitterrand's decision to institute a national memorial day for the victims of racism, anti-semitism and deportation scandalised the Front's supporters. Jean Madiran, the Director of *Présent* under a banner headline, 'France Humiliated', claimed that France was now being asked to shoulder the same burden of guilt as Germany for crimes against humanity. Mitterrand had, in his view, given way to the Jewish lobby in accepting that the Republic was a continuation of the Vichy state.[157] It was, argued Madiran, a 'mountainous deception' to argue that Marshal Pétain had participated in the extermination of the Jews or had even gone further than the Germans in this crime. Beneath Madiran's article, *Présent's* cartoonist, Chard, provided an image of the French people represented by a beret-clad youth being offered a coat emblazoned with swastikas by a pair of arms emanating from a cloud, with a Star of David on the sleeve.[158] Bruno Gollnisch, a member of the Front's Bureau Politique, wrote an open letter to the Prefect of the Rhône after receiving an invitation to a local ceremony. The burden of Gollnisch's complaint was that the Jews, or as he put it, one particular category of victims, was being remembered. He noted that the political authorities in Lyons had steadfastly refused to take part in any commemoration for the victims of the Revolutionary terror of 1793, which had killed ten times as many victims as the Gestapo officer, Klaus Barbie. And he railed against the leaders of the Jewish community; if there was a resurgence of anti-semitism, then it was their actions, he insisted, that were contributing to it.[159]

THE FRONT'S SELF-IMAGE

An analysis of the National Front's programme and ideology, the wording and emphasis of articles in what it calls 'the nationalist press' and the political statements of its leading protagonists, provides a clear indication of what sort of party it is. But how does the National Front view itself? For Bruno Mégret, it is a party of 'the nationalist Right'. Asked to define where the Party stands, he says:

> We are not on the extreme Right, because overall our ideas are moderate. I say that they are traditional ideas and what has actually happened

is that the whole of the political class has shifted towards the Left. Those who have remained faithful to themselves on the centre-Right today find themselves on the extreme Right of the board. But this is an optical illusion, not a real political position.[160]

Mégret argues that the old distinctions between Left and Right are no longer relevant. Previously, he says, the political process was a debate between Marxists and liberals over the social and economic organisation of a country. 'But today', he claims, there is a new debate 'between nationalism and cosmopolitanism, between identity and internationalism'.[161] Yvan Blot has described the Front as simply 'a national liberal party, nothing more, nothing less'.[162]

Le Pen himself sticks to the Party's original formulation of 1972: *la Droite sociale, populaire et nationale.*[163] For the National Front President, it is a Right that exalts work, defends the family, the old and the poor; it is faithful to its people; and it remains attached to its homeland, its roots and its traditions.[164] More recently, in the columns of *Le Figaro* and in his own Party publications, Le Pen has launched a strong campaign against the use of the appellation 'extreme Right' to describe the Front.[165] It is an intellectual subterfuge, he says, an attempt to give the Party a diabolical image. He describes the journalists who freely interchange the terms 'National Front' and 'extreme Right', as 'modern-day illusionists, remodelling the subconscious of the French people'.[166] And in conclusion, Le Pen returns to one of his oldest formulations, asserting that this media hypnosis is only seen as necessary because the National Front says out loud what people are thinking deep down.[167] After an examination of the Party's programme and ideology it should be clearer what the National Front itself is thinking, deep down, behind its public mask.

6 The Response of the Mainstream Parties

The rise of the National Front took all of the mainstream French political parties by surprise. After some ten years as a marginal political force, its initial electoral successes, in Dreux in 1983 and in the European elections of the following year, were generally explained away as a temporary fever in the French body-politic. In this view, Le Pen's emergence from relative obscurity was likened to similar eruptions in the past, like *Boulangisme* in the nineteenth century or more recently *Poujadisme*, where the extreme Right had surged forward, only to disappear from the scene, almost as quickly as they had come. The National Front was not treated seriously. Many on the Right believed that its success was solely linked to proportional voting (even the Municipal elections contained an element of proportional representation), and that the Front would quickly wither once confronted by the two-ballot majority voting system.

Nobody really imagined that Le Pen would become a permanent fixture of the French political scene. The mainstream parties of both Left and Right underestimated the National Front President. But they also failed to appreciate the powerful appeal of his anti-immigrant message in mobilising support, to the extent that, as we have seen in an earlier chapter, immigration became one of the central political issues of the 1980s. Thrown on to the defensive, to varying degrees, all of the mainstream parties attempted to steal Le Pen's thunder.

However, at the same time, they all remained deeply divided on how best to deal with the Front's challenge. During the early 1980s, while the Front's strengths were still unclear, the mainstream parties sought to exploit what they saw as a temporary phenomenon for their own political ends. Thus the UDF and RPR sought to make deals with Le Pen's supporters to wrest power from the Left. These sometimes took the form of declared electoral pacts, as in Dreux in 1983. Elsewhere, there were more, or less, explicit arrangements to stand down in each other's favour. (This was particularly the case in south-eastern France, where the UDF faced a severe challenge from the Front.) And after 1986, there were a host of deals, sometimes tacit, sometimes open, between Front representatives and their mainstream Right colleagues, to secure power on the newly-elected Regional Councils.

It wasn't just the mainstream Right who sought to use the National Front for short-term political advantage. President Mitterrand's decision to introduce a proportional voting system for the 1986 legislative elections was principally motivated by his desire to minimise his Socialist Party supporters' losses. But there was also a powerful subsidiary reason for electoral reform, since proportional representation would give seats to the National Front, and Mitterrand may have calculated that this would sow division within the UDF and RPR camp.

If Left and Right were both at fault in failing to appreciate the nature of the threat posed by Le Pen, they were similarly uncertain about the best means of combating him. Where was to be the principal focus of their counter-attacks? Should they confront Le Pen and his lieutenants in personal terms, or make the Party's ideas their principal objective? Were Le Pen's supporters to be a target of political attack? Were they to be considered beyond the political pale, or rather as simply misguided and disillusioned voters, capable of returning to the Republican fold?

Given the divisions within each political camp, it is impossible to speak of a single strategy on the part of either the Left or the Right to confront Le Pen. From the outset there were differing views, and a variety of approaches were counselled. However, over the course of time, clear patterns can be established. For the Right there was an initial period of seeking local deals. By the late 1980s, such alliances were rejected, as the true nature and threat posed by the Front became clearer. By the early 1990s the mainstream Right was pursuing a strategy of containment which effectively isolated the National Front, and Le Pen was unable to turn his electoral strength into any real political advantage.

On the Left too, there were attempts to exploit the Front's presence for partisan purposes. As we shall see, there were also some significant tactical errors, not least that of the Socialist Prime Minister Edith Cresson in seeking to place the Front at the very centre of the campaign for the 1992 Regional elections. As the Front began to establish itself in the political system, various attempts were made to mobilise popular support against Le Pen. There was SOS-Racisme (indirectly backed by Mitterrand himself) and organisations like Le Manifeste Contre le Front National, headed by the then Socialist Deputy Jean-Christophe Cambadelis. Here too, there were considerable disagreements as to how best to combat Le Pen, disagreements which at times divided President and Prime Minister, as well as creating strains between the Socialist government and sections of its supporters. But whatever the mistakes and tribulations of the Left, Le Pen's rise posed fundamental problems for the mainstream Right. They now had to fight on two fronts: the traditional battle against the Left – a bid for centrist votes – while also seeking to prevent their more right-wing supporters from drifting into the arms of Le Pen.

THE MAINSTREAM RIGHT

1983–88: Dealing with the Devil

The small town of Dreux, 80 kilometres west of Paris, has come to symbolise the start of the National Front's electoral march to political prominence. However, the Municipal election campaign there in 1983, together with its national repercussions, also provided the first evidence of the ambiguity of the mainstream Right's response to the National Front challenge. In Dreux, given the success of Jean-Pierre Stirbois, one of Le Pen's chief lieutenants, at the 1982 Cantonal elections, local RPR leaders insisted that the only way they could beat the incumbent Socialist mayor was to ally themselves with the National Front and bring Stirbois, together with some of his followers, on to a joint opposition list.

This caused some dissent within the mainstream Right's camp (at least at the local level) with two centrist politicians refusing to go along with the deal.[1] They both came from the small centre-right formation, the Centre des Démocrates Sociaux or CDS, one element of the UDF federation, and heir to the Christian Democratic tradition in French politics. While CDS leaders had no monopoly on expressing reservations about dealing with Le Pen, politicians from this tradition were to be among the most vocal opponents of any compromise with the National Front. The split in the mainstream Right in Dreux also illustrated something that was to become clearer as the years went on, namely that divisions over how to deal with Le Pen were not so much between the UDF and RPR, as within each formation, with powerful local interests often taking precedence over the concerns of national politics.

Whatever the situation in Dreux, the RPR leader, Jacques Chirac, insisted that there would be no deals in Paris, where Le Pen was contesting the Twentieth *arrondissement*. Speaking after the first round of voting, Chirac, who had disapproved of the arrangement in Dreux, noted that to bring Le Pen on to the mainstream Right's electoral list, 'would constitute an alliance against nature'.[2] But this is exactly what happened at the re-run of the Dreux election in September 1983 following the annulment of the earlier result, a narrow victory for the Socialist administration. Between ballots, Stirbois and his followers were incorporated into a single opposition list, which ultimately secured victory. The deal was immediately condemned by the former Health Minister, Simone Veil, who said that if she were a voter in Dreux, she would abstain at the second round, effectively encouraging the *Drouais* to follow her example.[3] She was supported by the leading CDS politicians like Bernard Stasi and Pierre Méhaignerie.

However, Veil and the CDS leaders, in expressing their outright opposition to any local deal with the National Front, were very much in the minority. While national RPR leaders generally maintained an embarrassed silence, insisting that this was very much a local matter and would be decided by local party officials, the President of the UDF group in the National Assembly, Jean-Claude Gaudin, sent a telegram to the RPR leader in Dreux, wishing his joint list every success. (Gaudin may already have been thinking about the potential threat that the Front might pose to his own political power-base in the south-east at the 1986 Legislative elections).[4] Jean-Pierre Soisson, a leading member of the Parti Républicain, urged the people of Dreux to back the new list and insisted that the alliance with the National Front should be interpreted as 'a disavowal of [the Left's] national policies, notably its economic policies'.[5] This theme was picked up by the RPR's Secretary-General, Bernard Pons, who, during a visit to Dreux to support the new joint list, asserted that 17 per cent of the voters of Dreux (Stirbois obtained 16.7 per cent at the first ballot) were not Front supporters; they had simply backed Stirbois to make a forceful demonstration of their opposition to Government policy.[6]

In the aftermath of the Right's victory in Dreux, Le Pen argued that his support was now essential if the RPR and UDF were to have any chance of beating the Socialists. But Pons insisted that there would be no national electoral deal and that Dreux was, as he put it, an '*épiphénomène*'.[7] However, the Gaullist leader, Jacques Chirac, made it quite clear that his refusal to countenance any pact in Paris was because of the fact that it was the capital – it would establish a bad example – and because, as Mayor of Paris, such a deal would involve himself and Le Pen directly. Chirac could not rule out local alliances on the Dreux model elsewhere.[8] Another leading Gaullist, Philippe Séguin, argued that the Dreux alliance was 'more silly than wicked' and that it wouldn't be repeated elsewhere. He described it as nothing more than 'a road-side incident'.[9]

The mainstream Right had failed the first test posed by the National Front's arrival on the political scene. The only thing its leaders could agree on was that there should be no national deal with Le Pen. Beyond this, with the exception of Simone Veil and a few centrist voices, there was little clarity in their arguments. The National Front was a bad thing, but then the Socialist Government was a bad thing too. If Le Pen was exploiting the immigration issue, this was only possible because of the laxity of the Left in dealing with the problem. Chirac had refused an alliance in Paris, but he had left the door open to deals elsewhere. The 'unnatural alliance' in Dreux had not been roundly condemned or rejected by the mainstream Right's national leadership. On the contrary, they had given it their tacit approval. Dreux had begun the process of legitimising the National Front as a party like any other. The Right's rhetorical flourishes against the Left often helped in this legitimation process. Chirac himself, for example, noted that the presence of Communist Ministers in the Government was much more dangerous to France than four members of the National Front on the Dreux Municipal Council.[10]

Indeed, as far as some people on the Right were concerned, this legitimation process did not have far to go. Claude Labbé, President of the RPR's group in the National Assembly, noted that:

> Le Pen exists, it is one of today's political realities. We have to take into account a political formation that exists, to work together, to act in concert with them, and not say 'I do not recognise you'.[11]

Labbé also argued that Le Pen himself was much closer to *Poujadisme* than to fascism. And he insisted that the Right would have to co-exist with the National Front, while stressing that co-existence did not imply any form of alliance.[12] However, Labbé's ambiguous comments seemed to be advocating just such an alliance, at least at the local level, and a few days later Bernard Pons attempted to issue a corrective by launching a strong attack against Le Pen and his political credentials.[13]

The question of the mainstream Right's relationship, if any, with the National Front would not go away. Indeed their predicament was underlined by the outcome of the European election of June 1984. The joint UDF-RPR list only obtained 43 per cent of the votes cast, with the National Front taking a little over 11 per cent. The mainstream Right would not have an overall majority in the country (essential at the second ballot of a Presidential election) without the support of Le Pen's voters. So how far should it go in attracting them?

Evidently the preferred circumstance was a two-ballot contest where the Front did not make it through to the second round. This had been the case at the by-elections at Aulnay-sous-Bois and Morbihan in 1983, and in both constituencies a significant number of Front voters rallied to the mainstream Right at the second ballot. But this might not always be the case. It was feared that in a close-run Presidential race, the electoral arithmetic might enable Le Pen to deny the mainstream Right the Elysée. Thus, to some extent, the National Front had to be tolerated, and, on occasion, accepted as a legitimate partner. And while national deals were repeatedly ruled out, local pacts and arrangements were by no means excluded.

Indeed, within the Right's own ranks there seemed to be a considerable number of people who favoured an outright pact with the National Front. A SOFRES opinion poll published in May 1984 indicated that 46 per cent of UDF sympathisers wanted some sort of understanding with the Le Pen at the next parliamentary elections, while 62 per cent of RPR sympathisers took a similar view. Some 37 per cent of RPR supporters expressed some element of sympathy with the National Front leader's views, as opposed to 24 per cent of UDF supporters.[14] Quite apart from indicating the significant pressures from within the mainstream Right to seek an accommodation with Le Pen, such polls also demonstrated the relatively rapid *banalisation* of the Front – its increasing acceptance as a normal feature of the political scene.

In an effort to try to win back those National Front supporters who had drifted into the Front's orbit, the leaders of the mainstream Right decided to make a clear distinction between Le Pen and the people who voted for him. There were to be no tainted votes. The Right could not afford to stigmatise any of Le Pen's supporters. (There would be no equivalent of the comments of the then-Socialist politician, Bernard Tapie, who in 1992 described Le Pen as a 'bastard' and those who voted for him as 'bastards' too.) Chirac, speaking after a Municipal by-election at Draguignan in February 1984, where Front voters generally opted for the mainstream Right's list at the second ballot (despite the refusal of local Front leaders to endorse such a choice), made it clear that he welcomed such transfers. Philippe Malaud, the leader of the small right-wing party, the Centre national des indépendants et paysans, or CNIP, argued on the eve of the European elections that Le Pen's score should be counted as part of the Right's total as a whole, since 'the majority of votes that will go to the National Front will not be extreme Right votes, but those of moderate electors exasperated by the policies of the *socialo-communiste* Government'.[15] Responding to Malaud's remarks, Simone Veil, who headed the mainstream Right's list at the European contest, urged her colleagues to seek to understand what 'this floating electorate wanted, who had voted for Le Pen without [necessarily] embracing the themes of the Far Right'.[16]

While continuing to attack Le Pen himself, Chirac determined to bid for the Front's supporters by advocating a tougher line on immigration and crime. The RPR leader went onto the offensive in July 1984 and hardened the tone of his remarks over the course of the ensuing months. At the end of October, for example, he noted that 'if there were fewer immigrants, there would be less unemployment, less tension in certain towns, and a lower social costs'.[17] In November he confirmed this shift to the right, linking the impact of abortion on France's falling birth-rate, with the threat of large-scale black immigration.[18] Chirac was making the sort of connections that were the common currency of Le Pen's rhetoric and his policy risked further legitimising Le Pen's message, with the uncertain prospect of recouping some of the ground lost to the National Front leader.

However, as the Cantonal elections of March 1985 approached, there were clear signs of changing attitudes on the part of the mainstream Right on the vexed question of alliances with the National Front. Simone Veil and Bernard Stasi, the first to reject any compromises with Le Pen, were now much less isolated. The former Prime Minister (and Presidential hopeful) Raymond Barre, who had once refused to regard Le Pen as a 'bogey-man', now urged voters not to give their support to such 'loud-mouths'. Leading RPR figures attempted to isolate the Front: Phillipe Séguin called for a written pact ruling out the possibility of governing with the support of National Front deputies should the Right win the parliamentary election due in 1986.[19] Jacques Toubon said that in the event of a Socialist and a National Front candidate being best-placed for a second ballot run-off, he would prefer to risk a Socialist victory by keeping the defeated RPR in the running, in an attempt to erect a barrier to the extreme Right.[20]

Chirac himself sought to dispel some of the ambiguity that had surrounded his Party's position towards the Front, insisting that there was now no question of any electoral deals, either at national or at local level.[21] Nonetheless there were still discordant voices. Jean-Claude Gaudin argued that UDF candidates might still step down in favour of better-placed National Front candidates where there was a danger of the Left winning a seat. While the official UDF position was that there would be no agreements and no standing down in favour of Le Pen's supporters, Gaudin took a more nuanced view, relying upon semantics to get his point across. He argued that he was in fact in favour of 'the retirement' of UDF candidates when out-distanced by the Front, rather than their *désistement*, a term that implied a withdrawal in favour of somebody else.[22]

Indeed the growing organisational strength of the Front meant that in several parts of the country, local UDF and RPR politicians found the shifting views of their national leadership unpalatable, to say the least.[23] Between the two rounds of voting, Jean-Claude Gaudin attempted unsuccessfully to get an RPR candidate to stand down in favour of a National Front supporter in one of the Marseilles constituencies; and while there were some local deals, for example that in the Drôme, between the UDF and the National Front, the overall results for Le Pen, at least in terms of council seats, were dismal.

The mainstream Right took some comfort from the results which indicated that despite its growing local implantation, the Front still faced considerable hurdles in a two-ballot contest, where a majority of the vote was needed to secure election. Despite some local problems the ban on dealing with the Front had generally proved effective. Indeed the Left's introduction of proportional representation for the 1986 parliamentary elections at least relieved the mainstream Right of the problem of electoral alliances. But with the National Front going into battle under its own flag, the mainstream opposition faced a severe threat in areas where Le Pen was strong.

This increased the temptation to adopt elements of Le Pen's agenda and even, on occasion, his rhetoric, especially on subjects like immigration where the mainstream Right believed a more muscular policy was required. Once again, centrist politicians in the UDF were uneasy: Bernard Stasi, vice-President of the CDS, warned his colleagues in a *Le Monde* article of the dangers of being contaminated by Le Pen's political style, a process which he believed was already underway, with dangerous consequence.[24]

However, whatever the differences there were among mainstream Right leaders on how best to tackle the problem posed by the National Front, they were all agreed on who was to blame for the phenomenon. It was the Left, in their view, who had to bear the principal responsibility. It was their weakness in dealing with immigration; and their failings on the economic front that had provided Le Pen with his opportunity. Whatever the merits of this polemical case, it did take on a greater validity in the immediate aftermath of the 1986 Legislative elections, where the Socialists' introduction of proportional representation was blamed for opening the doors of the National Assembly to the Front.

Conservative and centrist leaders were fascinated by what they saw as the similarity between their own problems with the National Front and the difficulties that the Socialist Party had suffered in trying to embrace the Communists. Stasi, for example, saw the Socialists' problems as an instructive 'counter-example': not only had the Socialists sought to deal with the Communist Party, but they had also become ideologically contaminated by it. Other people on the Right adopted a similar, though much less sophisticated, argument in an attempt to try to justify pursuing contacts with Le Pen's supporters. In their view, both Left and Right had their extremist formations. And if the Socialists chose to deal with the Communists – a party that owed its allegiance elsewhere – then why shouldn't the Right deal with the National Front, whose supporters were, after all, patriots? This point was made quite explicitly in 1987 by Michel Aurillac, the Minister of Cooperation in the Chirac Government, who when asked about the role of Le Pen in the French political system, insisted that nobody could be rejected out of hand and that at least Le Pen, unlike the Communists, had never taken his orders from abroad.[25]

Such comments were an indication that there were still many people on the Right who saw Le Pen as a lesser evil than the Communists, and thus more legitimate as a potential ally. Indeed, the whole question of alliances, whatever Jacques Chirac might say, was far from resolved. In 1986, while the question of dealing with the Front was no longer relevant at parliamentary elections (because of proportional representation), it was posed with added urgency at the regional level. Over the course of the next two years the budgets of several Regional Councils administered by the mainstream Right, including those of Picardie, Languedoc-Roussillon and Aquitaine, were adopted with the votes of National Front councillors.

Indeed, a number of events suggested that for at least some people on the mainstream Right, the National Front was very far from being beyond the pale. In April 1987, Deputies met in the Palais Bourbon to formally elect the *bureau* of the National Assembly. The National Front put forward Pascal Arrighi for one of the vice-Presidencies, who (though unelected at the second ballot) managed to obtain one hundred votes – a clear indication that some seventy Deputies of the mainstream Right were prepared (albeit at a secret ballot) to demonstrate their friendship for the Front.[26] With a return to the old two-ballot majority system for parliamentary elections, the Front was claiming that the witholding of its support could cost some 147 mainstream Right Deputies their seats – a calculation that many of them seem to have had in mind when voting for Arrighi. UDF and RPR activists participated in a number of National Front meetings, with two UDF deputies, Alain Griotteray and Jacques Médecin, along with the President of the CNIP, Philippe Malaud, attending the launch of Le Pen's Presidential campaign at a hall in Paris.[27] In July 1987 six UDF and RPR Deputies returned from a trip to South Africa. They had gone at the invitation of the Pretoria Government and were accompanied by three National Front Deputies. Their conclusion, that apartheid no longer existed, caused considerable embarrassment for mainstream Right leaders, who also had to cope with the fall-out from a municipal by-election in Grasse (the world's perfume capital in the Alpes-Maritimes) where the UDF mayor secured re-election by forming an alliance with the National Front.[28]

The mainstream Right's outlook was principally dictated by the electoral calendar. A Presidential election was due in 1988 where National Front voters might play a pivotal role at the second ballot, and there was every likelihood that a parliamentary election would follow the Presidential contest, whatever the outcome. The mainstream Right seemed uncertain of its strategy towards the Front. Nonetheless, some voices were raised against the drift and ambiguity that surrounded the mainstream

Right's position. Claude Malhuret, the Secretary of State for the Rights of Man, launched a strong attack on Le Pen and his ideology, arguing that Le Pen presented a facade of respectability behind which lurked a much-less respectable reality.[29] The Minister for Foreign Trade, Michel Noir, launched a similar attack barely a month later, asserting that he would rather lose an election than make compromises with the National Front.[30] Bernard Stasi welcomed Noir's forthright stand, saying that longstanding critics of contacts with the National Front, like himself and Simone Veil, now felt less lonely within the mainstream Right's camp.[31]

With the opinion polls indicating that Le Pen would probably get some 10 per cent of the vote in the forthcoming Presidential contest, but that only half of these voters might transfer to another candidate of the Right at the second round, Chirac believed it was essential to limit the growth of Le Pen's support. But there was no consensus on the Right as to how best to do this. Various strategies were being pursued at the same time.

For some, there was a temptation to incorporate the Front into a single right-wing camp: to apply a sort of 'national discipline' in terms of vote transfers, equivalent to the 'Republican discipline' long practised by the Left. In essence, this meant treating the National Front like any other political formation on the Right and forming alliances with it whenever necessary. Few, if any, national figures were prepared to explicitly back this approach, but in practical terms this policy was already in operation in several Regional Councils, not least that of Provence-Alpes-Côte d'Azur, where the majority was made up of 25 National Front councillors, 23 UDF, 17 RPR and seven assorted conservative councillors. Chirac sought to reaffirm that there was no overall alliance between the mainstream Right and the Front, arguing that such regional deals were born of necessity, the need to secure a working majority, and that no concessions were made to Le Pen's formation.[32] This was by no means the case. For one thing these regional alliances provided the Front with additional legitimacy and in some places concessions were indeed made to Le Pen's supporters. In Languedoc-Roussillon, for example, subsidies to bodies dealing with aid to the victims of crime were cut at the behest of the National Front, who claimed that the money was going to pay for jobs for Socialist Party functionaries.[33] Some budget cuts were also made in Picardie under National Front pressure.[34]

Some leaders on the Right argued for caution, preferring, like Raymond Barre, to remain silent rather than make the National Front the focus of political debate. But this is exactly what the National Front had become. One analyst noted that Le Pen was playing the role of an 'ideological bench-mark' on the Right; and since the candidates' policies were not so

Source: *Le Monde* 3 May 1988

very different, their attitude towards the National Front was at least one means of distinguishing them.[35] Barre's silence won few headlines, but it did have the advantage of doing nothing to antagonise Front voters, whose suppport he might need if he went through to the second ballot. Barre had promised to dissolve the National Assembly if elected; and with a reversion to the old electoral system, he was confident that the Front would be largely ejected from Parliament.

Interior Minister Charles Pasqua advocated a policy of winning back the Front's voters by pursuing tough policies on immigration and other issues championed by Le Pen. Of course, Le Pen himself consistently argued, probably with a large measure of justification, that voters would prefer the original strong line of the Front to any copy peddled by the mainstream Right. The Pasqua approach, faithfully pursued between 1986 and 1988, and again after 1993, risked legitimising many of Le Pen's themes as the mainstream Right adopted elements of the Front's political vocabulary and agenda. It was Charles Pasqua, who in a memorable phrase in May1988, declared that the Front and the mainstream Right shared the same values.[36] If, by this, he really meant that Le Pen had no monopoly on patriotism and the defence of the nation, then he chose his words rather badly. Indeed, the strategy of adopting hardline rhetoric and tough policies proved counter-productive when the Chirac Government failed to deliver on its promises. Its failure to bring forward a new Nationality Bill in advance of the 1988 election, simply provided Le Pen with added room to manoeuvre.

In contrast, those who favoured an outright rejection of Le Pen and all his works believed that they had not only seized the moral high ground, but that such a position made good practical sense. It would prevent the Left from exploiting any collaboration between the mainstream Right and Le Pen and would reassure centrist voters, securing at least one of the Government's flanks. However, their approach served to highlight the divisions within the Right and helped to keep Le Pen at the centre of the national debate.

This diversity of approach hampered the mainstream Right's response to the rise of Le Pen. Where there was rather more agreement, however, was in blaming the Socialists for the re-emergence of the extreme Right. Philippe Séguin's attitude was typical. He argued that:

> in matters of anti-racism or of hostility to the extreme Right, the majority has no lessons to learn from those who, by the introduction of proportional representation, have made the National Front what it is today.... It is the Socialist Party and Mr Mitterrand who carry the historic responsibility for this situation.[37]

François Guillaume, the Agriculture Minister, added an additional element to this argument, claiming that the Chirac Government had not been able to move ahead with legislation as quickly as it would have wished, because of the obstruction of the Socialists and President Mitterrand. Thus the electorate became impatient, and only Le Pen prospered.[38]

As far as electoral deals with the Front were concerned the way seemed to be open for local arrangements. Charles Millon, the *barriste* Deputy, insisted that one must continue to distinguish between local and national deals.[39] Chirac, asserting that he had always maintained a clear policy on this issue, insisted on the distinction between the Front's leaders, whose ideology was totally different from that of his own, and their voters, who for the most part had views close to those of the existing majority. There would be no national deal with the Front's leaders. But the Prime Minister accepted that 'at the local level there really was a problem that had to be taken into account by the local leaders of the different parties [of the mainstream Right].'[40] This was widely seen, not least by Le Pen himself, as providing a green light for local electoral deals.

The mainstream Right's problems were compounded following Le Pen's characterisation of the gas-chambers as 'a minor detail' of history. The Socialists called on them to renounce all deals with the Front and while most RPR and UDF leaders were shocked by Le Pen's pronouncements, they retorted that the Left were exploiting Le Pen for their own purposes. Jacques Blanc, the UDF President of the Languedoc-Roussillon Council, underlined that though he had concluded a local deal with the Front 'to liberate the region's economy', it was not 'a philosophical or ideological contract'.[41] While the Secretary-General of the Parti Républicain, François Léotard, argued that there should no longer be 'the slightest alliance' with the National Front, the President of the UDF, Jean Lecanuet, said that to break with the National Front at the Regional level would be 'an absurdity'.[42] In the wake of Le Pen's comments on the gas-chambers, some 53 per cent of UDF-RPR sympathisers opposed any electoral deal with the National Front, either for the Presidential election or the Municipal contest due in 1989. Nonetheless almost one-third of the mainstream Right's sympathisers still favoured such arrangements, whatever Le Pen's rhetorical excesses.[43] One consequence of Le Pen's remarks was to help tilt the balance in the power struggle within the CNIP. Philippe Malaud, who had backed a possible link-up with Le Pen's Party, was defeated by the supporters of Yvon Briant, who now sought a more independent line, hoping to win back right-wing voters to the mainstream fold. (Briant himself had been elected on the Front's list in 1986, but had since fallen out with Le Pen.)[44] The CNIP ultimately backed Chirac's Presidential bid, asserting that the National Front was becoming too extreme.

1988–93: Towards a Strategy of Containment

As the mainstream Right prepared for the Presidential election campaign of 1988, local deals with the National Front still continued. In Aquitaine, the Regional Council budget was passed with the support of Front councillors and in the Franche-Comté, the UDF retained the Presidency of the Council with Front votes. Locked in a Presidential race against a Socialist incumbent, the mainstream Right was also hampered by its own 'war of the chiefs' – the duel between Barre and Chirac – which was further complicated by the pressure from Le Pen on their right flank.

Raymond Barre refused to condemn those like Jean-Claude Gaudin who had formed regional alliances with the National Front. He argued that they had not compromised their principles and insisted that if they had accepted the ideas of the Front, then he would have been the first to regret it.[45] With only a few weeks of the campaign to go, Barre appealed to Front voters urging them to think again – an appeal which suggested that there was little wrong with their fundamental values, just with the political vehicle through which they sought to express them.[46]

Jacques Chirac, while insisting there could be no governmental agreement with Le Pen, had clearly decided that the mainstream Right's reserve of votes at the second ballot lay in the Le Pen camp.[47] On the one hand,

Chirac emphasised themes that would appeal to Front voters: in Marseilles, for example, the Prime Minister promised to resolve the problem of immigration within five years; and Pasqua expressed his personal preference for the restoration of the death penalty.[48] But Chirac also sought to win over National Front Deputies, not least by his refusal to dissolve the Assembly in the event of victory – something that would enable them to retain their seats for the immediate future. (With the defection to the RPR of Guy Le Jaouen, a Deputy for the Loire, the Front group in the National assembly stood at 32 members. Two more defections would prevent the Front from retaining the advantages of its own official group.) Chirac had also hinted two years earlier that outgoing Deputies who rallied to the Majority would have preference when it came to deciding on future candidates in their constituencies.[49] Yann Piat, then a National Front Deputy, claims that some months earlier overtures were made to her: she was told that if she left the Front and joined, in the first instance, the ranks of the CNIP, then she would ultimately receive the investiture of the RPR and UDF at the next legislative election.[50]

The scale of support for Le Pen at the first ballot of the Presidential contest appeared to confirm all of Chirac's worst nightmares. He was going to have to attract the bulk of the National Front leader's voters if he was to have any chance of defeating Mitterrand at the second round. It was in this context that Pasqua made the statement on 'shared values', referred to earlier. In a magazine interview he said that:

> There are certainly some extremists within the National Front, but essentially the Front has the same preoccupations and the same values as the majority. It just expresses them in a rather more brutal and noisy manner.[51]

This statement created considerable controversy within the mainstream Right, but ultimately did little to enhance Chirac's chances. Le Pen, relishing his apparent status as kingmaker (or, at least as the man who could help to deny his old enemy, Chirac, access to the throne) urged his supporters not to vote for Mitterrand, characterising him as *le pire* (the worst). But he hardly advocated a Chirac vote either, describing the outgoing Prime Minister as *le mal* (the bad).[52]

Mitterrand's subsequent victory and the legislative elections scheduled for June prompted the mainstream Right to rehearse the same anguished arguments about dealing with the National Front. However, there now seemed to be a growing realisation of the scale of the threat posed by Le Pen. The UDF and RPR went into the parliamentary campaign with a joint slate of candidates, with Pasqua insisting that there would now be no deals with the National Front, either at local or national level. Chirac and the Centrists had reached a broad consensus intended not only to forestall any deal with the Far Right, but also any temptation on the part of some centrists to seek an accommodation with the Left.[53] Chirac was also under pressure from more moderate elements within his own party who were tempted towards the smaller centrist formations.

Once again the specific local problems facing the UDF in the Bouches-du-Rhône led to an agreement between Gaudin and the National Front for mainstream candidates to stand down at the second ballot, in eight constituencies where they had either fallen below the threshold needed to continue, or where the Front candidate was better-placed. National UDF and RPR leaders attempted to play down the importance of this local deal, arguing it had little wider significance. There were certainly other local contacts between the mainstream Right and the National Front during the interval between the two rounds of voting, especially in constituencies in the Paris region.[54] However, the debates within the mainstream Right over the course of this intense electoral period seemed to be leading towards a fundamental shift in attitude towards the National Front.

All eyes were now on the Municipal elections of March 1989. True, some local deals were already being struck with the National Front, especially in the Bouches-du-Rhône. But in early September 1988, Raymond Barre proposed a change to the electoral law that would prevent the fusion of party-lists between the two ballots of the Municipal contest.[55] The aim was to prevent Front candidates from forming a joint list with the mainstream Right as they had done at Dreux. In areas where the Front might well out-distance the UDF and RPR at the first round of voting, it was hard to see how far Barre's proposal would have served to isolate the Front. In any case, it was not backed by the Socialists who feared the electoral impact that it might have for the Left, since their deals with the Communist Party would also be called into question. Nonetheless, it was an important indication of the way the wind was blowing.

Later in the same month, the RPR issued its strongest condemnation of both local and national deals with Le Pen's supporters.[56] This hardening of the RPR's position was assisted by the National Front leader's intemperate rhetoric, not least his *Durafour-crématoire* jibe.[57] Within days the RPR headquarters in Paris had taken disciplinary action against two constituency secretaries who had sought to make deals with the Front.[58]

While the mainstream Right's position was becoming less ambiguous towards the National Front, the nature of French political parties and the heavy weight given to local interests, meant that deals with the National Front could not be halted altogether. Nonetheless, there was a growing awareness of what Le Pen stood for. The very survival of his movement and its continuing, albeit slow, electoral growth, required it to be taken more seriously. The victory of Marie-France Stirbois at the Dreux by-election in December 1989, where she defeated an RPR candidate (even though both the Communist Party and the Socialist had urged their supporters to vote against the Front) provided renewed evidence of Le Pen's potential challenge, even with a two-ballot electoral system.

During the early 1990s, local electoral arrangements with the Front continued but, as before, they tended to be alliances of circumstance, born of electoral geography rather than any true ideological affinity. However, there were still those within the mainstream camp who expressed their enthusiasm for Le Pen's ideas. The UDF mayor of Nice, Jacques Médecin, whose dealings with the National Front prompted Jewish members of the City Council to resign, claimed that he was 99 per cent in agreement with Le Pen.[59] (Médecin resigned in September 1990 and fled to Uruguay to escape prosecution for corruption.) In November of the following year, another political maverick, Giscard's former Minister, Michel Poniatowski, also expressed his agreement with Le Pen, arguing that the Left was ten times worse than the Front.[60]

The balance within the mainstream Right was, however, clearly shifting towards a strategy of containment and an outright rejection of all alliances with Le Pen's formation. Chirac himself stressed that deals with the Front were not just morally wrong, they were also very much against the mainstream Right's own political interest. Moreover, Chirac's attitude towards the Front's electorate was also changing. In March 1990, he told an audience of RPR officials in Toulon that forty out of every hundred National Front voters came from the Left and would always vote against the mainstream Right. Some 15 per cent were, as he put it, '*pétainistes-nazilons-OAS*' who had always opposed Gaullism. The remaining 45 per cent he described as '*braves gens de droite*', who would ultimately vote for the mainstream Right, with or without electoral pacts.[61]

Giscard d'Estaing, whose longstanding refusal to condemn Le Pen in forthright terms had raised questions about his attitude towards the Front, insisted that his courtesy did not imply any surrender of principle with regard to the National Front leader.[62] And the dangers of ideological contamination were increasingly well understood, with Charles Pasqua and Philippe Séguin (as part of their call for a renewal of Gaullism) warning that UDF and RPR leaders risked 'aligning themselves without thinking' with the policies of Le Pen.[63]

If attitudes were changing among mainstream Right leaders, then the cloak of ambiguity towards the National Front still remained. The idea of a 'Republican front' – an electoral alliance of all anti-Le Pen forces – while backed by some people, nonetheless proved elusive.[64] A Cantonal by-election at Villeurbanne in June 1990 resulted in a straight second-round fight between a National Front and a Socialist candidate. The Mayor of Grenoble, Alain Carignon, was the only leading RPR or UDF figure to call on mainstream Right voters to transfer their allegiance to the Socialist contender.[65] In Charles Pasqua's view, a 'Republican front', at any level, would only enable the Left to cling on to power.[66] Philippe Séguin argued that such an alliance would risk boosting Le Pen's share of the electorate to thirty or forty per cent.[67] Carignon was disciplined by the RPR for breaking ranks.

The Regional elections of 1992 provided a crucial test of the main-stream Right's evolving position. National Front support had helped the mainstream Right to control several Councils, and whatever the claims to the contrary, the Front had exacted a price, obtaining some influence in return for its favours.[68] The question now was whether such alliances would be renewed. The calculations of Jacques Blanc, the UDF President of the Languedoc-Roussillon Council, were typical. He had presided over the Region's affairs since 1986, with the help of eight National Front Councillors. However, circumstances had changed. For one thing, half of the Front's councillors had left Le Pen's party over the course of the inter-vening years, making the Front a less powerful prop to his majority. And while in 1986 the Front was still eager to maintain a veneer of respectabil-ity, Le Pen's rhetorical excesses and the Front's increasingly hardline views made it an even less respectable partner. Even in the National Front's heartland of the south-east, Jean-Claude Gaudin, the UDF President of the Provence-Alpes-Côte-d'Azur Council, declared that he would renounce his former deals with the National Front.[69] In part Gaudin felt constrained by the terms of the UDF-RPR pact, the charter of the Union pour la France which ruled out such alliances. However, his change of heart probably owed more to the potential threat from the Left's front-runner in the Region, Bernard Tapie, the owner of the Marseilles football club who sought to present himself to centrist voters as the only real barrier to the Front's progress. All the evidence suggested that while the Left would fare badly, Le Pen's supporters would do well – yet another reason for the mainstream Right to take a tougher stance towards the Front's challenge.[70]

Therefore, while there was still some local bargaining in the aftermath of the 1992 Regional elections, the National Front's ability to pressurise the mainstream Right was much reduced. It became only one of 'a multi-coloured mosaic' of parties out of which regional coalitions could be fashioned.[71] This paradoxical weakening of the Front's bargaining power, even as its electoral strength increased, was confirmed at the 1993 Legislative elections. It is tempting to argue that the mainstream Right has at last dropped its ambiguities and wholeheartedly backed a strategy of containment. After 1993 Le Pen certainly felt isolated and vented his anger against the Balladur Government at every opportunity. However, caution is still needed in explaining the mainstream Right's apparent change of heart. For one thing it is due in large part to a change in circumstance – the Left's weakness, rather than its own strength. The temptation to 'deal with the devil', at least at the local level, still exists.

In addition, despite its isolation, the themes championed by the National Front remained very much on the political agenda, pushed through by the Balladur Government, as the vanguard of its legislative programme. Such themes as immigration and insecurity have become important concerns for both the UDF and RPR's own electorate. And having determined to occupy this part of the political battlefield, the mainstream Right is unlikely to give ground which could easily be exploited by Le Pen. Indeed, in an interview in November 1993, Charles Pasqua insisted that the only way to stop the rise of the National Front was to prove that the Government was absolutely firm on matters such as law and order.[72]

The attempt by Pasqua and Séguin to renew the RPR and to fashion a revived, popular Gaullism, depended to a significant extent on championing the themes dear to Le Pen's supporters. This inevitably ran the risk of legitimising the Front's own policies and bolstering Le Pen's appeal. While Pasqua is a muscular, populist politician (a sort of French Norman Tebbit), Séguin is a much more reflective individual whose approach is based on the need to return to authentic Gaullist values (those of de Gaulle himself): notably the defence of French independence, opposition to hasty European integration and again, like Pasqua, the need to broaden the RPR's appeal.[73] It is tempting to see such moves as in some ways a response to the challenge posed by Le Pen. However, the debates within the RPR have much more to do with the neo-liberal direction of the Party under Chirac, the true nature of Gaullism, and the RPR's relationship with the UDF, than they do with the rise of the National Front. And while it has become commonplace to accuse Le Pen of poaching the RPR's popular support, leading experts on Gaullism, like Jean Charlot, argue persuasively that Gaullism's popular appeal has been waning for a long time, probably since 1968 and certainly since before the creation of the RPR. Indeed, today, it is the National Front that probably has the most broadly-based electorate of all the major parties.[74]

Others have more explicitly sought to incorporate elements of the Front's appeal into the mainstream Right's own ideological armoury. The political movement launched in May 1992 by the then UDF Deputy for the Vendée, Philippe de Villiers, Combat pour les Valeurs, similarly depends upon a no-nonsense, 'back to basics' approach, championing traditional moral values. Like Séguin and Pasqua, de Villiers was firmly in the anti-Maastricht camp during campaigning for the September 1992 referendum. But unlike them, de Villiers is not so much a conservative or populist, as a true reactionary. He has used his Vendéean connection to emphasise the sacrifice of those who opposed the French Revolution – an important theme in Le Pen's own interpretation of French history. Like Le Pen he resolutely opposes abortion and champions the family. Nonetheless, while he is against the creation of a multicultural society, he insists on distinguishing himself from Le Pen, arguing that just because the National Front President uses certain words and phrases, there is no reason to exclude them from the wider political vocabulary.[75]

While de Villiers' movement remains a marginal force within the mainstream Right as a whole, the National Front at first cynically welcomed his endeavours. Bruno Mégret, for one, has described Combat pour les Valeurs as 'an extra element of division within the UDF-RPR camp' and de Villiers himself as 'a pilot fish for the National Front in bourgeois circles'.[76] Le Pen insisted that he had no ideological disagreements with de Villiers:

> Monsieur de Villiers is a charming man who supports ideas very close to our own, but nonetheless we would say his position is ambiguous, because at the same time as he affirms his support for the 'battle for values' – that's the name of his movement – in the Party in which he is a member, he also rubs shoulders with those who are responsible for the very policies that he fights against. I'll give you an example: he is one of the main opponents of abortion, yet abortion is the work of Mr Chirac and Mr Giscard d'Estaing. And now Mr de Villiers is in Giscard's party and is an ally of Chirac.[77]

Whatever the ambiguities of his position, de Villiers demonstrated that he was not quite such a marginal figure at the European elections of 1994. He outdistanced Le Pen's own list, and clearly hoped to use his support as a bargaining counter to gain leverage over whichever mainstream Right candidate won through to the second ballot of the Presidential contest in 1995. As we have already seen, National Front leaders initially sought to interpret the rise of de Villiers in terms favourable to themselves. But this effort proved short-lived and as the Presidential election campaign began in earnest, de Villiers came under increasing attack from Le Pen and his lieutenants.[78] The success of de Villiers was to provide an additional complication to the calculations of the various contenders for the Presidency. But it was especially galling to the National Front, for it would significantly weaken Le Pen's ability to play a similar role.

THE LEFT: WRONG ANSWERS TO THE RIGHT QUESTIONS

Just as the mainstream Right underestimated the durability and significance of the Le Pen phenomenon, so too did the Left. It was only by the late 1980s, when the National Front had established itself within the political system, that the Socialist Party began to fully appreciate the scale of the problem confronting it. While a section of Le Pen's support undoubtedly came from among those who had voted for Mitterrand in 1981, the Left, unlike the mainstream Right, was not explicitly seeking to win back National Front voters. Given the Socialists' traditions and outlook, Le Pen and all his works were anathema; a throwback to the fascism of the 1930s. Both Le Pen and his supporters were beyond the pale. Bernard Tapie's inelegant comment in January 1992, that if Le Pen was a bastard, 'then all those who voted for him were equally bastards', expressed what many on the Left were feeling.[79] At the 1992 Regional elections,where Tapie, the President of the Olympique de Marseille football club, carried the Left's standard in direct opposition to Le Pen in Provence-Alpes-Côte-d'Azur, the Socialist Prime Minister, Edith Cresson, placed the Front at the very centre of the Socialists' campaign.

But this resolute opposition to the National Front did not enable the Left to avoid the ambiguities of policy that hampered the mainstream Right. As we have already seen, successive Socialist governments agonised over immigration policy, struggling to reconcile a tough stance on illegal immigration with liberal policies on integration. However, France's growing Muslim minority provided a new sort of challenge; and when the 'Headscarves Affair' brought the issues of tolerance, integration and multiculturalism into the school classroom, many Socialists (traditionally a Party where schoolteachers were over-represented) felt their secular Republican 'faith' challenged.

The Communists also reflected the fundamental ambiguity that characterised virtually the whole of the French political class. On the one hand, Communist spokesmen denounced Le Pen in terms that harked back to the rhetoric of the Popular Front of the1930s. For André Lajoinie, the PCF Presidential candidate in 1988, 'Le Pen was an escape route for the bourgeoisie and the worst enemy of the working class. His sole aim was to sow division and confrontation among the workers, to prevent them uniting against their common enemy, the forces of capitalism.'[80]

However, if Le Pen was condemned for fostering racism and division, then local Communist officials periodically expressed the sort of anti-immigrant attitudes that had helped to establish the issue on the agenda at the beginning of the 1980s. This was especially the case during the 'Headscarves Affair' when the Communist Party's official position was to criticise strongly what it saw as Education Secretary Lionel Jospin's hesitation in defending the principle of the separation of religion from State education.[81] Some Mayors in the Paris region expressed their unease over immigration in forthright terms. The views of André Deschamps, the Mayor of Clichy-sous-Bois, were typical of this undercurrent. He said that integration was not about the veil and other forms of traditional dress: 'when all these Arabs, Blacks and Asiatics are in suits or jeans. That is the way I would like to see them in the streets.'[82]

Some two years later the Party published a document entitled 'Immigration: The View of the Communists' which was strongly criticised by those, like Anicet Le Pors, on its reformist wing. The document, while denouncing xenophobia and the poison of racism, stressed that immigration was a real problem and that there were clear abuses in the application of the rules governing family unification, which should be tightened up. Where there are drugs, violence and delinquency, it asked, 'should one close one's eyes when immigrants are involved, so as not to be considered a racist?' The PCF's answer was 'absolutely not'.[83] Le Pors believed that this text contained elements which might provoke hostility to immigrants and should be withdrawn. As a bizarre footnote to the Communist Party's ambiguities, it was revealed in July 1993 that some PCF activists had even been flirting with ideologues of *la nouvelle droite*, like Alain de Benoist.[84] Furthermore, a fringe journal, *l'Idiot international*, which for a time received the Communist Party's financial backing, became a focus for the interchange of ideas between certain Communist activists and the Far Right.[85] Admittedly such connections were a marginal phenomenon, but they were, nonetheless, deeply embarrassing for the PCF leadership, who belatedly threatened to expel anyone who had had dealings with the extreme Right.

The National Front even caused problems for the newest arrival on the French political scene, the Greens. They of course backed proportional representation, whatever solace this might give to Le Pen. But at times, for Les Verts in particular, political independence proved more important than support for an anti-National Front coalition. In November 1990, the

Greens' Conference at Strasburg backed a motion that proposed that the Party should give no advice to its voters at the second ballot of an election, even where a National Front candidate was present and the Greens' candidate had been eliminated.[86] This stand caused some unease among the Party's rank and file and embarrassed its leadership. Within the week, its principal spokesman, Antoine Waechter, and the Greens' seven European Deputies were compelled to issue a statement clarifying the Party's position, asserting that Green candidates were resolutely opposed to the National Front, at whatever stage of voting.[87]

Whatever the problems for the Communists and other small formations like the Greens, it was the Socialists who saw themselves as the chief bulwark against Le Pen and all the values that he stood for. After all, Socialist governments were in power for eight out of the ten years after Le Pen's first electoral breakthrough in 1983. Nobody disagreed on the need to combat the National Front; but there were considerable differences as to the best means or tactics for going about it. Indeed, during the mid-1980s there were considerable suspicions that President Mitterrand, at least, saw the National Front as a political phenomenon to be exploited, to sow confusion and division within the mainstream Right.

The chief charge against President Mitterrand is related to his decision to bring in proportional representation for the 1986 Legislative elections. The mainstream Right has consistently argued that it was Mitterrand who facilitated Le Pen's entry into the National Assembly. Communist leaders have also condemned the President's tactics, Lajoinie arguing that Mitterrand sought to use the National Front as a means of winning over centrist politicians into a new centre–Left alliance. For Lajoinie, the President was playing a dangerous game, making him little more than 'the sorcerer's apprentice'.[88]

For his critics, Mitterrand's behaviour certainly lends some support to these charges. Proportional representation had been part of his programme in 1981, so why was its introduction left until 1985 when the National Front had already begun its ascent? Undoubtedly the principal factor was the Socialist Party's own predicament: proportional representation was intended to minimise an unpopular Government's losses. But there is strong anecdotal evidence to suggest that if a side-effect of the new voting system was a strengthening of Le Pen and consequently difficulties for the mainstream Right, then this too, at least for some in the President's circle, would have political advantages. Mitterrand himself is quoted as saying that in 1986 he 'considered that a victory for the RPR and its allies represented a greater risk to the country than the election of some National Front Deputies'.[89]

Mitterrand's statement indicates a longstanding aspect of the President's position (shared by many in the Socialist Party) – namely his reluctance to distinguish between the extreme Right and the mainstream Right. Indeed, the latter could be worse than the former. This view was not supported by one of the Party's most strident campaigners against the Front, the former Socialist Deputy, Jean-Christophe Cambedelis. He argues that in the early days

> The President and many Socialist leaders believed that in the final analysis there was no such thing as the extreme Right. The extreme Right is part of the Right as a whole; the mainstream Right is within the extreme Right. That is to say that, at root, Le Pen is nothing more than the most visible expression of a set of political ideas which have always been present on the French Right, which has always been conservative, xenophobic and nationalist, and therefore one shouldn't wage a specific campaign against the National Front. The real divergences within the Party were not about using the National Front to weaken the Right, they were more that one shouldn't fight the extreme Right too strongly because such a strategy would get the mainstream Right off the hook.[90]

Cambedelis does not share the view that the President's introduction of proportional representation made the National Front what it is today. He insists that it merely facilitated the expression of a current of opinion that already existed. What is clear is that when Mitterrand sought to revert to a proportional voting system in the early 1990s, this step was strongly (and successfully) opposed by the then Prime Minister, Michel Rocard, for whom limiting the National Front's parliamentary representation was an important factor in sticking with the two-ballot system.[91]

The President's hostility to the mainstream Right explains his opposition to Rocard's attempts to seek a consensus on the issues of immigration and racism, through 'round-table' talks with the opposition. As Gérard Grunberg, a member of Rocard's staff, remembers, there were differences between the Elysée and the Matignon, with the President rejecting this search for consensus. He argues that François Mitterrand wished to proceed in a wholly different manner, for example, wanting to state explicitly that he was in favour of the vote for immigrants at municipal elections. Grunberg believes that the President opposed the round-table approach because he had a horror of anything that smacked of consensus or compromise with the Right.[92] Grunberg also partly explains the President's sympathy for the anti-racist movement SOS-Racisme in terms of political psychology: Mitterrand, he says, 'loves youth, he is an oppositional figure, attracted by protest and activism'.

The Elysée was one of the principal backers of SOS-Racisme, one of the few political movements, other than the National Front (and to some extent the Greens), to catch the public imagination during the 1980s. Indeed, Mitterrand's decision to speak out on the desirability of local voting rights for immigrants in April 1985, an issue which had been quietly dropped from the political agenda after the Socialists took office, seems in part to have been linked to SOS-Racisme's rise and his personal desire to take a principled stand on the issue. (Even though such a speech ran the risk of inflaming the very racist passions that the President insisted he wished to contain.)

SOS-Racisme, launched at the end of 1984, with its stickers proclaiming the slogan, *touche pas à mon pote* (hands off my mate), stood in the fore-front of the campaign against Le Pen. Its President, Harlem Désir, was born in Paris, though his father, a teacher, came from French Guyana. While there were many in the movement who were close to the Socialist Party, the aim of SOS-Racisme was to pursue a campaign independent of both existing political formations and anti-racist groups. One of its earliest achievements was to unite Jewish and Arab students under the same banner.

SOS-Racisme became a significant media success, organising rock concerts and other events to proclaim its anti-racist message. But there were some question-marks concerning its whole approach. Not everyone agreed with the Socialist Deputy, Julian Dray (one of the movement's founders), who argued that SOS-Racisme's struggle would provide a new axis for the recomposition of the Left in France – a battle for equal rights.[93] Some people on the Left were far from convinced that the organisation was pursuing the correct strategy. For one thing, Désir did not shrink from wholesale criticism of the policies of Socialist governments when he thought it necessary. In 1990 he condemned Prime Minister Michel Rocard for talking a great deal about integration, while doing very little on the ground. Désir took exception to Rocard's statement that France could no longer be 'a country of immigration', and he condemned the Government for adopting Communist legislation against racism too hastily. He claimed that the passage of the new measures looked to the public like a political manoeuvre, since the ground had not been prepared in advance.[94]

Indeed, the latter years of the Socialist Administration saw growing tensions between SOS-Racisme and the Government. A major demonstration against racism in Paris in January 1992 provided ample evidence of the growing rift: many of the slogans were directed against Edith Cresson and her fellow Ministers. In the face of this criticism and relegated to marching in the body of the procession, rather than at its head, the Socialist leadership refused to take part in the march.[95] Those, who like Julien Dray, were among its sponsors, took a different tack. They seemed to have decided to take the long view, looking ahead, beyond the Socialists predicted defeat in 1993, to a recomposition of the Left, in which the agenda of SOS-Racisme would play its part. At a similar march, almost a year later, the Socialist Party was again largely absent – only Jean-Christophe Cambadelis and Julian Dray taking a prominent place in the cortège.

Cambadelis is an interesting figure, since he has consistently argued for an explicit political campaign against the National Front. Some people have criticised SOS-Racisme for initially promoting a multicultural model of society, inappropriate to French traditions.[96] (In one sense this created a situation where the National Front and SOS-Racisme were each nourished by the other's propaganda.) However, Cambadelis took issue with their whole approach:

> The divergence which I have with SOS-Racisme is that I believe we must pursue the struggle by designating the enemy and not like today by simply having the positive virtue that we are all anti-racists.[97]

In September 1990 Cambedelis launched an organisation – Le Manifeste Contre Le Front National – to pursue just this strategy. The aim was to fight the National Front at the grassroots; to win back the suburbs and to go into territory where traditionally the Socialist Party itself has been weak. In Cambedelis' own words, Le Manifeste hopes:

> to create throughout France an organisation sufficiently solid and capable to confront, mobilise against, and study the National Front and to say: 'You will not pass, we are here.' Its purpose is to fight in the cities and towns, to reconquer the ground lost, but to fight, not against racism in general, but specifically the National Front.[98]

The Manifeste was also notable in that unlike much of the anti-racist movement, which saw Le Pen in terms of the anti-fascist struggle of the 1930s, Cambedelis believed that the National Front was a rather different phenomenon, *national-populiste* in character.[99]

By the early 1990s the Socialist Government had determined to place the National Front at the very centre of its political struggle. Edith Cresson signalled the new offensive in January 1992 by deciding to take Le Pen to court for describing the Government as 'a pack of thieves, racketeers and gangsters'.[100] Le Pen was determined to capitalise on the Socialist Government's problems – it had been afflicted by a series of scandals and *affaires* – and Cresson was just as eager to try to deflect attention elsewhere. However, the Socialists' qualifications to lead the anti-Le Pen struggle were significantly tarnished: as we have already seen, there were growing strains between the Government and the wider anti-racist movement. It was in this context that Bernard Tapie characterised Le Pen's voters as 'bastards', doing little to improve the terms of the political debate.[101] The Prime Minister followed up with a strong attack on the mainstream Right, whom she characterised as providing a trampoline on which the Front had bounced to prominence.[102] For the Right, Eduard Balladur responded that the Government was simply 'fanning the National Front flames'.[103]

The campaign for the 1992 Regional elections became ever more hysterical, and violence by left-wing demonstrators at National Front meetings more frequent. The Government was forced to distance itself from these attacks, insisting that the Front was a legal political formation and had every right to hold its meetings. The Socialist Party's Executive Bureau also asserted that its campaign was not to be summed up as a battle against the National Front. But the tone of Government pronouncements had helped to create this climate, and its emphasis on Le Pen was suspected by many of masking the emptiness of many of its own proposals.[104]

A responsible appeal by the Socialist Deputy, Gérard Fuchs, for a pact at the Regional Council level between all the mainstream parties to recognise the right of relative majorities to govern, and thus to avoid the need for any deals with the National Front, fell on deaf ears.[105] And even before the ballot, one Socialist election expert was warning of the error in the Party's strategy, insisting that the emphasis on the National Front actually put off prospective Socialist voters rather than mobilising them.[106] Nonetheless, not everyone agreed that the focus on the National Front was a mistake. Cambedelis believes that the offensive against Le Pen was correct. In his view, the Socialist Party's 'strategic error', lay elsewhere:

> Our strategic errors were not specifically related to the National Front, they were strategic errors in relation to the world that we were supposed to represent. From the moment that we decided to turn around and apply a policy of austerity (which was an economic necessity) and to go for a long-term policy, we did much to promote a deflation of salaries; and we took in hand the problems of the suburbs (insecurity, for example) much too late. From then on we were not able to resolve the problems which would help us to continue to organise the social groups that we were supposed to represent. We let them go. That was the real error.[107]

All of France's mainstream political parties, then, made errors in their response to the rise of Jean-Marie Le Pen. Initially they underestimated the potential strength and durability of his support. The Right also overestimated its ability to win back National Front voters. Le Pen was playing upon emotionally charged themes; and to some extent it was territory long-abandoned by the mainstream formations. In April 1988, in the wake of Le Pen's strong showing at the first round of voting in the Presidential election, the leading Socialist politician, Jean-Pierre Chevènement, warned of 'the grave error in abandoning the tricolour flag to Le Pen'.[108] He argued that there was what he called, 'a crisis of the national idea', especially on the Left. However, as one of the more cogent commentators on the Front has pointed out, the errors here were equally shared:

> Political formations who carry in their traditions an idea of the nation –
> I am thinking of the Gaullist and Socialist families – have shown them-
> selves incapable of counterposing their conceptions of the nation to
> those of the National Front.[109]

At times, it seemed as though the National Front was the only party with a coherent image of the nation; and it was the nationalism of Barrès, rather than that of Michelet or the Jacobins that was on offer – a closed, exclusive nationalism rather than an open one.[110]

When the established parties have tried to fight Le Pen on his own ground – for example, that of immigration – they have been either hopelessly hampered (like the Left) by the conflicting pressures of toughness and tolerance, or (like the Right) they have sought to outbid the National Front leader – a policy that has merely served to legitimise his position and increase his support.

But the struggle to limit the political advance of the National Front was also hampered by the temptations of political expediency, as much as by fundamental strategic and tactical errors. The mainstream Right in particular oscillated between principle and pragmatism. Furthermore, the traditional and deep division within the French political system between Left and Right greatly complicated the issue. It proved impossible to obtain a 'Republican consensus' among the democratic mainstream parties to create a barrier to halt Le Pen's advance. As we have already seen in Chapter 4, it was equally impossible to find common ground among the mainstream parties on immigration policy. This mutual hostility of '*Les Deux Frances*' was an important factor in facilitating the National Front's advance. Left and Right viewed each other with mutual suspicion. For many on the Right, the National Front (at least in the early years) occupied a similar position to that held by the Communists on the Left. If it was OK for the Socialists to bring the Communist Party into Government in 1981 (indeed for many the Socialist Government itself was in some sense illegitimate), then why was it so terrible for the mainstream Right to conclude the odd electoral deal with the National Front? After all, according to this line of argument, Le Pen's supporters were at least patriotic Frenchmen, while the Communists were seen as owing their allegiance to a foreign power.

Even on the Left, consensus was difficult. The much-weakened Communist Party remained suspicious of its erstwhile Socialist ally. In addition, the Communists had to cope with pressures from their grassroots, many of which were in areas of high immigrant population, where the National Front was making spectacular advances. The attempts of the Left when in power to take a firm stand on immigration ruffled the feathers of the anti-racist movement and ultimately led to a distancing of SOS-Racisme from the Government. While SOS-Racisme represented a popular attempt to combat the National Front, its own local roots were limited and, as we have seen, there were serious questions about its strategy.

Others have raised more fundamental questions about the whole approach used to counter Le Pen, arguing that attempts to exclude the National Front leader from the political debate and efforts to turn him into the fount of all evil have backfired: Le Pen has instead become something of a martyr; and this has served once again to justify much of the National Front's own rhetoric. One noted commentator, Pierre-André Taguieff, has even gone so far as to speak of 'a crisis of anti-racism' in France, arguing that the anti-racist movement of the 1980s was essentially a movement created from the top, down; both highly politicised and heavily dependent upon the media. Happenings and great events replaced daily, local work. And the '*juvénilisation*' of the anti-racist movement, symbolised by SOS-Racisme, quickly achieved its limits.[111]

There was also a significant element of political myopia on the part of French political leaders when approaching the problems posed by the National Front. It was not just the extent to which the Right sought short-term advantage by dealing with Le Pen. Neither was it simply a question of the Left's temptation to use the National Front for similar short-term gains. In neither case was there any real attempt to stand outside the problem. Few people were able to see the rise of the National Front as a part of a broader, political problem in European society. There seemed to be little interest in similar movements, and the responses to them, elsewhere in Western Europe, despite Le Pen's own prominence on the European stage.

Conclusion: The National Front in a European Perspective

One of the great ironies of the National Front's politics is that, despite its wholesale antipathy towards the European Union, it is Europe that has provided Jean-Marie Le Pen with one of his most effective platforms. The proportional voting system used in France and most other countries for elections to the European Parliament has served the Front well. It has consistently been represented in the Strasburg parliament since 1984, when it won ten seats. Indeed, after the 1994 European elections, it sent 11 Members of the European Parliament (MEPs) to Strasburg, though this was the result of the French parties as a whole being granted more seats. The Front's own vote actually fell slightly.[1]

The parliamentary stage in Strasburg has enabled Jean-Marie Le Pen to pose as a leader of European stature. Until 1994 it enabled the National Front President to organise his own parliamentary group with likeminded parties. For a time the Front chose the Movimento Sociale Italiano – or MSI – as its principal European ally, but after the 1989 elections, Le Pen opted for a deal with the German Republikaner. Presiding over a parliamentary group gave Le Pen additional status; the far-Right grouping being able to present its own motions in the Strasburg parliament. Membership of the European Parliament also afforded Le Pen immunity from prosecution, though this was on occasion lifted, forcing the National Front President to confront his critics in the French courts. Above all, the National Front President's activities in Strasburg helped to keep Le Pen in the public eye. There were the debates on the lifting of his parliamentary immunity; the Front's characteristic interventions on issues like racism and immigration; or the European Right's much-criticised trips to member-states where it had no representation. The result was the same: Le Pen captured the headlines. The National Front leader may not have coined the assertion that there is no such thing as bad publicity, but he has clearly never doubted its wisdom. As one Front publication put it, referring to the Party's success in the 1984 European ballot, 'the European adventure had begun'.[2]

A EUROPEAN PLATFORM

The National Front's arrival in Strasburg in 1984 marked a significant stage in the Party's electoral advance. It would be two years before National Front deputies would take their seats in the National Assembly in Paris, and in the meantime Le Pen was eager to make the most of the new-found opportunities that Strasburg provided. The National Front was the largest far-Right party in the European Parliament, and in July 1984 the ten Front MEPs joined with their five Italian colleagues from the MSI, and one Greek Deputy from the National Political Union (EPEN), to form a parliamentary group – the so-called Groupe des Droites Européennes. Jean-Marie Le Pen became its President.

Le Pen hailed the establishment of this group as a victory over the traditional European political parties. This was the first officially recognised Far-Right grouping in the Strasburg Parliament's history. Its very creation proved, at least according to the Group's own newsletter, that a European patriotism and nationalism could exist without contradicting or compromising the individual parties' love of their own homelands or nations.[3] This dual thrust was encapsulated in the newsletter's title, *Europe et Patries*. Its layout and design revealed the National Front's dominant position within the group. It was similar to other Front bulletins and newsletters and the device that it carried, to the right of its mast-head, was the Front's tricolour flame surrounded by a circle of European stars.

However, European patriotism and chauvinistic nationalism proved uneasy bedfellows. After the 1989 European elections, the German Republican Party (Republikaner Partei), led by Franz Schönhuber, a former member of the Waffen-SS, won six seats and Le Pen hoped to bring them into a single, enlarged, far-Right grouping. For the Republicans and the Italian MSI, however, the lure of old-style nationalism proved stronger than the cause of European cooperation. They were deeply divided over the future of South Tyrol, which once formed part of Austria, until it was ceded to Italy after the First World War. The extreme nationalists of the Republican Party accused the Italians of persecuting the German-speaking population of the region. Le Pen made several efforts to resolve this war of words. The National Front President was motivated by simple arithmetic rather than sentiment. The single Belgian MEP – Karel Dillen of the Vlaams Blok – who insisted that he was not Belgian, but Flemish – had made it clear that he wanted to go into a group with the German Republicans. The rules governing the creation of a European Parliamentary group were clear: if Le Pen sought to form an alliance with the MSI alone, he would need 18 parliamentary seats to form a two-nation group. He only had 14; but a deal with the Republicans and the 'Flemish' deputy would give him 17 seats – well above the threshold of 12 needed for a three-nation group. Le Pen went ahead and established a so-called 'Technical Group of the European Right': the Germans were in, the Italians out.[4]

Not everyone was happy with the arrangement. Jean Madiran, the editorial director of *Présent,* made it clear that he did not like the German Republicans and that, in his view, the Front's long-standing links with the Italian MSI had been betrayed.[5] The row between the German and Italian parties continued for some time, with Schönhuber calling the MSI 'fascists', while Gianfranco Fini, the MSI's Secretary-General, claimed that Mr Schönhuber was 'more extreme than Hitler'.[6]

In the wake of the 1994 European election Le Pen's problems were of a very different nature. Far-Right parties had made significant gains in Belgium and Italy; the MSI's tally rising from four to 13 seats. Overall, the elections despatched some 27 far-Right MEPs to the European Parliament – more than enough to form a parliamentary group.[7] However, once again the arithmetic caused Le Pen problems. His German Republican allies lost all of their seats and the MSI – now part of the governing coalition in Italy – had embarked upon a quest for respectability and was unwilling to sit alongside the French National Front. Le Pen's only potential allies were from Belgium: the 'Flemish' Vlaams Blok now had two deputies and the Belgian National Front – representing Francophone nationalism – had one. But this only gave Le Pen 14 seats and the Parliament's rules now required a minimum of 21 seats for a two-nation group. Le Pen's frustration was increased by the fact that Phillipe de Villiers – whose list Majorité pour l'autre Europe took 13 seats – was able to form his own European Parliamentary group, linking up with four Danish and two Dutch anti-Maastricht MEPs. This group, presided over by the financier Jimmy Goldsmith, was named Europe des Nations, a title which provided an echo of Le Pen's own much-trumpeted call for a Europe of independent and sovereign nations. Just as in the Palais Bourbon, the mainstream Right was now stealing some of the National Front President's best lines.

Le Pen's inability to form a parliamentary group was potentially only a temporary setback. When Austria acceded to the European Union in January 1995 it was allocated 21 parliamentary seats. They were distributed on the basis of the existing level of representation of each of the parties in the Austrian parliament. This meant that the extreme-right Austrian Freedom Party, the FPÖ of Jörg Haider, gained five MEPs in Strasburg. In theory, if Haider were willing to deal with Le Pen, this would have given the National Front leader the 16 seats he needed to form a three-nation group. However, initial soundings from the FPÖ suggested that Haider was cautions about becoming involved with Le Pen, especially when the Frenchman's star seemed to be waning. For Le Pen himself, the loss of a European Parliamentary group of his own is not the disaster it might first appear: the status and legitimacy it conferred were far more important ten years ago; and Le Pen is now well-established. Moreover, it has been suggested that the absence of a highly visible parliamentary group may well facilitate closer ties between the far Right and groupings of the mainstream Right.[8]

Prior to 1994, Le Pen sought to use his Presidency of the Far-Right grouping in the European Parliament to reinforce his links with similar parties elsewhere in Europe – even those who do not have any representation in Strasburg. The pages of *Europe et Patries* contained regular updates about the activities of the Front's allies. In addition to news from Flanders, Germany and Greece, there was information about the Freedom Party in Austria, the Spanish Frente Nacional of Blas Piñar, and the Dutch Centre Democrats. The Italian MSI – whatever their differences in 1989 – still received strong coverage. Four pages of a special issue of *Europe et Patries,* to mark ten years of the European Right's adventure in Strasburg, were devoted to the MSI, while all of the other parties were given half as much space.[9] Despite the official cold-shoulder (at least in public) from the MSI's leadership (now operating under the banner of the National Alliance), Le Pen lost no time in trying to associate himself with the Party's successes. Le Pen hailed the entry of neo-fascist ministers into the Italian government, following Silvio Berlusconi's election victory in March 1994, as an example that would inspire the European Right as a whole. He claimed that it was a symbol that the postwar period had ended; and that to lead a country it was necessary to look ahead to the future, and not to polemicise over the painful events of the recent past.[10]

Le Pen's parliamentary group also sought to spread its message by holding its meetings in a variety of countries, and even by pursuing its own diplomatic missions beyond the European Union's frontiers. Le Pen made his much-publicised visit to Baghdad in November 1990, following the invasion of Kuwait, in the company of Gianfranco Fini of the MSI, Chrysanthos Dimitriadis of the Greek EPEN and Emil Schlee of the German Republicans.[11] In December of the same year the Group went to to the Southern Sahara, via Las Palmas and care of the Moroccan Air Force. Subsequently Le Pen met with King Hassan in Rabat. In April of the following year Le Pen led his Group on a visit to Zagreb for a series of political briefings, during which, according to *Europe et Patries*, they were able to express their support for the Croatian people's aspirations to liberty and independence.

However, the extreme right-wing Group's voyages of discovery did not please many of the other Members of the European Parliament. Trips to Ireland, Denmark and other countries which had not returned far-Right MEPs, were seen as questionable at best. A trip to Corfu, where the MEPs were put up in a five-star hotel for four days, while apparently holding only four hours of meetings, prompted calls for strict cash limits on MEPs' travel budgets. One longstanding critic of Le Pen, the British Labour MEP Glyn Ford, asserted that 'this monthly trekking around Europe can at best be described as political tourism and at worst as political provocation'.[12] Le Pen sought to explain away the Corfu affair as a 'storm in a glass of ouzo'. He argued that the European Community's aim was to bring the peoples of Europe together. What better way was there to do this, he asked, than to go to see where they live and work?[13] The European Right had to cancel similar meetings in Edinburgh and Dublin following public pressure which forced hoteliers to refuse them accommodation. In May 1994 the leaders of the other Parliamentary groups refused permission to allow EC funding for a meeting of the European Right which had been switched from the Algarve to the Azores.[14]

Le Pen's 'political tourism' nonetheless provided observers with useful opportunities to gauge who the National Front's friends really were, not least in Britain. Le Pen visited London for a meeting of his European Right Group in December 1991. Despite press reports that Le Pen was to meet with British National Party leaders during his stay, his chief contacts were with fringe intellectual groups beyond the margins of the Conservative Party. The trip was hosted by an obscure group – the Western Goals Institute – a sort of right-wing political public relations agency, which is run by several former members of the Federation of Conservative Students. Western Goals is reported to have strong links with more radical elements within the Monday Club, on the right wing of the Conservative Party.[15]

The policies advanced by the European Right grouping were broadly similar to those peddled by the Front itself: an emphasis on countering immigration, agricultural protectionism, and outright opposition to the march of European federalism. The European Right strongly denounced what it claimed was the 'militant anti-racism' of the European Parliament – a reference to its studies into racism and xenophobia in Europe. The far Right regularly uses the Parliament's annual debates on this issue to put forward its own propositions, arguing in January 1994, that 'anti-racism is one of the greatest hoaxes perpetrated on contemporary Europe' and that 'racism and xenophobia are marginal phenomena'.[16]

Given the fact that *Europe et Patries* is produced by members of Le Pen's own team, it is not surprising that it stresses the similarity between the French National Front and the various other national right-wing groupings on which it reports. The electoral performance of these parties is mixed. But it is clear that if the National Front was in the vanguard of the European far Right's advance during the 1980s, its leading position has been taken by others during the 1990s – the National Alliance in Italy and by the Freedom Party in Austria. In comparison, Le Pen's formation seems to be marking time, and the formerly ascendant German Republikaner are now in electoral retreat.

The rise of the Front clearly mirrors developments elsewhere in Western Europe during the past two decades. Indeed, one leading French political scientist has suggested that far too little attention has been paid in France to this broader European context. From this perspective, the Front can be seen as 'an international phenomenon with a French specificity'.[17] But how far are international comparisons instructive? And are there any lessons that Le Pen's formation could learn from its more successful European counterparts?

FELLOW-TRAVELLERS ON THE EUROPEAN RIGHT

In October 1994 Jean-Marie Le Pen greeted the results of the Austrian general election, together with those of the local elections in Belgium, with evident relish. For the National Front President, the success of the Austrian Freedom Party and the advance of the two nationalist parties in Belgium marked 'the awakening of the European people ... translated into massive votes in favour of those who, despite demonisation, rise against the dangers of cosmopolitanism and world-wide policies'.[18] Le Pen felt sure that French voters would follow their lead. The task, he said, was to 'build a brotherly Europe of homelands and peoples', adding the inherently contradictory slogan, 'nationalists of all countries, unite'.[19]

Seen from the Front's headquarters in Paris, however, these results, especially the spectacular success for Haider's FPÖ, must have caused just a little envy. Le Pen's own favoured European partners – the German Republikaner – were sliding. A poor performance in the European elections was followed by a weak showing in the Bavarian State elections in September 1994, where they won no seats in an area of traditional strength. Then there was the dismal setback at the October 1994 general election. The Republikaner barely scraped 2 per cent of the vote. In terms of seats, it was three straight zeros in a row.

Worse still for Le Pen, the Italian MSI, who had shunned any dealings with the Front in Strasburg, were now in government and their leader, Gianfranco Fini, seemed to be going from strength to strength, remaining outside the cabinet and basking in a large measure of popularity as financial scandal battered at the doors of Prime Minister Silvio Berlusconi's government.

The problem for Le Pen was to emulate the Italian and Austrian examples, but to avoid the fate of the German Republicans. But to what extent were the varying degrees of success achieved by these extreme-right parties primarily a product of their own strategies? Or, did they depend upon the political context and the balance of political forces in the system in which they worked? It is tempting to see the rise of the European far Right as a coherent and comparable phenomenon. In one sense this is correct. All of these parties – the French National Front, the Belgian Vlaams Blok, the German Republikaner, the Austrian FPÖ, and the National Alliance in Italy – have risen in response to a sense of domestic crisis, a growing disenchantment with existing politics and politicians. All, to varying degrees, display a strident nationalism and they have all manifested a strong dose of ethnic exclusionism, playing upon the issue of immigration to mobilise support.

While it is quite possible to draw up a typology that would seek to differentiate between these parties, ascribing to them labels like 'populist nationalist' or 'neo-fascist', it is by no means clear what such an exercise achieves. Where do you place the idiosyncratic ultra-nationalism of the Flemish Vlaams Blok, for example? And such a typology fails to account for the dynamic nature of politics. Individual parties may well change and develop. The National Front, for example, is a qualitatively new type of formation on the French far Right. The Italian MSI has proudly carried its neo-fascist credentials for many years, but there is now a wide-ranging debate within the party, with Fini and other modernisers eager for the old MSI effectively to be submerged into the more broadly based National Alliance.[20] Fini himself argues that if forced to define himself in these terms, he would choose the label of 'post-fascist', signifying that the fascist experience ended in 1945.[21] Such transformations may be as much a product of generational as they are of doctrinal change. To the liberal observer the new parties may be no more appealing than their progenitors. And although a label like 'neo-fascist' may convey opprobrium or disapproval, it is perhaps, less useful as an analytical term, fifty years after the collapse of Nazi Germany and Fascist Italy.[22]

In a sense, what unites these parties is far more important than their individual political itineraries or the specific details of their programmes. They are responding to a similar set of challenges; a similar crisis in the liberal democratic consensus. One recent study seeks, and I believe succesfully so, to assimilate all these movements under the banner of 'radical right-wing populism'. The majority of such parties, the author asserts,

> are radical in their rejection of the established socio-cultural and socio-political system and their advocacy of individual achievement, a free market, and a drastic reduction of the role of the state, without, however, openly questioning the legitimacy of democracy in general. They are right-wing first in their rejection of individual and social equality and of political projects that seek to achieve it; second in their opposition to the social integration of marginalized groups; and third in their appeal to xenophobia, if not overt racism and anti-Semitism. They are populist in their unscrupulous use and instrumentalization of diffuse public sentiments of anxiety and disenchantment and their appeal to the common man and his allegedly superior common sense.[23]

But if Fini, Haider, Le Pen and Schönhuber are all here, and if all are responding to a similar set of challenges, why are some parties spectacularly more successful than others? The answer, not surprisingly, lies to a large extent in the different contexts within which they operate. Past ideological affinities are not necessarily an obstacle. The Italian Alleanza Nazionale, or National Alliance, joined the conservative coalition that came to office after the 1994 general election, having undergone only cosmetic changes to its image. Certainly two of the five National Alliance ministers in Berlusconi's government had never belonged to the MSI. But as one commentator has noted, it is difficult, at this stage, to take Fini's repudiation of fascism at face value:

> At the moment, Alleanza Nazionale is little more than a front for the MSI, which provided the election workers, the organization and the overwhelming majority of the Alleanza's parliamentary candidates. No doubt, Fini would like to transform the movement into something like an Italian version of the Gaullist Party. But history is still a formidable obstacle.[24]

History is not, however, an obstacle to a share in power. Nor does it necessarily hamper a radical right-wing populist party's advance. And quite apart from their 'respectable' following, most of these formations attract support from the skinhead sub-culture and the amateur fascists and collectors of Nazi memorabilia. On their rightward fringes, it is sometimes hard to draw a clear line between their own supporters and those of more clandestine and violent groupings. The far Right's electoral progress suggests that in many countries there is considerable ambivalence towards the past, and that a party's bad image can be overlooked.

Indeed, even mention of Fascist and Nazi leaders of the 1930s, while provoking controversy, seems to do little damage to a party's prospects. In Austria, Jörg Haider has done well despite temporary setbacks, notably following his praise for Hitler's employment policies.[25] Moreover, the only country where history really does seem to present problems for the far Right is Britain, itself very much a limiting case. One of the most potent factors militating against the success of such movements in the United Kingdom is that despite their protestations of British patriotism, 'they are perceived as foreign and disloyal in the light of the Second World War'.[26]

But the British example does highlight one crucial factor in the European far Right's advance. Its forward progress is, in many countries, closely related to the ability of mainstream politicians – conservative or otherwise – to deal with the issues of immigration and asylum. In Britain, successive Conservative Governments have 'talked tough' on immigration. And legislation in a similar vein, has given little room, except at a very localised level, for the far Right to exploit this theme.[27] However, in both Germany and France, governments were slow to grapple with the issue. Of course, in Germany the problem of asylum-seekers was exacerbated by the strains and expectations arising from reunification.[28] But belatedly, in both countries, governments took a firmer grip on the issue. Germany's tougher asylum laws, passed in May 1993, seem to have contributed, in part, to the Republicans' decline. As we have seen, in France too, the Government's efforts to steal the far Right's thunder – spearheaded by Charles Pasqua – seem to have halted Le Pen's advance.

It would, of course, be wrong to see any of these parties as simply a single-issue movement linked to immigration. However, in programmatic terms, while offering a bundle of policies, few of these parties have yet developed to a stage where they have been able to turn their nationalist concerns into a coherent programme for government. Thus they continue to need emotive issues, like immigration, around which to rally support.

Of course, another great rallying cry of radical right-wing parties is the call to throw out the corrupt old guard. A 'clean hands policy' and opposition to the established political order figure prominently in the politics of many far-Right parties. Indeed, in Italy the degree of corruption was such that the old political establishment was swept away in what, in many ways, resembled a peaceful revolution. The success of the FPÖ in Austria can also be seen as a response to the peculiarly frozen political system of the postwar period. Austria also provides an interesting comparison with France: Heider, like Le Pen, managed to bring the issues of immigration and asylum-seekers on to the agenda, forcing the established parties to bring in legislation to address the popular concern. But the Austrian coalition reaped few rewards and the FPÖ's advance continued despite Heider's relative defeat in the anti-immigration petition his Party sponsored in January 1993.[29]

But if Italy and Austria demonstrate that in a favourable context the far Right can make significant gains, they also illustrate one of the essential conditions for such an advance, namely the availability of willing coalition partners to give them a leg-up into office. In Italy, the National Alliance, the Northern League and Berlusconi's Forza Italia were forced by the new electoral system to cooperate if any of them were to have a share in office. By contrast, Heider was unable to capitalise on his Party's success in Austria, due to the absence of any viable coalition partner.

This last lesson is one that is not lost on Le Pen. His own Party's performance in regional and local councils has demonstrated the necessity of having mainstream politicians who are eager to cut a deal. It is both the mainstream Right's cold-shouldering of the Front together with the Balladur Government's success in stealing some of Le Pen's rhetorical clothes, that have posed fundamental problems for the National Front President.

THE RESISTIBLE RISE OF JEAN-MARIE LE PEN

The French National Front has now reached a critical stage in its brief history. Irrelevant for most of its first decade of existence, ideological and organisational renewal during the late1970s and early 1980s turned it into the fourth largest political formation in France – one that was able to exert a significant influence on the tone, and to some extent the agenda, of the political debate. Le Pen's 14.62 per cent share of the vote at the 1988 Presidential election represents a benchmark that, as yet, the Party has not yet matched. Nonetheless, its most recent election results have been respectable: 12.4 per cent at the 1993 Legislative elections, and 10.5 per cent at the European Assembly elections the following year. The Front seems to have reached a sort of electoral plateau. Some of its results are better than preceding elections of the same type, others are slightly worse. But as the Party geared itself up to fight the 1995 Presidential election campaign, it appeared strangely isolated and, to all intents and purposes, marginalised.[30] The Front only seemed capable of winning seats at European Assembly and at Regional Council elections – arguably the least important ballots in terms of the French domestic scene. It had to face up to a fundamental paradox: its electoral successes now brought it little influence.

So, can the National Front escape this paradox? Does Le Pen's movement have a future? And what sort of future will it be once Le Pen himself ultimately steps down? The answers to these questions can only be tentative. At least part of the response can be derived from a review of the factors that contributed to the Front's initial rise.

It has become commonplace to speak of a pervasive crisis afflicting both French political life and the standing of its politics and politicians over the past two decades. In part, as the American scholar, Stanley Hoffmann has pointed out, this crisis is often set against the warm nostalgic glow emanating from the myth that has grown up around *les trentes glorieuses*, the thirty postwar years, during which

> reconstruction, state planning and the opening of borders transformed the aging (*sic*) and paralyzed nation of peasants and shopkeepers into a major industrial and exporting power, and a predominantly urban country with a growing population.[31]

If the myth of thirty golden years of plenty doesn't bear too close scrutiny, no matter. As Hoffmann points out, it still serves 'to reinforce unhappiness with the twenty years of economic difficulties that followed the first world oil shock of 1973'.[32] Rising unemployment, urban alienation, and disillusionment with mainstream politics, all contributed to the National Front's growing tally of votes. Indeed, others have suggested that the relatively late modernisation of French society, and thus the relatively late implantation of modern value systems, meant that with the onset of economic crisis, there was a ready market for those appearing to offer a more traditional political recipe.[33]

The diminished status of politicians – a widespread phenomenon throughout western Europe – was in large part caused by their inability to find effective answers to the complex economic and social problems of the day. In France things were made worse by the taint of corruption, with the Socialist Party in particular proving that it had little to learn in this sphere from previous conservative administrations.[34] The twice-tried constitutional experiment of *cohabitation* – the co-existence of a President of the Left with a Government of the Right – may also have served to blur the distinctions between the main political parties. The National Front routinely claimed that it was the only real opposition party, irrespective of the political allegiance of the Prime Minister of the day. The victory of the Left in 1981 raised all sorts of expectations within its own constituency that could not be realised. The switch to a rigorous austerity programme and the collapse of the alliance between the Socialist Party and the Communists served to increase the disorientation and disillusionment of a large section of the Left's popular following.[35] On the other side of the political spectrum, the arrival of the Left in power led to a radicalisation of the Right. It is no coincidence that some of the Front's early success, especially in 1984, was due to its ability to win over disillusioned voters from the mainstream Right, especially the RPR, many of whom reverted to their former allegiance in 1986.[36]

The exact contours of the political crisis afflicting France have not yet been carefully defined. There is often as much sentiment in the debate as hard political fact. Nonetheless, there is a growing feeling that politics isn't what it was.[37] There is a sense that the political system is passing through a transitional phase. This is perhaps as much a product of the growing realisation of France's declining international standing, as it is of any domestic political crisis. Nonetheless, the collapse of the Communist Party during the 1980s, followed by the Socialists' débâcle of 1993, the stagnation of the mainstream Right, together with the emergence of new political forces like the Greens and the National Front, have posed fundamental challenges to the established party-system of the Fifth Republic. As one author has suggested, the traditional political cultures of both Left and Right are in crisis:

> On the Right, the Catholic values of order and social harmony are collapsing with the rapid decline in Christianity. The Gaullists, forgetting their working class and nationalist tendencies, are giving themselves over, body and soul to neo-liberalism. Finally on the Left, the political culture of equality and social solidarity, which for many years served as a vehicle for the Communist Party and the trade union movement is disintegrating, and the Socialist Party, whose organisation is still too weak, is powerless to prevent this. Many sections of society, left without political and social reference points and subjected to the dark anxieties of recessionary times, are ready to be tempted by the first populist siren that comes their way.[38]

However, it would be unfair to suggest that the National Front was merely the beneficiary of favourable circumstances. Le Pen has played skilfully the cards he has been given. He was especially fortunate to be able to take advantage of the intensive electoral calendar between 1983 and 1986.[39] It was, above all, the Front's ability to crystallise the growing sense of alienation and the increasing fear of crime and drug-abuse into a single 'all-embracing' issue – immigration – which brought Le Pen electoral success. The other political parties first underestimated the Front's staying-power. Both Left and Right struggled to elaborate a strategy that would, at one and the same time, marginalise Le Pen, while seeking to address the issues that he raised. Both the Left and the Right displayed varying degrees of principle and opportunism. The problems were especially acute for the mainstream Right, who during much of the 1980s – at least at a local level – were motivated by one essential calculation: if the Front's backing, or that of its voters, was needed to secure electoral victory, then, in their view, it was better to deal with Le Pen's supporters than to suffer defeat at the hands of the Left. Fundamentally Le Pen's influence depended upon this calculation of the overall correlation of forces between Left and Right.

By the early 1990s the Front's advance had slowed considerably. The Party had become part of the political landscape and Le Pen no longer made the sort of headlines or attracted the degree of attention that he had commanded during the 1980s. Critically the overall power balance in

Source: *Le Monde* 4 February 1994

French politics had shifted very much against the Left. This meant that the backing of Le Pen's supporters was no longer vital in securing majorities in Regional Assemblies. With the mainstream Right back in power after 1993 and with the end of the Mitterrand years fast approaching, the Balladur Government was able to mount a two-pronged assault both to galvanise its own supporters and to try to win back some of the votes lost to the National Front. Of central importance, here, was the plain-speaking rhetoric of Interior Minister Charles Pasqua. While the debate surrounding the changes to the Nationality Law raised considerable emotion, their practical impact was much less than the degree of controversy suggested. Of far greater significance was Pasqua's tightening-up of the immigration laws. The whole tone of the French political debate was changing. As one commentator noted:

> during much of 1992 and 1993, what was most striking about French political life was its regression into a kind of shrill, defensive and protectionist nationalism, which recalled previous episodes of chauvinism in French history.[40]

Le Pen may have made immigration an issue, but the mainstream Right had now toughened up its own message, not just on immigration, but on a variety of issues like Europe and international trade, where it has to some extent stolen Le Pen's nationalistic rhetoric. Inevitably this has reduced the National Front President's own room for manoeuvre.

While Pasqua was talking tough on immigration, the Prime Minister, Eduard Balladur, was applying his own very special remedy to France's political ills. Chosen by the RPR leader, Jacques Chirac, as a caretaker Prime Minister, Balladur emerged as one of the most popular politicians in France. Chirac had not wanted to embroil himself for a second time in what he regarded as a pointless and potentially damaging stint at the Matignon, while Mitterrand remained at the Elysée. It may have been a significant miscalculation. Chirac's eye was on the Presidential race in 1995. He clearly controlled many of the levers of the RPR machine. But questions were asked as to who might be the better candidate; and Balladur's modest and businesslike approach quickly made him the most popular presidential contender on the Right.[41]

Balladur's rise to prominence casts him as the 'new man' in the mainstream Right's camp. There is a certain irony here. Balladur's own career as a civil servant goes back to the Pompidou era; he is no recent arrival in the corridors of power. In contrast, Le Pen's novelty has worn off. Indeed, there are growing indications that the Front – at least in its present form, and with its present leader – may have reached the limits of its success.

The most recent study by SOFRES for *Le Monde* and RTL indicates that three-quarters of those questioned believe that Le Pen is a danger to democracy.[42] Even if Le Pen's championing of themes like immigration and crime wins him support from beyond the Front's narrow constituency, it is difficult for this support to be converted into votes. The success of de Villiers' list in the 1994 European elections confirms that there is a wider constituency for an appeal to traditional values and nationalism, but that a significant fringe of the mainstream Right's voters are simply not prepared to opt for Le Pen.

The National Front's advance may have slowed, but during the past fifteen years it has put down local roots and created an impressive national organisation. This is not going to simply wither away overnight. There has always been a niche in the Fifth Republic's politics for a party attracting a significant protest vote. For much of the period since 1958 this was the part played by the Communist Party. Le Pen's movement, like the Communists of old, seems intent on creating its own counter-culture: its press, its fairs and functions, its camps and educational activities. And the National Front's diverse electorate, very different from that of a traditional French Far-Right party, also suggests that it, too, may well have taken on such a role.[43]

But can the Front be anything more than a vehicle for protest? Much depends on what happens after Le Pen steps down. Up to now his role has been crucial. Through his strength of personality (and his grip over the Front's finances), he has been able to bind together many of the fractious currents of the extreme Right. In historical terms it is a significant achievement. But with the passage of time, many of these differences between the far Right's various families are coming to appear less and less relevant.

Le Pen himself is reluctant to speculate on the future and is happier to stress his own personal role:

> If I were to disappear, a Congress would be held, and it would have the major task of keeping the Party together. It is still heterogeneous at the moment and it will be a most difficult task. I obviously have the charisma of being the founder. Lots of people have a personal attachment to me. It avoids them having to ask themselves difficult questions. It enables them to say – I don't agree, but that doesn't matter. What's important is the personal attachment I have to the [National Front] President. So it will be a difficult time, but Gaullism has survived de Gaulle.[44]

Le Pen's principal lieutenants are mainly in their forties. Le Pen has no designated successor. In 1993, when questioned about who might take over the reins of the Party in the future, he mentioned three names: those of Bruno Mégret, Bruno Gollnisch and Carl Lang. While Mégret and Lang effectively occupy the number two and three positions in the Front's party machine, Le Pen's mention of Gollnisch was noteworthy. The Far-Right daily newspaper, *Présent*, certainly took this as a promotion for the former university Law professor, who joined the Front in 1983, served as a Deputy between 1986 and 1988 and is today one of its representatives in Strasburg.[45] Gollnisch is one of the Front's three Vice-Presidents and has responsibility for international issues. All three of the men mentioned by Le Pen come from a new generation of far-Right politicians – more technocratic, outwardly more respectable, and much influenced by the thinking of the *nouvelle droite*. (Mégret was born in 1949, Gollnisch in 1950 and Lang in 1957). In this sense, they are far removed from the era of Vichy and *Algérie Française*.

Such leaders would clearly not be content to allow the Front to remain a mere vehicle of protest. Their task will be to break out from the new, albeit more lavishly appointed, political ghetto in which the Front finds itself increasingly trapped. Mégret, for one, clearly believes that the Front must still change considerably, suggesting that: 'the National Front today is very different from what it will be tomorrow'.[46]

However, with every likelihood of a mainstream-Right President emerging from the election of 1995, the National Front's future strategy is hard to plot. The Front is clearly not going to come to power on its own. One option might be to seek an Italian-style compromise. The MSI has succeeded in escaping from its old neo-fascist image, at least to the extent that it is now one of the elements of Italy's governing coalition. It is not impossible to imagine a National Front headed by the likes of Mégret or Gollnisch coalescing, at some point in the future, with the fringes of the mainstream Right. Such a development would depend fundamentally upon what happens on the wider French political scene – what schisms and personality clashes occur within the mainstream camp, and what the overall balance of power is between Left and Right.

Nonetheless, for the moment the National Front is very much on its own. Under Jean-Marie Le Pen the Party has come a long way. But the signs are that one period in its development is now at an end. The road ahead is uncertain. The Front's immediate goal for 1995 is to equal or better Le Pen's showing at the previous Presidential election of 1988. The Front may be marginalised, but Le Pen could still hope for a brief revival in his Party's influence. After a long honeymoon period Balladur's Government began to show signs of weakness. In October 1994 the battle over who should be the mainstream Right's candidate at the Presidential election broke out in earnest, despite the Prime Minister's efforts to dampen down the fires. This 'war of the chiefs' contributed to the mainstream Right's defeat in both 1981 and 1988, and it might well have given Le Pen renewed room to manoeuvre in 1995. Le Pen's calculation was that the mainstream Right's candidate was going to need the support of at least some of his voters at the second ballot to obtain an absolute popular majority. Le Pen believed he could make a good showing. As the autumn of 1994 turned into winter, Prime Minister Balladur's Government caught a bad chill: some of his Ministers have been beset by corruption charges, and the continuing violence in Algeria, and the renewed debate on the wearing of the Islamic headscarf in French schools only served to highlight issues on which the National Front could capitalise.

However, in January 1995, when Jacques Delors – widely seen as the most promising Socialist Presidential contender – decided against running in the race for the Elysée, the nature of the contest was fundamentally altered. With no viable Left-wing candidate it would be fought out exclusively on the Right. But both Prime Minister Eduard Balladur, and the Mayor of Paris Jacques Chirac, knew that the critical electoral battleground was on the RPR's left flank. Whoever was to win the Elysée would need to gather votes from the centre-Right and indeed, at the second ballot, from centre-Left voters as well. If de Villiers gathered a significant slice of the conservative vote, his support at the second round of voting could help to tip the balance in favour of one candidate or another. But it was increasingly difficult to see how Le Pen could hope to influence the election's outcome.

The 1995 Presidential election could well mark Le Pen's political swansong, even if he were to do relatively well. Indeed, the Municipal elections due in June of the same year will probably provide a more accurate reflection of where the National Front's political fortunes really stand. Up to now, Le Pen's stewardship of the Party has been a relative success. While power, as such, has eluded the National Front, its influence on the political agenda, especially during the 1980s, has been considerable. However, more recently, to borrow from Bertold Brecht, the rise of Jean-Marie Le Pen has looked rather more resistible.[47] After much hesitation, some behind-the-scenes dealing, and a number of false starts, the mainstream Right appears to have got the measure of this new upstart formation. If the Front is ultimately to prosper further, it may need both a new leader and a new, and more attractive, political strategy.

Appendix

Map 1   Regions and Departments

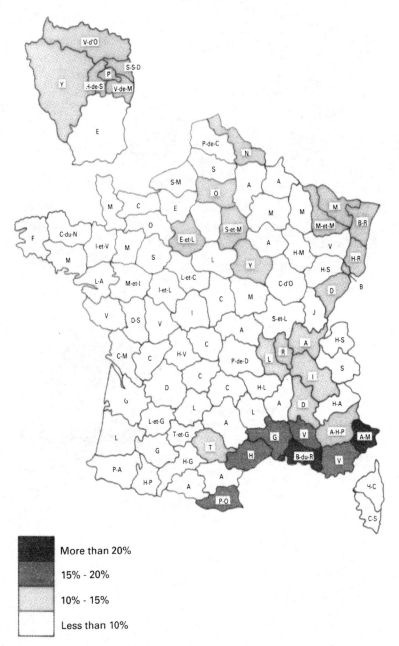

Map 2 Percentage of votes gained by the National Front in the 1986 Legislative election. (Adapted from *Le Monde*.)

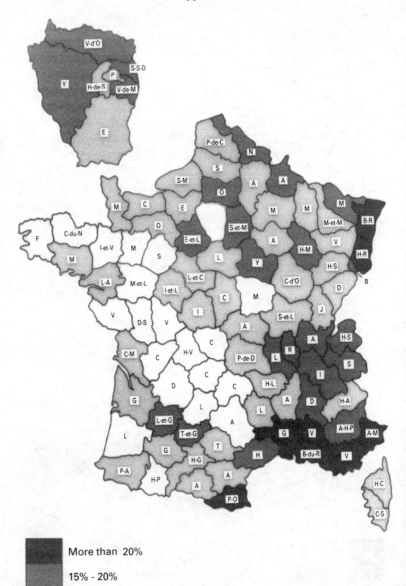

Map 3 Percentage of votes gained by Jean-Marie Le Pen in the 1988 Presidential election. (Adapted from *Le Monde*.)

Map 4   Percentage of votes gained by the National Front in the first round of the 1993 Legislative election. (Adapted from *Le Monde*.)

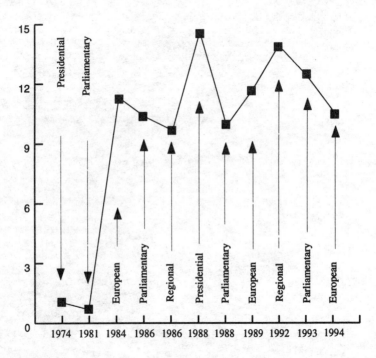

Fig. 1 The National Front's electoral progress, as a percentage of votes cast.
(Adapted from *Le Monde.*)

Notes

INTRODUCTION: THE NATIONAL FRONT'S WORLD

1. *Les Chouans*, a name given to many of the armed bands that rose up against the Revolutionary regime, their name derived from that given to the leader of one group, Jean Chouan. See J.-C. Martin, *Blancs et Bleus dans la Vendée déchirée* (Paris: Découvertes-Gallimard, 1990). The events in the Vendée are also an important reference point today for Philippe de Villiers, the traditionalist, some would say reactionary conservative leader, who ran his own list at the 1994 European elections obtaining 12.33 per cent of the vote, to Jean-Marie Le Pen's 10.51 per cent.
2. *Présent*, 28 September 1993.
3. See E. Weber, France, *Fin de Siècle* (Cambridge, Mass.: Harvard University Press, 1986), pp. 112–13.
4. See J. Martin, *L'Empire Triomphant 1871/1936, Tome 2, Maghreb, Indochine, Madagascar, îles et comptoirs* (Paris: Denoël, 1990), pp. 85–116.
5. Interview conducted at the Front's headquarters in Paris, 27 September 1993.
6. Indeed, in an interesting 'might have been', two experts, one of whom participated in the Vedel Commission study into the electoral system, calculated the results using varying elements of proportionality. In one case, the Front emerged with 18 seats to the Communists' 11. Under the second scheme the Front had 8 seats, the Communists 6 seats. M. Balinski and L. Mann, *'Si le mode de scrutin avait été modifié ...'*, *Le Monde*, 3 April 1993.
7. Vladimir Zhirinovsky's Liberal Democratic Party unexpectedly won nearly 23 per cent of the vote at the Russian general election of 12 December 1993.
8. See Chapter 3.
9. Le Pen consistently refuses to describe the National Front as being on the Far Right or the extreme Right, insisting that it is merely a component of the broader right-wing camp.
10. Press conference, 24 March 1993. For press coverage, see *L'écho républicain*, 25 March 1993.

1 THE EMERGENCE OF THE NATIONAL FRONT

1. Quoted in H. Lottman, *The People's Anger: Justice and Revenge in Post-Liberation France* (London: Hutchinson, 1986), pp. 272–3. Another estimate suggests some 9000 summary executions, to which must be added 767 people executed after condemnation by a court. See J.-P. Rioux, *La France de la Quatrième République, Volume I – L'Ardeur et la nécessité, 1944–1952* (Paris: Le Seuil, 1980), pp. 54–7.

2. This obscurity is difficult to imagine given the fascination during the 1980s of much of the news media with the Vichy regime and collaboration. It was Marcel Ophuls' film in 1969, *Le Chagrin et le Pitié*, which marked a significant step in the reawakening of interest in the war years. For a discussion of this phenomenon, see H. Rousso, *Le Syndrome de Vichy 1944–198...* (Paris: Éditions du Seuil, 1987).

3. See Pierre Milza, *Fascisme français: Passé et Présent* (Paris: Flammarion, 1987), pp. 276–333. For a detailed discussion of French neo-fascism during this period, see J. Algazy, *La Tentation néo-fasciste en France 1944–65* (Paris: Fayard, 1984). Also J.-P. Rioux, 'Des clandestins aux activistes (1945–65)', in M. Winock (ed.), *Histoire de l'extrême droite en France* (Paris: Seuil, 1993), pp. 215–41.

4. Milza (1987), pp. 278–9.

5. For a comparison of the electoral strength of *Poujadisme* and the National Front, see Chapter 2. For a discussion of the Poujadist phenomenon, see Milza (1987), pp. 299–308.

6. For a discussion of the phenomenon of *Algérie Française*, see Milza (1987), pp. 309–24. See also J.-P. Rioux (1993), pp. 232–41.

7. See P. Williams and M. Harrison, 'Algerian Independence: the April 1962 Referendum' in P. Williams, *French Politicians and Elections 1951–1969* (Cambridge: Cambridge University Press, 1970), pp. 127–36.

8. Quoted in J. Algazy, *L'extrême-droite en France (1965 à 1984)* (Paris: L'Harmattan, 1989), p. 22.

9. For a detailed discussion of *Occident* and its activities, see Algazy (1989), pp. 45–64. An indispensable handbook covering the various factions, groupings, journals, and individuals on the Far Right, from 1945 to the present day, is J.-Y. Camus and R. Monzat, *Les Droites Nationales et Radicales en France* (Lyon: Presses Universitaires de Lyon, 1992).

10. During the summer of 1969, Far-Right journals like *Découvertes, Le Soleil*, and *Défi* – the latter run by the former OAS activist Pierre Sergent, later to be one of Le Pen's strongest critics from within the National Front – all ran articles calling for the formation of front organisations to unify the Far Right and broaden its appeal. 'We have been beaten for so many years because we are divided', wrote Sergent. Quoted by Algazy (1989), p. 89.

11. The MSI did well at the 1971 local election, scoring 13.9 per cent and in some areas much higher (Catania 27 per cent, Palermo 19.5 per cent). See F. Sidoti, 'The Extreme Right in Italy: Ideological Orphans and Countermobilization', in P. Hainsworth (ed.), *The Extreme Right in Europe and the USA* (London: Pinter, 1992), pp. 151–74. In Germany, the National Democratic Party (NPD) entered seven Land parliaments and won 61 seats between 1966 and 1968. However, its score of 4.3 per cent and no seats at the 1969 Federal elections proved disappointing to its supporters. See E. Kolinsky, 'A Future for Right Extremism in Germany?', in P. Hainsworth (ed.) (1992), pp. 61–94. In Britain, the National Front, formed in 1967 in an attempt to create an electoral force out of the various currents on the Far Right, fared best at local rather than national contests. Nonetheless, at a parliamentary by-election at West Bromwich in 1973, it won some 16 per cent. Its local election peak came in 1977, when in some areas of London its average score ranged between 12 and nearly 18 per

cent. See M. Walker, *The National Front* (London: Fontana, 1978), pp. 133–203.

12. J. Algazy (1989), p. 103.
13. *Ordre nouveau hebdo*, No. 5, 2–8 September 1972, quoted by Algazy (1989), p. 117.
14. Roger Holeindre, a member of the Front's leading circles (with membership of both the *Secrétariat général* and the *Bureau politique*) also runs the Cercle National des Combattants – an associated grouping representing the interests of ex-servicemen, with a strong nostalgia for Algeria. He began his far-Right career in the OAS, and ran security for Tixier-Vignancour's Presidential campaign in 1965. Pierre Durand, also a member of the Front's *Bureau politique*, is co-director of the daily *Présent*.
15. See R. Chiarini, 'The "Movimento Sociale Italiano": A Historical Profile', in L. Cheles, R. Ferguson & M. Vaughan (eds), *Neo-Fascism in Europe* (London: Longman, 1991), pp. 19–43.
16. For a description of the meeting, see Algazy (1989), p. 122.
17. A. Rollat, *Les hommes de l'extrême droite, Le Pen, Marie, Ortiz et les autres* (Paris: Calmann-Lévy, 1985), p. 71.
18. See Algazy (1989), p. 163.
19. *Le National,* February 1979.
20. For a discussion of the early shifts in the National Front's ideology, see J. Wolfreys, 'An Iron Hand in a Velvet Glove: The Programme of the French Front National', *Parliamentary Affairs*, 46 (1993), 415–29.
21. The PFN has been increasingly marginalised. Many of its cadres have moved into the CNIP, emphasising this more respectable formation's role as a bridge between the Far Right and the mainstream. Alain Robert himself joined the CNIP in 1981 and in 1986 was elected a Regional Counsellor on the RPR list for Seine-Saint-Denis. *Le Monde*, 19/20 January 1992.
22. For a discussion of the *solidaristes* and their influence within the National Front, see Chapter 2, pp. 36–7.
23. On GRECE and the 'New Right' in general, see Anne-Marie Duranton-Crabol, *Visages de la Nouvelle Droite Le G.R.E.C.E. et son Histoire* (Paris: Presses de la Fondation Nationale des Sciences Politiques, 1988), P. Milza (1987), pp. 366–96, I. Barnes, 'The Pedigree of GRECE (I)', *Patterns of Prejudice*, 14 July 1980, 14–24, continued in *Patterns of Prejudice*, 14 October 1980, 29–39.
24. A. de Benoist, *Vu de droite* (Paris: Editions Copernic, 1977).
25. For an excellent discussion of the New Right in Britain and the USA, see A. Gamble, *The Free Economy and the Strong State: The Politics of Thatcherism* (London: Macmillan, 1994), pp. 34–68.
26. On Gramsci's thought, see L. Kolakowski, *Main Currents of Marxism: Its Origins, Growth, and Dissolution: Volume III, The Breakdown* (Oxford: Clarendon Press, 1978), pp. 220–52. Also A. Sassoon, *Gramsci's Politics* (London: Croom Helm, 1980).
27. Quoted in Milza (1987), p. 369.
28. *Défence de l'Occident,* 170, December 1979, pp. 28–9, quoted by Algazy (1989), p. 244.
29. A.-M. Duranton-Cabrol (1988), p. 24.
30. Quoted in Milza (1987), p. 376.

31. Pierre-André Taguieff has written exhaustively on the ideology of the 'New Right'. See e.g. 'La Stratégie culturelle de la Nouvelle Droite', in R. Badinter (ed.), *Vous avez dit fascismes?* (Paris: Arthaud/Montalba, 1984), pp. 13–152; and 'Nouvelle Droite: Une doctrine anti-égalitaire', *Après-demain,* April 1983, 21–8.

32. See the full-page article by R. Monzat, 'Le rituel SS de la Nouvelle Droite', *Le Monde,* 3 July 1993.

33. See Chapter 2.

2   LE PEN: THE MAN AND HIS PARTY

1.   J.-M. Le Pen, *Les Français d'abord* (Paris: Carrère/Lafon, 1984), p. 34. In fact Le Pen's father's death was a tragic wartime accident. He was killed in the summer of 1942 when the nets of his fishing boat caught on a mine which exploded. See the recent critical biography of Le Pen, G. Bresson and C. Lionet, *Le Pen* (Paris: Seuil, 1994).

2.   Le Pen (1984), p. 35.

3.   Ibid.

4.   *Libération,* 28 September 1987.

5.   Le Pen (1984), p. 36.

6.   Le Pen (1984), p. 39.

7.   E. Plenel and A. Rollat, *L'effet Le Pen* (Paris: Editions la Découverte/Le Monde, 1984), p. 223.

8.   Le Pen (1984), p. 40.

9.   Ibid., p. 44.

10. Ibid., p. 46.

11. Ibid., p. 46.

12. The classic study of *Poujadisme* remains that of S. Hoffmann, *Le Mouvement Poujade* (Paris: Librarie Armand Colin, 1956).

13. *Présent,* 27 March 1993.

14. D. Porch, *The French Foreign Legion: A Complete History* (London: Macmillan, 1991), p. 585.

15. A. Horne, *A Savage War of Peace: Algeria 1954–1962* (New York: The Viking Press, 1978), pp. 197-207.

16. Cited by E. Plenel and A. Rollat (1984), p. 225.

17. Le Pen's broadcast on *L'heure de vérité, Le Monde,* 15 February 1984.

18. For a discussion of the *Libération* attack and Le Pen's response, see *Le Point,* 18 February 1985.

19. *Le Monde,* 30 April 1957.

20. *International Herald Tribune,* 8 October 1993.

21. Le Pen (1984), p. 48.

22. Quoted in *Le Monde,* 7 December 1989.

23. Le Pen (1984), p. 53.

24. *Le Monde,* 25 October 1985.

25. Ibid.

26. *Le Monde,* 16 October 1985.

27. *Le Monde,* 18 October 1985.

28. *Le Monde,* 17 October 1985.
29. *Playboy* (French Edition), No. 23, July 1987.
30. Author's interview, September 1993.
31. *Le Monde,* 8 October 1987.
32. By far the best discussion of the National Front's currents and inner work-ings is provided by G. Birenbaum, *Le Front national en politique* (Paris: Editions Balland, 1992), pp. 244–53.
33. *Le Monde,* 15 February 1984.
34. Plenel and Rollat (1984), pp. 11–14.
35. P. Sigoda, *'Les cercles extérieurs du RPR', Pouvoirs,* No. 28, 1984, pp. 143–58.
36. Plenel and Rollat (1984), pp. 68–71.
37. Birenbaum (1992), p. 60.
38. Sigoda (1984), p. 148.
39. I. Barnes, 'Pedigree of GRECE', *Patterns of Prejudice,* Vol. 14, No. 3, July 1980.
40. *Le Monde,* 17 December 1985.
41. Y. Piat, *Seule, tout en haut à droite* (Paris: Fixot, 1991), pp. 106–7. Piat, who had known Le Pen during her childhood, left the Party in 1988 and joined the *Parti républicain.* She was murdered in February 1994, appar-ently the subject of a gangland contract. For her murder, see *Le Monde,* 27/28 February 1994 and for the subsequent arrests, see *Le Monde,* 18 June 1994.
42. Piat (1991), p. 118.
43. Ibid., pp. 122–3.
44. Ibid., p. 171.
45. *Le Monde,* 1 October 1988.
46. Author's interview, September 1993.
47. *Le Figaro,* 19 September 1983.
48. Author's interview, September 1993.
49. J.-Y. Camus, 'Political Cultures within the Front National: The Emergence of a Counter-Ideology on the French Far Right', *Patterns of Prejudice,* Vol. 26, No. 1/2, 1992.
50. Piat (1991), p. 115.
51. *Le Monde,* 8 February 1992.
52. B. Hennion, *Le Front national: l'argent et l'establishment* (Paris: Éditions La Découverte, 1993), pp. 208–17.
53. *Le Monde,* 8 February 1992.
54. *Le Monde,* 5 February 1992.
55. Piat (1991), p. 143.
56. *Le Monde,* 8 February 1992.
57. Ibid.
58. J.-C. Masclet, *Les règles du financement de la vie politique,* published in the series *Problèmes Politiques et Sociaux,* No. 667–8, 15–29 November 1991.
59. *Journal Officiel,* 6 November 1993, 15403. This could well drop by about 5 per cent as an austerity measure, see *Le Monde,* 5 November 1993.
60. Author's interview, September 1993.
61. *Identité,* No.4, November/December 1989. For a discussion of *Action française,* the right-wing intellectual group founded in response to the

Dreyfus Affair, see A. Cobban, *A History of Modern France, Volume 3: 1871–1962* (Harmondsworth: Penguin, 1965), pp. 86–9.

62. Interview with Pierre-André Taguieff in *Le Monde*, 10 April 1991.
63. For take-over, see *Présent*, 30 September 1993. For Mégret's concerns, see *Libération*, 22 May 1992. Le Pen was speaking in an interview with the author, December 1993.
64. Author's interview, September 1993.
65. *Le Guide du Responsable, Livre I* (Paris: Editions nationales), 5.
66. *Le Monde*, 8 February 1994. The article also reported attempts to 'fix' the vote of the delegates for the Central Committee. There were, it seems, several lists circulating at the Congress with ready-made selections of candidates for delegates to copy.
67. See the article by Olivier Biffaud, *Le Monde*, 5 February 1994.
68. See *'La Lettre de Jean-Marie Le Pen'*, No. 201, July 1994, 7.
69. Birenbaum (1992), p. 86.
70. What Birenbaum classifies as the 'moderns', Birenbaum, (1992), pp. 75–6.
71. Piat (1991), p. 210.
72. *Le Monde*, 3 July 1986.
73. Piat (1991), p. 153.
74. Quoted in *Le Monde*, 1 October 1987.
75. *Le Monde*, 29 April 1992.
76. *Le Figaro*, 18 May 1992.
77. *Le Monde*, 17 February 1994.
78. *Le Monde*, 7 July 1990.
79. *Le Monde*, 8/9 July 1990.
80. Reported in *Libération* and quoted in *Le Monde*, 20 May 1992.
81. *Le Monde*, 1 September 1990.
82. *Le Monde*, 4 September 1990.
83. *Le Monde*, 19 October 1993.
84. *Le Monde*, 31 October/1 November 1993.

3   THE ELECTORAL RISE OF THE NATIONAL FRONT

1. For the exploitation of the theme of immigration during the campaign, see *Le Monde*, 13 March 1983. For an analysis of the campaign, see J. Marcus and C. Dorgan, 'French Politics and the Municipal Elections of March 1983', *The Political Quarterly*, 54 (1983) 307–12.
2. *Le Monde*, 9 March 1983.
3. In Vernouillet (Eure-et-Loire) and Châteauneuf-sur-Charente (Charente) National Front candidates scored 11.6 per cent and 10.2 per cent. See Gerard Le Gall, *'Un recul du "bloc au pouvoir" moindre en 1983 qu'en 1977'*, *Revue politique et parlementaire*, 903 (1983), 11–41.
4. For an analysis of the Aulnay-sous-Bois result, see *Le Monde*, 15 November 1983.
5. SOFRES opinion poll in *Le Monde*, 25 May 1984.
6. J. Jaffré, 'Les fantassins de l'extrême droite', *Le Monde*, 14 February 1984.

7. See P. Perrineau, 'Le Front National: 1972–1992', in M. Winock (ed.), *Histoire de l'extrême droite en France* (Paris: Seuil, 1993).

8. S. Hoffmann, *Le Mouvement Poujade* (Paris: Armand Colin, 1956), passim.

9. A. Rollat in *Le Monde*, 12 March 1985.

10. J. Jaffré, 'Front National: la relève protestataire', in E. Dupoirier and G. Grunberg (eds), *Mars 1986: la drôle de defaite de la gauche* (Paris: Presses Universitaires de France, 1986). Also G. Le Gall, 'Mars 1986: des elections de transition?', *Revue politique et parlementaire*, 922 (1986) 6–18.

11. SOFRES poll in *Le Monde,* 14 March 1987.

12. SOFRES poll in *Le Monde*, 4 November 1987.

13. *Le Monde*, 1 December 1987.

14. J. Jaffré, 'Le Pen ou le vote exutoire', *Le Monde*, 12 April 1988.

15. *Le Monde,* 26 April 1988. For analysis, see J. Marcus, 'French Politics after the Elections', *The World Today,* (October 1988), 173–6. Also P. Perrineau, 'Le Front national et les élections: L'exception presidentielle et la règle législative', *Revue politique et parlementaire,* 936 (1988), 34–41.

16. Bull-BVA-CNRS poll in *Le Monde*, 11 May 1988.

17. As Pascal Perrineau emphasised in an interview with the author, the apparent coincidence between the decline of the Communist Party and the rise of the FN is a complex phenomenon and difficult to approach in a quantitative manner. While there is little evidence for direct transfers of PCF voters to the Front, there is strong circumstantial evidence, at the very least, to suggest that the Front has to some extent come to replace the PCF in its 'tribune role', in areas of former Communist strength. One suggestion is that disillusioned former Communist voters may take refuge in abstention for some years before drifting into a vote for Le Pen. See E. Plenel and A. Rollat, *L'effet Le Pen* (Paris: La Découverte/Le Monde, 1984), pp. 118–23 and pp. 159–65. See also F. Platone and H. Rey, 'Le FN en terre communiste' in N. Mayer and P. Perrineau (eds), *Le Front national à découvert* (Paris: Presses de la Fondation nationale des sciences politiques, 1989).

18. SOFRES poll in *Le Monde*, 6 January 1989. See also N. Mayer and P. Perrinneau, 'La puissance et le rejet ou le lepénisme dans l'opinion', in O. Duhamel and J. Jaffré (eds), *SOFRES: L'état de l'opinion 1993* (Paris: Seuil, 1993).

19. *Le Monde,* 28 September 1988.

20. In the 6th constituency in Bouches-du-Rhône the Front was down 12.3 per cent and in Seine-Saint-Denis 5.3 per cent. In both cases the candidates were former Front deputies who had been elected in 1986. *Le Monde*, 24 January 1989.

21. *Le Monde*, 14 March 1989.

22. P. Perrineau, 'Le Front national: les cléfs de la défaite', *Revue politique et parlementaire*, 940 (1989), 19–24.

23. G. Le Gall, 'Un triple avertissement: pour l'Europe, la démocratie et les Socialistes', *Revue politique et parlementaire*, 942 (1989) 11–20.

24. *Le Monde*, 28 November 1989. At the first ballot in 1988, Stirbois took 15.8 per cent.

25. *Le Monde*, 5 December 1989.

26. F. Gaspard, 'L'evolution du F.N. à Dreux et dans les environs (1978–1989)', *Revue politique et parlementaire*, 945 (1990), 62–9.

27. SOFRES poll in *Le Monde*, 25 October 1991.

28. J. Marcus, 'France: Punishing the Socialists', *The World Today* (June 1992), 99–100. Also G. Le Gall, 'Elections: les handicaps du pouvoir face à 1993', *Revue politique et parlementaire*, XXX (1992) 3–13.

29. J. Jaffré, 'La défaite des socialistes et l'insatisfaction des electeurs', *Pouvoirs*, 62 (1992), 135–49.

30. J. Marcus, 'France: The Right Triumphs', *The World Today* (May 1983), 82–3.

31. N. Mayer and H. Rey, 'Avancée électorale, isolement politique du Front national', *Revue politique et parlementaire*, 964 (1993), 42–8.

32. A SOFRES study produced for *Le Monde* and RTL. See *Le Monde*, 4 February 1994.

33. The National Front stood down its candidate in only one seat, the canton of Creil-Sud, in favour of Ernest Chénière (RPR), the former principal of a college who had been instrumental in raising the whole issue of Islamic girls wearing the headscarf. In making his decision, Le Pen praised his 'courageous and honourable position'. See *Le Monde*, 25 March 1994.

34. Fernand Le Rachinel re-elected in Canisy (Manche) at the first ballot, and Eliane de La Brosse in Toulon (Var), and Marie-France Stirbois in Dreux Ouest (Eure-et-Loir), at the second. The Front lost one seat. Another, that of Jacques Peyrat, was not at issue in 1994. Thus it emerged from the Cantonal elections with four Departmental Council seats in total. *Le Monde*, 29 March 1994.

35. For the Front's own gloss on the results, see *La Lettre de Jean-Marie Le Pen*, No. 193, March 1994.

36. Quoted in *Le Monde*, 31 March 1994. Peyrat resigned from the National Front in September 1994, following Le Pen's designation of Jean-Pierre Gost, the Front's Departmental Secretary for the Alpes Maritimes Federation, to head the Nice list at the 1995 Municipals. *Le Monde*, 3 September 1994. Another local councillor, Michel Moulin, followed Peyrat. Of the seven FN Municipal Councillors elected for Nice in 1989, only three remained inside the Party. Reported by AFP on 11 October 1994.

37. For the results of the European elections, see *Le Monde*, 14 June 1994. The Party lost votes in many of the places where it had achieved its best scores in 1989: Alpes-Maritimes, Var, Bouches-du-Rhône, Pyrénées-Orientales. It increased its vote slightly in some 22 Departments, including Alsace, Centre, Champagne-Ardenne, Lorraine, Nord-Pas-de-Calais, Haute-Normandie and Picardie.

38. Bruno Mégret, 'Les leçons du 12 Juin', *La Lettre de Jean-Marie Le Pen*, No.199, June 1994, 3.

39. Of 100 voters who opted for de Villiers' list in 1994, 56 had voted for either Barre or Chirac at the first round of the 1988 Presidential ballot. See the SOFRES post-electoral opinion poll, June 1994. While the SOFRES study finds some 8 per cent of de Villiers' support coming from Le Pen voters of 1988, the BVA exit-poll suggests a rather higher figure of some 13 per cent of de Villiers' support coming from those who had voted for Le Pen at the legislative elections of 1993. All these figures should be treated with caution, and much more work needs to be done on the make-up of de Villiers' support and its longer-term significance.

40. Rossi was writing in a forthcoming edition of the Republican Party's own magazine, the *Journal des Républicains*. Quoted by Agence France-Presse, 23 September 1994.

41. Indeed, a recent study of the electorates of Le Pen and de Villiers suggests significant differences between them. The two men are not competing over the same ground. In June 1994 De Villiers' support was strongest in north-western France, especially in the Pays de la Loire. De Villiers' voters tended to be older, practising Catholics, and more middle-class, while Le Pen's electorate is younger, more popular in character and more heterogeneous both geographically and politically. See Pascal Perrineau, '*La dissidence villiériste*', *Le Monde*, 19 november 1994.

4   IMMIGRATION AS A POLITICAL ISSUE

1. *Figaro-Magazine*, 26 October–1 November 1985, 123–33.

2. *Le Matin*, 28 October 1985.

3. Fabius was speaking on the television programme *L'heure de vérité* on 5 September 1984. He was commenting on the relationship between the Far Right and the mainstream Right parties: 'The Far Right – they're offering the wrong answers to valid questions.... An electoral system can't make a political party.... On the other hand I think you can limit or even stop the development of a movement by refusing to become allied with it.... It was by no means necessary for the parties on the Right to ally themselves with the Far Right in order to run things in Corsica. What I find shocking is that these ideas of the Far Right are in some way becoming commonplace and, little by little, they're filtering down, even into the forces of the traditional Right'. See *Le Monde*, 7 September 1984.

4. For a considered and realistic presentation of the issues, see the book by the former Socialist deputy, G. Fuchs, *Ils resteront: Le défi de l'immigration*, (Paris: Syros, 1987).

5. *Le Monde*, 18 October 1985.

6. Quoted in *Le Monde*, 11 June 1991.

7. *Le Monde*, 2 July 1991.

8. *1981–85: Une nouvelle politique de l'immigration*. Published by the Ministère des Affaires Sociales et de la Solidarité Nationale, June 1985, 17–23.

9. Algerians 795 920 (21.6 per cent), Portuguese 764 860 (20.8 per cent), Moroccans 431 120 (11.7 per cent), Italians 333 740 (9.1 per cent), Spanish 321 440 (8.7 per cent), Tunisians 189 400 (5.1 per cent), Africans (sub-Sahara)138 080 (3.7 per cent), Turks 123 540 (3.4 per cent), South East Asians 105 520 (2.9 per cent).

10. *1981–85: Une nouvelle politique de l'immigration*. (1985) 18.

11. See C. Wihtol de Wenden, *Les Immigrés et La Politique* (Paris: Presses de la Fondation Nationale des Science Politiques, 1988), 264–6.

12. *L'Humanité*, 7 January 1981.

13. Speech quoted in *Communist Affairs*, Vol. 1, (1), 1982, 325.

14. See M. Schain, 'Racial Politics: The Rise of the National Front', in J.S. Ambler (ed.), *The French Socialist Experiment* (Philadelphia: ISHI, 1985), pp. 129–35.

15. See the article by P. Jarreau, 'Cher Mustapha ...', *Le Monde*, 13 March 1983.

16. *Le Monde*, 15 July 1983.

17. Whitol de Wenden (1988), 278–88.

18. Interview in *Le Monde*, 3 August 1983.

19. *Le Monde*, 2 September 1983.

20. *L'Express*, 25 May 1984.

21. Quoted by P. Favier and M. Martin-Roland, *La Décennie Mitterrand. Vol. 2. Les épreuves* (Paris: Seuil, 1991), p. 580.

22. See A. Hochet, '*L'Immigration dans le débat politique français de 1981 à 1988*', *Pouvoirs*, No. 47, 23–30.

23. *Le Monde*, 16 March 1988.

24. See P. Weil, '*Immigration et Insertion*', *Le Journal des Elections*, May 1988, 22.

25. See P. Weil, '*Un débat récurrent: l'immigration*', in D. Chagnollaud (ed.), *Etat Politique de la France: Année 1991* (Paris: Quai Voltaire, 1992), pp. 165–72.

26. *Le Figaro*, 16 March 1987.

27. Ibid.

28. *Le Point*, 31 August 1987 and *Le Monde*, 8 September 1987.

29. Interview in *Le Monde*, 9 January 1988.

30. Mitterrand's New Year message, *Le Monde*, 3 January 1989.

31. *Le Monde*, 3 June 1989.

32. *Le Monde*, 9 July 1991.

33. Wihtol de Wenden (1988), p. 284.

34. *Le Monde*, 18 October 1987.

35. Speech on 20 April 1985, see *Le Monde*, 23 April 1985 for reactions.

36. *Le Monde*, 18 May 1980.

37. *Le Monde*, 7 October 1989.

38. LICRA, the Ligue Internationale Contre le Racisme et l'Antisémitisme, is one of France's oldest and most significant independent anti-racist groups. Its traces its origins to the Ligue Contre les Pogroms, founded in 1927 to campaign against anti-semitic persecution in Russia.

39. See the evidence of Ligue des Droits de l'homme, in the *Rapport de la Commission Nationale Consultative des Droits de l'Homme:1991. La Lutte Contre Le Racisme et la Xénophobie* (Paris: *La Documentation française*, 1992), pp. 224–32.

40. *Le Point*, 16 October 1989.

41. *Le Monde*, 25 October 1989.

42. *Le Monde*, 26 October 1989.

43. *Le Monde*, 28 October 1989.

44. *Le Monde*, 29 November 1989. The *Conseil d'Etat* seemed to leave the issue open, arguing that, 'The wearing of religious symbols was not, in itself, incompatible with the lay character of public schools.' However, such symbols as the headscarf could be banned if they were used to proselytise, provoke, or if they infringed the liberty or the dignity of a child. Three years

later (2 November 1992) the Conseil d'Etat seemingly took a contradictory step, when it annulled a clause in a school's regulations banning the wearing of the headscarf.

45. *Le Monde,* 30 November 1989.
46. Kofi Yamgnane, Secretary of State for Social Affairs and Integration quoted in *Le Monde,* 10 October 1991.
47. *Le Monde,* 17 March 1990.
48. *Le Monde,* 13 October 1993.
49. *Le Monde,* 12 November 1993.
50. *Le Monde,* 21 September 1994. See also the special supplement 'La France et l'Islam', *Le Monde,* 13 October 1994.
51. Robert Solé, writing in *Le Monde,* 13 September 1994.
52. See the IFOP opinion poll in the special supplement 'La France et l'Islam', *Le Monde,* 13 October 1994, vi–vii. While emphasising the continuing gulf between the positive perception of Islam held by French Muslims and the overwhelmingly negative view held by the population at large, the poll showed that over 60 per cent of those with Muslim origins regarded the Algerian Islamic Salvation Front (FIS) as a threat to democracy, and 70 per cent believed that FIS did not represent Islamic values as they understood them.
53. *Le Monde,* 11 June 1993.
54. AP News Agency, 11 May 1993.
55. Interview in *Le Monde,* 2 June 1993.
56. Interview in *Le Figaro,* 5 April 1993.
57. Marsaud was one of those who sought to 'toughen' up the legislation, see *Le Figaro,* 16 June 1993.
58. Author's interview, December 1993.
59. *Le Monde,* 4 December 1985.
60. Reuter's News Agency, 14 September 1985.
61. *Le Figaro,* 20 June 1991.
62. *Libération,* 21 June 1991.
63. *Le Monde,* 21 June 1991.
64. See *'L'exemple de la Goutte-d'Or ou les mauvais comptes du maire de Paris',* *Le Monde,* 22 June 1991.
65. *Le Figaro-Magazine,* 21 September 1991.
66. See N. Mayer, 'Carpentras and the Media', *Patterns of Prejudice,* Vol. 26, 1/2, 1992, 48–63.
67. Quoted in N. Hansson, 'France: The Carpentras Syndrome and Beyond', *Patterns of Prejudice,* Vol. 25, (1), 1991, 32–45.
68. For Le Pen's comments, see *Le Monde,* 13/14 May 1990.
69. *Le Monde,* 11 May 1990.
70. See M. Marrus, 'French Antisemitism in the 1980s', *Patterns of Prejudice,* Vol. 17, (2), April 1983, 3–20.
71. J. Shields, 'Antisemitism in France: The Spectre of Vichy', *Patterns of Prejudice,* Vol. 24, No. 2–4, Winter 1990, 5–17.
72. See the analysis by Roland Cayrol in *La Lutte Contre Le Racisme et La Xénophobie: 1992 – Rapport de La Commission Nationale Consultative des Droits de l'Homme* (Paris: *La Documentation Française,* 1993), 59–76.
73. Cayrol (1993), p. 70.

74. Cayrol (1993), p. 75.
75. See *'Racisme: la droite contre-attaque'*, in *L'Express*, 4 September 1987.
76. *Le Monde*, 21 November 1987.
77. *Le Monde*, 24 November 1987.
78. *Le Monde*, 19 December 1987.
79. *Le Monde*, 5 April 1990.
80. Pasqua denied any suggestion that his measures might create hostility to Muslim immigrants, taking the opportunity to stress again that the best means of avoiding xenophobia was for French Muslims to fit in. See the interview with Pasqua in *Le Figaro*, 12 August 1994, and for a discussion of his measures and their possible impact on French Muslims, see the articles by Henri Tincq and Patrick Jarreau in *Le Monde*, 12 August 1994.

5   THE NATIONAL FRONT'S PROGRAMME AND IDEOLOGY

1. See S. Mitra, 'The National Front in France – A Single-Issue Movement?', *West European Politics*, (11) April 1988, 47–64.
2. *300 Mesures pour la renaissance de la France: Front national programme de gouvernement* (Paris: Editions Nationales, 1993). (Subsequently cited as Programme 1993.)
3. J.-M. Le Pen, *L'Espoir* (Paris: Albatros, 1989), p. 12. (Subsequently cited as Le Pen, 1989.)
4. Le Pen, 1989, p. 12.
5. J.-M. Le Pen, *Les français d'abord* (Paris: Editions Carrère, 1984), p. 12. (Subsequently cited as Le Pen, 1984).
6. Ibid., p. 71.
7. Ibid., p. 75.
8. Ibid., p. 73.
9. Ibid., p. 18.
10. M. Winock, *Nationalisme, antisémitisme et fascisme en France* (Paris: Seuil, 1982), p. 45.
11. Le Pen, 1984, p. 177. Churchill actually said, 'No one pretends that democracy is perfect or all-wise. Indeed, it has been said that democracy is the worst form of Government except all those other forms that have been tried from time to time'. House of Commmons, 11 November 1947.
12. Quoted by Pierre-André Taguieff, in N. Mayer and P. Perrineau (eds), *Le Front national à découvert* (Paris: Presses de la Fondation Nationale des Sciences Politiques, 1989), p. 197.
13. Le Pen, 1989, p. 152.
14. Author's interview, September 1993.
15. See B. Mégret, *'Le nouveau clivage'*, in *Identité*, No. 4, November/December 1989, 18–21.
16. Le Pen, 1984, p. 82.
17. Ibid., p. 79.
18. Ibid., p. 183.
19. Ibid., pp. 131 and 79.
20. Ibid., p. 115.

21. *Le Monde,* 1 August 1987.
22. *Le Monde,* 6/7 March 1988.
23. Le Pen, 1984, p. 100.
24. Le Pen, 1989, p. 14.
25. Le Pen, 1984, p. 168.
26. Ibid., p. 164.
27. Le Pen, 1989, p. 22.
28. Ibid., p. 21.
29. Le Pen, 1984, p. 110.
30. Poll in *Le Monde*, 25 October 1991. For Chirac's comments, see *Le Monde*, 21 June 1991; and for Giscard, see *Le Monde,* 21 September 1991.
31. *Le Monde*, 19 November 1991.
32. *Le Monde,* 19 June 1985.
33. See the *Rapport Milloz: Le coût de l'immigration* (Paris: Editions Nationales, 1990), P. Milloz, *Les étrangers et le chômage en France* (Paris: Editions Nationales, 1991), and J.-Y. Le Gallou and P. Olivier, *Immigration: Le Front national fait le point* (Paris: Editions Nationales, 1992).
34. *Présent,* 16 June 1993.
35. *Présent,* 3 August 1993.
36. *Présent,* 26 February 1993.
37. *Présent,* 29 April 1993.
38. J.-M. Le Pen, *'L'âme des peuples', Identité,* No. 12, March/April/May 1991, 3.
39. B. Mégret, *'L'économie au service de la nation', Identité,* No.17, Autumn 1992, 21.
40. Le Pen, 1984, p. 133.
41. Le Pen, 1989, p. 117.
42. See *Le Monde,* 12 June 1985.
43. Programme 1993, pp. 227–78.
44. Author's interview, September 1993.
45. B. Mégret, *'L'économie au service de la nation', Identité,* No. 17, Autumn 1992, 20–21.
46. *La Lettre de Jean-Marie Le Pen,* No. 178, June 1993.
47. *Présent,* 25 June 1993.
48. *Présent,* 11 June 1993.
49. Programme 1993, 200–1.
50. Le Pen, 1989, p. 136.
51. Le Pen, 1984, p. 94.
52. Le Pen, 1989, p. 18.
53. *Le Monde*, 11 April 1987.
54. Le Pen, 1984, p. 95.
55. Author's interview, December 1992.
56. Programme 1993, pp. 61–2.
57. Le Pen, 1989, p. 17.
58. *Le Monde,* 20 September 1983.
59. Le Pen, 1984, p. 113.
60. See G. Ignasse, *'Le SIDA et la vie politique française', Pouvoirs* (58) 1991, 93–102.
61. Quoted in G. Ignasse, 1991, 97.
62. *Le Monde*, 8 May 1987.

63. *Le Monde,* 11 January 1984.
64. *Le Monde,* 3 May 1990.
65. Author's interview, September 1993.
66. See E. Plenel and A. Rollat, *L'effet Le Pen* (Paris: La Découverte/Le Monde, 1984), p. 231, views reaffirmed during Le Pen's 1993 trip to Latin America. See *Le Monde,* 29 December 1993.
67. *Le Monde,* 18 September 1986.
68. Programme 1993, p. 401.
69. Jean-Yves Le Gallou in *Le Figaro,* 18 June 1991.
70. *Le Monde,* 12 June 1991.
71. Le Pen, 1984, p. 87.
72. J.-Y. Le Gallou, *'Préserver notre identité', Identité,* No. 13, June/July/August 1991, pp. 20–3.
73. *Le Monde,* 10 December 1991.
74. Programme 1993, p. 71.
75. Ibid., p. 81.
76. Ibid., p. 82.
77. *Présent,* 31 July 1993.
78. Programme 1993, p. 88.
79. *La Lettre de Jean-Marie Le Pen,* No.180, July 1993, 3.
80. *La Lettre de Jean-Marie Le Pen,* No. 180, July 1993, 3.
81. *Le Monde,* 20 January 1993.
82. Y. Blot, *'Baroque et politique', Identité,* No.12, March/April/May 1991, 29. For a fuller discussion of this thesis, see Y. Blot, *Baroque et politique: Le Pen est-il néo-baroque?* (Paris: Editions Nationales, 1992).
83. Y. Blot (1991), p. 30.
84. *La Lettre de Jean-Marie Le Pen,* No.179, July 1993, 10.
85. *Présent,* 23 September 1993.
86. Programme 1993, p. 93.
87. Ibid., p. 97.
88. Ibid., p. 329.
89. J.-M. Le Pen, *'Agir pour rester libre', Identité,* No.18, Spring 1993, 3.
90. Ibid.
91. Le Pen, 1984, p. 159.
92. Le Pen, 1989, pp. 88–9.
93. See the communiqué published in *Présent,* 4 August 1993.
94. Programme 1993, p. 346.
95. Ibid., p. 341.
96. *Le Monde,* 24 October 1990.
97. See the communiqué published in *Présent,* 14 September 1993.
98. See the interview with Antony on his return from Croatia, *National-Hebdo,* 6–12 August 1993.
99. *Le Monde,* 22 August 1993.
100. Reuters News Agency, 26 January 1993.
101. *Libération,* 1 February 1993.
102. Programme 1993, p. 349.
103. Ibid., 350.
104. Le Pen speaking on 21 June 1990, quoted in *Le Monde* 11 January 1992.

105. At the first round of voting in the Algerian Legislative election on 26 December 1991, the Islamic Salvation Front, or FIS, looked set to be heading for victory, but on 12 January 1992, the High Security Council suspended the second round of voting. For a good background, see 'Hapless Democratic Experiment', *The Guardian*, 28 January 1992.
106. *Minute-La France*, 7 January 1992. *Le Monde*, 11 January 1992.
107. *Le Monde*, 15 January 1992.
108. *Le Monde*, 5 March 1991.
109. Le Pen, 1984, p. 148.
110. Programme 1993, 320.
111. Le Pen, 1984, pp. 146–7.
112. Programme 1993, p. 317.
113. *Le Monde*, 14 January 1992.
114. Interviewed in *Le Figaro*, 13 August 1990.
115. *Le Monde*, 2 October 1990.
116. *Le Monde*, 18 January 1991.
117. *Le Monde*, 25 January 1991.
118. *Le Monde*, 26 February 1991.
119. *Le Monde*, 24 August 1990.
120. *Le Monde*, 14 August 1990.
121. *Le Monde*, 24 August 1990.
122. Ibid.
123. *Le Monde*, 19/20 August 1990.
124. *Le Monde*, 17 January 1991.
125. *Le Monde*, 20 February 1991.
126. Author's interview, September 1993.
127. Author's interview, September 1993.
128. Le Pen, 1984, p. 146.
129. Interviewed in *The Jerusalem Report,* 27 February 1992, pp. 23–6.
130. See *Libération*, 16 September 1987.
131. *National-Hebdo* 1–7 October 1992.
132. *Présent,* 15 June 1993.
133. *Présent,* 2 March 1993.
134. *National-Hebdo,* 11–17 March 1993.
135. *National-Hebdo,* 6–12 August 1992.
136. *National-Hebdo*, 13–19 August 1992.
137. Le Pen, 1984, p. 171.
138. Ibid., p. 171.
139. *Le Monde*, 15 February 1984.
140. *Le Monde,* 15 February, 1984.
141. Quoted in *Le Monde*, 29 August 1991.
142. *Le Monde*, 7 December 1989.
143. Jean-Marie Le Pen, speaking on 13 September 1987 to the Grand Jury RTL-Le Monde, see *Le Monde,* 15 September 1987.
144. *Le Monde*, 25 May 1990.
145. Quoted in *Le Monde,* 10/11 September 1989.
146. *Le Monde,* 10/11 September 1989.
147. Quoted in *Le Monde,* 12 August 1989.

148. *Le Monde,* 7 February 1992.
149. *Ibid.*
150. *Le Monde,* 27 November 1992.
151. For example, see *Le Monde* 30 June/1 July 1991. National Front cadres display a high degree of suspicion towards Jews. A survey of delegates at the Front's 1990 Congress found that 88 per cent agreed with the proposition that 'Jews have too much power in France'. Among the electorate as a whole the proportion agreeing with this statement was 21 per cent. See C. Ysmal, *'Les cadres du Front national: les habits neufs de l'extrême droite',* in O. Duhamel and J. Jaffré (eds), *SOFRES. L'état de l'opinion 1991* (Paris: Seuil, 1991), p. 193.
152. See *The Jerusalem Report,* 11 February 1993.
153. *Présent,* 11 May 1993.
154. *Le Monde,* 20 September 1988.
155. Author's interview, September 1993.
156. *Présent,* 25 May 1993.
157. *Présent,* 17 July 1993.
158. Ibid.
159. *Présent,* 20 July 1993.
160. Author's interview, September 1993.
161. Author's interview, September 1993.
162. Interviewed in the *Quotidien de Paris,* 29 July 1989 and quoted in *Le Monde,* 1 August 1989.
163. Le Pen, 1984, p. 67.
164. Ibid.
165. *Le Figaro,* 19 September 1993.
166. *La Lettre de Jean-Marie Le Pen,* No. 176, May 1993, 9–10.
167. Ibid.

6 THE RESPONSE OF THE MAINSTREAM PARTIES

1. *Le Monde,* 11 February 1983.
2. *Le Monde,* 12 March 1983.
3. Speaking in a television interview, 5 September 1983.
4. *Le Figaro,* 7 September 1983.
5. Ibid.
6. *Le Monde,* 9 September 1983.
7. *Le Monde,* 18/19 September 1983.
8. *Le Monde,* 20 September 1983.
9. *L'Express,* 30 September 1983.
10. *Le Monde,* 20 September 1983.
11. *Le Monde,* 16 February 1984.
12. Ibid.
13. *Le Monde,* 18 February 1984.
14. *Le Monde,* 25 May 1984.
15. *Le Monde,* 9 June 1984.
16. *Le Monde,* 14 June 1984.

17. *Le Monde,* 31 October 1984.
18. *Le Monde,* 6 November 1984.
19. *Le Monde,* 2 March 1985.
20. *L'Express,* 1 March 1985.
21. *Le Monde,* 2 March 1985.
22. *Le Monde,* 8 March 1985.
23. *Le Monde,* 7 March 1985.
24. *Le Monde,* 20 December 1985.
25. *Le Monde,* 21 March 1987.
26. *Le Monde,* 4 April 1987.
27. Ibid.
28. *Le Monde,* 14 July 1987. The Mayor, Hervé de Fontmichel, was subsequently expelled from the Radical Party, see *Le Monde,* 17 July 1987.
29. *Le Matin,* 17 April 1987.
30. *Le Monde,* 15 May 1987.
31. *Le Monde,* 22 May 1987.
32. *Le Monde,* 27 May 1987.
33. *Le Monde,* 14 February 1987.
34. *Le Monde,* 18/19 January 1987.
35. Jean-Luc Parodi, quoted in *Le Point,* 4 May 1987.
36. *Le Monde,* 2 May 1988.
37. *Le Monde,* 1 August 1987.
38. Ibid.
39. Ibid.
40. *Le Monde,* 4 August 1987.
41. *Le Monde,* 17 September 1987.
42. *Le Monde,* 25 September 1987.
43. SOFRES poll in *Le Monde,* 4 November 1987.
44. *Le Monde,* 17 December 1987.
45. *Le Monde,* 16 February 1988.
46. *Figaro-Magazine,* 9 April 1988.
47. See the advice given to the Chirac camp by the BVA polling organisation, *Le Monde,* 15 April 1988.
48. *Le Monde,* 12 March 1988.
49. *Le Point,* 4 April 1988.
50. Y. Piat, *Seule, tout en haut à droite* (Paris: Fixot, 1991), pp. 164–5.
51. Interviewed by the extreme-Right journal, *Valeurs Actuelles,* 2 May 1988.
52. *Le Monde,* 3 May 1988.
53. *Libération,* 18 May 1988.
54. See the comments of Hugues Portelli, *Le Journal des Elections,* No. 3, June 1988, 7.
55. *Le Monde,* 7 September 1988.
56. *Le Monde,* 10 September 1988.
57. For this and other anti-semitic comments, see Chapter 5.
58. *Le Monde,* 14 September 1988.
59. *Le Monde,* 13 April 1990.
60. *Le Monde,* 5 November 1991.
61. *Libération,* 16 March 1990.
62. *Le Monde,* 22 May 1990.

63. *Le Monde,* 12 April 1990.
64. The RPR Mayor of Grenoble, Alain Carignon, had called for just such an alliance on 9 June. See also the article on the debate within the Right on the response to Le Pen's rise, *Le Monde,* 7 June 1990.
65. *Le Monde,* 13 June 1990.
66. *Le Monde,* 12 June 1990.
67. *Le Monde,* 13 June 1990.
68. See the article on the Languedoc-Roussillon Council in *Le Monde,* 22 September 1990.
69. *Le Monde,* 14 January 1992.
70. See Jérôme Jaffré, 'La Droite et ses tentations', *Le Monde,* 24 January 1992.
71. Claude Patriat, *'Pouvoirs régionaux en chantier: Le réglage régional des majorités nationales?'* in Philippe Habert, Pascal Perrineau and Colette Ysmal, *Le Vote Eclaté* (Presses de la Fondation Nationale des Sciences Politiques: Paris), 1992, pp. 307–26.
72. *Le Monde,* 17 November 1993.
73. See the interview with Professor Jean Baudouin on *'Séguinisme'* in *Le Monde,* 13 October 1993 and, for recent developments within the Gaullist movement, see the article by Peter Fysh, 'Gaullism Today', *Parliamentary Affairs,* Vol. 46, No. 3, July 1993, 399–415.
74. Author's interview with Jean Charlot, December 1993.
75. *Libération,* 18 May 1992.
76. *Libération,* 20 May 1992.
77. Author's interview with Le Pen, 15 December 1993.
78. Compare Mégret's article in *La Lettre de Jean-Marie Le Pen,* No.199, June 1994, 3 with Le Pen's attack on de Villiers, *Le Monde,* 15 November 1994.
79. *Le Monde,* 30 January 1992.
80. *Le Monde,* 15 September 1987.
81. *L'Humanité*, 26 October 1989.
82. *Le Monde,* 4 November 1989.
83. *Le Monde,* 30 June/1 July 1991.
84. *Le Monde,* 3 July 1993.
85. *Le Monde,* 11/12 July 1993.
86. *Le Monde,* 4/5 November 1990.
87. *Le Monde,* 13 November 1990.
88. *Le Monde,* 16 March 1990.
89. Quoted by P. Favier and M. Martin-Roland, *La Décennie Mitterrand: Vol. 2, Les épreuves* (Paris: Seuil, 1991), pp. 308–9.
90. Author's interview with Jean-Christophe Cambedelis, September 1993.
91. Author's interview with Gérard Grunberg, former *conseiller politique* in Rocard's private office, September 1993.
92. Author's interview with G. Grunberg.
93. *Le Monde,* 7 April 1990.
94. *Le Monde,* 8 May 1990.
95. *Le Monde,* 28 January 1992.
96. Pascal Perrineau interviewed in *Le Monde*, 12 February 1992.
97. Author's interview, September 1993.
98. Author's interview, September 1993.

99. For a discussion of the classification of the Front, see Pierre-André Taguiefff, *'Mobilisation national-populiste en France: vote xénophobe et nouvel anti-sémitisme politique'*, *Lignes*, No. 9, March 1990, 91–136. See also Michel Winock, *'Le retour du national-populisme'*, in M. Winock, *Nationalisme, antisémitisme et fascisme en France* (Paris: Editions du Seuil, 1990), pp. 41–9. There are, as yet, few studies of the response to Le Pen's movement on the Left, but among the first is Nonna Meyer, *La Mobilisation anti-Front National*, in *L'engagement politique: Crises ou Mutation?*, (Paris: Presses de la FNSP, 1993).
100. *Le Monde*, 21 January 1992.
101. *Le Monde*, 30 January 1992.
102. *Le Monde*, 29 February 1993.
103. *Le Figaro*, 6 March 1992.
104. *Le Monde*, 6 March 1992.
105. *Le Monde*, 10 March 1992.
106. Gérard Le Gall interviewed in *Le Monde*, 11 March 1992.
107. Author's interview, September 1993.
108. *Le Monde*, 27 April 1988.
109. Pascal Perrineau, interviewed in *Le Monde*, 12 February 1992.
110. See Michel Winock, *'Nationalisme ouvert et nationalisme fermé'* in M.Winock, *Nationalisme, antisémitisme et fascisme en France* (Paris: Editions du Seuil, 1990), pp. 11–40.
111. Interview with Pierre-André Taguieff in *Le Monde*, 10 April 1991.

CONCLUSION: THE NATIONAL FRONT IN A EUROPEAN CONTEXT

1. The number of seats allocated to French parties as a whole rose from 81 to 87. The Front won 10.51 per cent as against 11.73 per cent in 1989. For a discussion of the results and the significance of Phillipe de Villiers' rival list, see Chapter 3.
2. *Europe et Patries*, No. 49, November 1992, 4.
3. *Ibid.*
4. *Le Monde*, 21 July 1989.
5. *Le Monde*, 25 July 1989.
6. *Le Monde*, 10 October 1989.
7. For an analysis of the outcome of the elections, see 'The performance of Far-Right parties in the European Parliament elections', *Institute of Jewish Affairs: Intelligence Report*, No.12, June 1994.
8. For the implications of Austria's accession for the Far Right, I am indebted to the British Labour Party MEP Glyn Ford. Telephone interview, July 1994.
9. *Europe et Patries*, No. 56, August–September 1993.
10. *Le Monde*, 13 May 1994.
11. For a discussion of Le Pen's stance during the Gulf Conflict, see Chapter 5. Schönhuber broke with Le Pen soon after the Baghdad trip, claiming that he

hadn't been informed of its purpose and scope. *Le Monde*, 9/10 December 1990. Nonetheless, relations between the German Republicans and the National Front seemingly remained cordial.

12. *The Guardian*, 21 June 1993.
13. Jean-Marie Le Pen, writing in *Europe et Patries,* No. 54, June 1993, 9.
14. *The Guardian*, 12 May 1994.
15. *The Independent*, 5 December 1991. See also *Searchlight*, January 1992, 5.
16. See 'Fascist polemics in anti-racism debate', *Searchlight*, January 1994, 23, and the European Parliament's 1991 report, published as G. Ford, *Fascist Europe: The Rise of Racism and Xenophobia* (London: Pluto Press, 1992).
17. For this formulation I am indebted to Serge Hurtig, interviewed at the *Ecole Nationale des Sciences Politiques* in Paris, September 1993.
18. Le Pen, quoted in *The Independent,* 11 October 1994. The Freedom Party of Austria (FPÖ) achieved its highest vote ever in the general election on 9 October. It won 22.6 per cent and 42 of the 183 parliamentary seats, compared with 16.6 per cent and 33 seats at the previous election in 1990. See *Le Monde,* 11 October 1994. In Belgium in the local elections of 10 October 1994, the far-Right Francophone Front national did well in Wallonia and in Brussels, while the Flemish Vlaams Blok became the largest party in Antwerp, with 28 per cent. See *Le Monde*, 14 October 1994.
19. *The Independent*, 11 October 1994.
20. Reuters News Agency reported on 22 September 1994 that Fini intended to disband the MSI and that a closing Congress would be held in January 1995. See also *The International Herald Tribune*, 26 October 1994.
21. Interview with Gianfranco Fini in *Le Monde*, 18 June 1994.
22. See Robert O. Paxton, 'Fascismes d'hier et d'aujord'hui', *Le Monde*, 17 June 1994.
23. Hans-Georg Betz, *Radical Right-Wing Populism in Western Europe* (London: Macmillan, 1994), p. 4.
24. A. Lyttelton, 'Italy: The Triumph of TV', *The New York Review of Books,* 11 August 1994, p. 29.
25. Haider praised 'the orderly labour policies of the Third Reich' in the Provincial Parliament of Carinthia in June 1991 and was forced to step down as Provincial Prime Minister. See J. Bunzl, 'National Populism in Austria', *Patterns of Prejudice*, Vol. 26, Nos. 1/2, 1992, 28–36.
26. See Tony Kushner, 'The Fascist as "Other"? Racism and Neo-Nazism in Contemporary Britain', *Patterns of Prejudice,* Vol. 28, January 1994, 33. Kushner rightly notes that an undue emphasis on the overtly party-political aspects of the Far Right can mean that significant problems of racist violence can be overlooked, even in societies like Britain, where organised far-Right political activity is marginal.
27. There was considerable media coverage of the victory of Derek Beackon of the British National Party in a local council by-election on the Isle of Dogs in London's Dockland in September 1993. See *The Guardian,* 17 September 1993. The seat was quickly lost at local elections in May 1994. See *The Institute of Jewish Affairs, Intelligence Report*, No. 7, September 1993 and No.10, May 1994.

28. See W. Bergmann, 'Xenophobia and Antisemitism after the Unification of Germany', *Patterns of Prejudice,* Vol. 28, January 1994, 67–80.

29. See R. Mitten, 'Jörg Haider, the Anti-immigrant Petition and Immigration Policy in Austria', *Patterns of Prejudice*, Vol. 28, April 1994, 27–47.

30. This growing sense of isolation was reflected in the views of several National Front figures whom I interviewed during the autumn of 1993. Mégret's hope of a 'political rupture' is tantamount to an admission that the Front's forward electoral march faces serious obstacles.

31. S. Hoffmann, 'France: Keeping the Demons at Bay', *The New York Review of Books*, 3 March 1994, 10–16.

32. Hoffman (1994), 10.

33. This suggestion came from the distinguished electoral analyst, Colette Ysmal. Author's interview, December 1993.

34. As early as September 1984, opinion polls were giving some indication of the low standing of politicians. One poll suggested that 82 per cent of those questioned didn't believe that politicians told the truth. See the SOFRES study contained in *'Les Français jugent la classe politique'*, *Le Monde,* 6 September 1984.

35. For a discussion of the transfer of votes from the Left to Le Pen, see F. Platone and H. Rey, *'Le FN en terre communiste'*, in N. Mayer and P. Perrineau (eds), *Le Front National à découvert* (Paris: Presses de la Fondation Nationale des Sciences Politiques, 1989).

36. A point emphasised by Colette Ysmal in an interview with the author and identified in a series of electoral studies. See, for example, P. Perrineau, *'Les ressorts du vote Le Pen,* in P. Habert and C. Ysmal (eds), *L'election Presidentielle* 1988 (Paris: Le Figaro/Etudes Politiques, 1988), p. 21. On the early attraction of some of the mainstream Right's electorate by Le Pen, see also G. Le Gall, *'Une élection sans enjeu avec conséquences'*, *Revue Politique et Parlementaire*, No. 910, May–June 1984, 40–7.

37. R. Rémond, *La politique n'est plus ce qu'elle était* (Paris: Calmann-Lévy, 1993).

38. P. Perrineau, *'Les ressorts du vote Le Pen'*, in P. Habert and C. Ysmal (eds), *L'Election Presidentielle 1988: Résultats, analyses et commentaires* (Paris: Le Figaro/Etudes Politiques, 1988).

39. See J. Charlot, *Les partis politiques et le système des partis en France* (Paris: Ministère des Affaires Etrangères, 1992).

40. Hoffmann (1994), 12.

41. See *The Economist*, 21 May 1994.

42. *Le Monde*, 4 February 1994.

43. Here I am indebted to conversations over several years with Serge Hurtig.

44. Author's interview, December 1993.

45. *Présent,* 27 July 1993.

46. Author's interview, September 1993.

47. See the parable of the rise of Hitler written in 1941, B. Brecht, *The Resistible Rise of Arturo Ui* (London: Methuen, 1993).

Select Bibliography

Algazy, J., *L'extrême droite en France (1965 à 1984)* (Paris: L'Harmattan, 1989).

Anderson, M., *Conservative Politics In France* (London: George Allen & Unwin, 1974).

Ambler, J.S., *The French Socialist Experiment* (Philadelphia: ISHI, 1985).

Barnes, I.R., 'The Pedigree of GRECE (I)', *Patterns of Prejudice*, 3 (1980), pp. 14–24.

——, 'The Pedigree of GRECE (II)', *Patterns of Prejudice*, 4 (1980), pp. 29–39.

——, 'The Ideas of the French Far Right', *Patterns of Prejudice*, 1 (1982), pp. 3–12.

Barreau, J.-C., *De l'immigration en général et de la nation française en particulier* (Paris: Le Pré au Clercs, 1992).

Bell, D.S, and Criddle, B., 'Presidential Dominance Denied: The French Parliamentary Election of 1986', *Parliamentary Affairs*, 39 (October 1986), 477–88.

Betz, H.-G., 'The New Politics of Resentment: Radical Right-Wing Populist Parties in Western Europe', *Comparative Politics*, (25) July 1993, 413–27.

——, *Radical Right-Wing Populism in Western Europe* (London: Macmillan, 1994).

Beyme, C. von. (ed), *Right-wing Extremism in Post-war Europe* (London: Frank Cass, 1988).

Birenbaum, G., *Le Front National en politique* (Paris: Balland, 1992).

Birnbaum, P., *'La France aux Français': histoire des haines nationalistes* (Paris: Seuil, 1993).

Boussard, I., 'Maastricht: Le refus des agriculteurs et des ruraux', *Revue Politique et Parlementaire*, No. 961, September–October 1992, pp. 25–8.

Bréchon, P., and Mitra, S.K., 'The National Front in France: The Emergence of an Extreme Right Protest Movement', *Comparative Politics*, (25) October 1992, pp. 63–82.

Bresson, G., and Lionet, C., *Le Pen* (Paris: Seuil, 1994).

Camus, J.-Y., 'Political cultures within the Front National: The Emergence of a Counter-Ideology on the French Far Right', *Patterns of Prejudice*, 26 (1992), pp. 5–16.

Camus, J.-Y., and Monzat, R., *Les droites nationales et radicales en France* (Lyon: Presses Universitaires de Lyon, 1992).

Chagnollaud, D., (ed.), *Etat politique de la France, année 1991* (Paris: Quai Voltaire, 1992).

Charlot, J., *Les partis politiques et le systéme des partis en France* (Paris: Ministère des affaires Etrangères, 1992).

——, 'Les rapports de forces électoraux entre les partis', *Revue Politique et Parlementaire*, No. 958, March–April 1992, 19–23.

Charlot, M., 'L'émergence du Front national', *Revue Française de Science Politique*, 36 (February 1986), 30–45

Cheles, L., Ferguson, R., and Vaughan, M. (eds), *Neo-Fascism in Europe* (London: Longman, 1991).

Cobban, A., *A History of Modern France, Volume 3: 1871–1962* (Harmondsworth: Penguin, 1965).

Commissions Nationale Consultative des Droits de l'Homme, 1990. La Lutte Contre Le Racisme et La Xénophobie (Paris: La Documentation Française, 1991).

——, *1992. La Lutte Contre Le Racisme et La Xénophobie, Exclusion et Droits de l'Homme* (Paris: La Documentation Française, 1993).

Dorgan, C., and Marcus, J., 'The French Cantonal Elections: Local Skirmish or National Test?' *The World Today*, May 1982, 185–93.

Dorgan, C., and Marcus, J., 'French Politics and the Municipal Elections of March 1983', *The Political Quarterly*, (54) July–September 1983, 307–12.

Dreyfus, F.G., 'Letter from France: After the Referendum of 20 September', *Government and Opposition*, (28), Winter 1993, 82–6.

Duhamel, A., 'L'Image du Front national auprés des français', SOFRES, June 1993.

Duhamel, O., Dupoirier, E., and Jaffré, J. (eds), *SOFRES L'état de l'opinion 1988* (Paris: Seuil, 1988).

Duhamel, O., and Jaffré, J. (eds), *SOFRES L'état de l'opinion 1993* (Paris: Seuil, 1993).

Dupoirier, E., and Grunberg, G. (eds), *Mars 1986: la drôle de défaite de la gauche* (Paris: Presses Universitaires de France, 1986).

Duranton-Crabol, A.-M., *Visages de la nouvelle droite: Le G.R.E.C.E. et son histoire* (Paris: Presses de la Fondation Nationale des Sciences Politiques, 1988).

Eatwell, R., 'Poujadism and Neopoujadism: From Revolt to Reconciliation', in P. Cerny (ed.), *Social movements and Protest in France* (London: Frances Pinter, 1982).

Etienne, B., *La France et l'islam* (Paris: Hachette, 1989).

Favier, P., and Martin-Roland, M., *La Décennie Mitterrand: Vol. 1. Les ruptures* (Paris: Seuil, 1990).

——, *La Décennie Mitterrand: Vol.2. Les épreuves (1984–88)* (Paris: Seuil, 1991).

Ford, G., *Fascist Europe: The Rise of Racism and Xenophobia* (London: Pluto Press, 1992).

Frears, J.R., *Political Parties and Elections in the French Fifth Republic* (London: C. Hurst & Co., 1977).

——, *France in the Giscard Presidency* (London: George Allen & Unwin, 1981).

Fuchs, G., *Ils resteront: Le défi de l'immigration* (Paris: Editions Syros, 1987).

Gaffney, J.(ed.), *The French Presidential Elections of 1988* (Aldershot: Dartmouth, 1989).

Gaspard, F., 'Immigration: Loi du sol ou loi de sang?', *Revue Politique et Parlementaire*, No. 921, January–February 1986, 53–6.

——, 'L'évolution du F.N. à Dreux et dans les environs (1978–1989)', *Revue Politique et Parlementaire*, No. 945, January–February 1990, 62–9.

Habert, P., and Ysmal, C., *L'election présidentielle 1988* (Paris: Le Figaro/Etudes Politiques, 1988).

Habert, P., Perrineau, P., and Ysmal, C. (eds), *Le vote éclaté, les élections régionales et cantonales des 22 et 29 mars 1992* (Paris: Figaro/Presses de la Fondation Nationale des Sciences Politiques, 1992).

Habert, P., Perrineau, P., Ysmal, C. (eds), *Le Vote Sanction: Les élections législatives des 21 et 28 mars 1993* (Paris: Département d'études politiques du Figaro & Presses de la Fondation Nationale des Sciences Politiques, 1993)

Hainsworth, P., *The Extreme Right in Europe and the USA* (London: Frances Pinter, 1992).

Hall, P., Hayward, J., and Machin, H. (eds), *Developments in French Politics* (London: Macmillan, 1994).

Hansson, N., 'France: The Carpentras Syndrome and Beyond', *Patterns of Prejudice*, 1 (1991), 32–45.

Harris, G., *The Dark Side of Europe: The Extreme Right Today* (Edinburgh: Edinburgh University Press, 1990).

Hennion, B., *Le Front national, l'argent et l'establishment* (Paris: La Découverte, 1992).

Hoffmann, S., *Le Mouvement Poujade* (Paris: Armand Colin, 1956).

Hollifield, J., and Ross, G. (eds), *Searching for the New France* (London: Routledge, 1991).

Howorth, J., and Ross, G. (eds), *Contemporary France: A Review of Interdisciplinary Studies, Vol. 3* (London: Frances Pinter, 1989).

Ignasse, G., 'Le SIDA et la vie politique française', *Pouvoirs* (58), 1991, 93–102.

Jacob, J., 'L'extrême-droite revue et corrigée par Jean-Marie Le Pen', *Revue Politique et Parlementaire*, No.927, January–February 1987, 35–7.

Jaffré, J., 'La défaite des socialistes et l'insatisfaction des électeurs', *Pouvoirs*, (62), 1992, 135–149.

——, 'La droite restaurée', *Pouvoirs*, (66), 1993, 141–55.

Kolakowski, L., *Main Currents of Marxism: Its Origin, Growth, and Dissolution. Volume III, The Breakdown* (Oxford: Clarendon Press, 1978).

Lancelot, A., (ed.), *1981: Les élections de l'alternance* (Paris: Presses de la Fondation Nationale des Sciences Politiques, 1986).

Le Gall, G., 'Une élection sans enjeu avec conséquences', *Revue Politique et Parlementaire*, No. 910, May–June 1984, 9–47.

——, 'Mars 1986: des élections de transition?, *Revue Politique et Parlementaire*, No. 922, March–April 1986, 6–18.

——, 'Printemps 1988: retour à une gauche majoritaire', *Revue Politique et Parlementaire*, No. 936, July–August 1988, 14–24.

——, 'Novations et paradoxes des Municipales 89', *Revue Politique et Parlementaire*, No. 940, March–April 1989, 8–13.

——, 'Un triple avertissement: pour l'Europe, la démocratie et les Socialistes', *Revue Politique et Parlementaire*, No. 942, July–August 1989, 11–20.

——, 'Elections: les handicaps du pouvoir face à 1993', *Revue Politique et Parlementaire*, No.958, March–April 1992, 3–13.

——, 'Une répétition des élections du printemps 1992', *Revue Politique et Parlementaire*, No. 964, March–April 1993, 6–18.

——, 'Cantonales 94: la fin de la disgrâce de la gauche', *Revue Politique et Parlementaire*, No. 970, March–April 1994, 5–14.

Le Pen, J.-M., *L'Espoir* (Paris: Editions Albatros,1989).

——, *Les Français d'abord* (Paris: Editions Carrère, 1984).

——, *Droite et Démocratie Economique* (Paris, 1984).

——, *Pour La France: Programme du Front National* (Paris: Editions Albatros, 1985).

Marcus, J., 'France: The Resurgence of the Far Right', *The World Today*, December 1984, 507–13.

——, 'Mitterrand's Half-Time Verdict', *The World Today*, June 1985, 103–4.

——, 'France's Year of Dualism', *The World Today*, May 1987, 81–4.

——, 'French Politics after the Elections', *The World Today*, October 1988, 173–6.

——, 'France: Punishing the Socialists', *The World Today*, June 1992, 99–100.

——, 'France: The Right Triumphs', *The World Today*, May 1993, 82–3.

Marrus, M. R., 'French Antisemitism in the 1980's', *Patterns of Prejudice*, 2 (1983), 3–20

Mayer, N., and Perrineau, P. (eds), *Le Front national à découvert* (Paris: Presses de la Fondation Nationale des Sciences Politiques, 1989).

——, *L'engagement politique: Déclin ou mutation?* (Paris: Presses de la Fondation Nationale des Sciences Politiques, 1994).

Mayer, N., and Rey, H., 'Avancée électorale, isolement politique du Front national', *Revue Politique et Parlementaire*, No. 964, March–April 1993, 42–8.

Mayer, N., 'Carpentras, machine arrière', *Commentaire*, No. 53, Spring 1991, 75–80.

——, 'Carpentras and the Media', *Patterns of Prejudice*, 1/2 (1992), 48–63.

——, 'Ethnocentrism and the National Front Vote in the 1988 French Presidential Election', unpublished paper delivered to the conference on Racism, Ethnicity and Politics in Contemporary Europe, Loughborough University, 24–6 September 1993.

Milza, P., *Fascisme français: Passé et présent* (Paris: Flammarion, 1987).

Monzat, R., *Enquêtes sur la droite extrême* (Paris: Le Monde-Editions, 1992).

Noiriel, G., *Le Creuset Français: Histoire de l'immigration XIXe–XXe siècles* (Paris: Seuil, 1988).

Perrineau, P., 'Le Front National: un électorat autoritaire', *Revue Politique et Parlementaire*, No. 918, July–August 1985, 24–31.

——, 'A l'ombre des législatives ... les élections régionales', *Revue Politique et Parlementaire*, No. 922, March–April 1986, 19–27.

——, 'Le Front national et les élections: L'exception présidentielle et la règle législative', *Revue Politique et Parlementaire*, No. 936, July–August 1988, 34–41.

——, 'Front national: l'écho politique de l'anomie urbaine', in *Esprit: La France en Politique 1988* (Paris: Esprit Fayard Seuil, 1988).

——, 'Le Front national: Les clefs de la défaite', *Revue Politique et Parlementaire*, No. 940, March–April 1989, 19–24.

Pfister, T., 'Le nouveau paysage politique: les trois Frances', *Revue Politique et Parlementaire*, No. 935, May–June 1988, 5–14.

Plenel, E., and Rollat, A., *L'effet Le Pen* (Paris: La Découverte/Le Monde, 1984).

Piat, Y., *Seule, tout en haut à droite* (Paris: Fixot, 1991).

Rémond, R., *Les droites en France*, Fourth Edition (Paris: Aubier Montaigne, 1982).

——, *La politique n'est plus ce qu'elle était* (Paris: Calmann-Lévy, 1993).

Rollat, A., *Les hommes de l'extrême droite* (Paris: Calmann-Lévy, 1985).

Ross, G., Hoffmann, S., and Malzacher, S. (eds), *The Mitterrand Experiment* (Cambridge: Polity Press, 1987).

Rousso, H., *Le syndrome de Vichy 1944–198 ...* (Paris: Seuil, 1987).

Schain, M., 'Party Politics, the National Front and the Construction of Political Legitimacy', *West European Politics* (10), April 1987, 229–52.

Shields, J.G., 'Le Pen and the French Radical Right', *Patterns of Prejudice*, 1 (1986), 3–10.

—— 'Antisemitism in France: The Spectre of Vichy', *Patterns of Prejudice*, 2/4 (1990), 5–17.

——, 'The Front National and the Politics of Discrimination in France', *Institute of Jewish Affairs Analysis*, No. 2, June 1992.

Showstack Sassoon, A., *Gramsci's Politics* (London: Croom Helm, 1980).

Searls, E., 'The French Right in Opposition 1981–1986', *Parliamentary Affairs*, 39 (October 1986), 463–76.

Sirinelli, J.-F. (ed.), *Histoire des droites en France,1. Politique* (Paris: Gallimard, 1992).

——, *Histoire des droites en France, 2. Culture* (Paris: Gallimard, 1992).

——, *Histoire des droites en France, 3. Sensibilités* (Paris: Gallimard, 1992).

Smith, G., *Politics in Western Europe*, Fifth Edition (Aldershot: Dartmouth, 1989).

Sternhell, Z., *La droite révolutionnaire 1885–1914: Les origines Françaises du fascisme* (Paris: Seuil, 1978).

——, *Ni droite, ni gauche: L'idéologie fasciste en France* (Paris: Editions Complexe, 1987).

Subileau, F., and Toinet, M.-F., 'La participation aux régionales: une divine surprise?', *Revue Politique et Parlementaire*, No. 958, March–April 1992, 14–18.

Taguieff, P.-A., (ed.), *Face au racisme. Vol. 2, Analyses, hypothèses, perspectives* (Paris: La Découverte, 1991).

——, *Sur la Nouvelle droite* (Paris: Descartes & Cie, 1994).

Tristan, A., *Au Front* (Paris: Gallimard, 1987).

Tuppen, J., *Chirac's France, 1986–88* (London: Macmillan, 1991).

Walker, M., *The National Front* (London: Fontana, 1977).

Weber, E., *France, Fin de Siècle* (Cambridge, Mass.: Harvard University Press, 1986).

Wihtol de Wenden, C., *Les immigrés et la politique* (Paris: Presses de la Fondation Nationale des Sciences Politiques, 1988).

Wilkinson, P., *The New Fascists* (London: Pan Books, 1983).

Williams, P.M., *Wars, Plots and Scandals in Post-war France* (Cambridge: Cambridge University Press, 1970).

——, *French Politicians and Elections 1951–1969* (Cambridge: Cambridge University Press, 1970).

Winock, M., *Nationalisme, antisémitisme et fascisme en France* (Paris: Seuil, 1982).

—— (ed.), *Histoire de l'extrême droite en France* (Paris: Seuil, 1993).

Wolfreys, J., 'An Iron Hand in a Velvet Glove: The programme of the French National Front', *Parliamentary Affairs*, (46) July 1993, 415–29.

Ysmal, C., 'Recul et divisions de la droite modérée', *Revue Politique et Parlementaire*, No. 936, July–August 1988, 25–33.

——, 'Modérés: Le double défi de la gauche et de l'extrême droite', *Revue Politique et Parlementaire*, No. 940, March–April 1989, 14–18.

——, 'Le RPR et l'UDF face au Front national: concurrence et connivences', *Revue Politique et Parlementaire*, No. 913, November–December 1984, 6–20.

Index